Gender
Intelligence

Gender
Intelligence

WITHDRAWN

Breakthrough Strategies for Increasing Diversity and Improving Your Bottom Line

Barbara Annis & Keith Merron

An Imprint of HarperCollins*Publishers*
HARPER
BUSINESS
www.harpercollins.com

HarperCollins books may be purchased for educational, business, or sales promotional use. For information, please e-mail the Special Markets Department at SPsales@harpercollins.com.

FIRST EDITION

Charts by Barbara Annis & Associates

Designed by Sunil Manchikanti

Library of Congress Cataloging-in-Publication Data has been applied for.

ISBN 978-0-06-230743-9

14 15 16 17 18 OV/RRD 10 9 8 7 6 5 4 3 2 1

To my husband, Paul Reed Currie, whose amazing support, love, and integrity I always admire and treasure.

And to my wonderful children, Lauren, Sasha, Stéphane, and Christian; my bonus children, Zachary, Kelly, and Jeremy; and my grandchildren, Colin, Cameron, Alaia, Brydan, Jake, Riley, and Grayson.

—*Barbara*

To my extraordinary children, Josh and Maya, who each in their own way walk on this earth with grace, kindness, and extraordinary integrity.

To my ex-wife, Tina Benson, for her loving support and powerful example of partnership, and for being the wonderful mother she is to our children.

And to my father, Jules Merron; my mother, Gail Grewe; and my step-mom, Chrissa Merron, for believing in me throughout my whole life.

—*Keith*

Contents

Preface

When Barbara began her journey in 1987 and Keith joined her in 2002, our sincerest intention and desire was to empower women in the workplace and help them navigate their careers. Time seems to pass so quickly when you're this deeply consumed in your work.

The world has changed in so many remarkable ways in that span of time. And in collecting the information and stories for this book, we realized how much we have changed as well.

Early on in her practice, Barbara was making the same mistakes most consultancies and heads of organizations were making—missteps many are still making today in their pursuit of gender equality and diversity. As with so many others back then, her focus was on coaching and training women to adapt to the world of business, to take charge of their careers as men would, and to advance—no matter how inauthentic and uninviting it felt.

Keith joined Barbara twelve years ago after having spent the previous twenty years consulting to leaders to help them create organizations that are more vibrant, adaptive, collaborative, and inclusive. Together, they began to focus on more system-wide approaches to producing a transformation in the balance of men and women and the spirit of inclusiveness.

We learned a great deal along the way, most important, that *gender* as it relates to the workplace is not about women only, but about women and men together. And as we grew in our own Gender Intelligence, we became even more motivated to share with leaders and organizations what we had discovered to be the true sustainable path—the final and most profound leg of our collective journey to gender diversity and inclusiveness.

That insight we had back then became our unifying theme and the driving force behind all our efforts, and it stands today at the heart of our practice and message. When men and women bring their genuine selves to the workplace and embrace each other's authenticity, they discover the true meaning of gender diversity and success, equals not in number alone, but also in value and contribution.

Through Gender Intelligence, we have helped many organizations break the code on gender equality. We have guided toward true diversity by teaching them to view gender from a strength-through-differences standpoint rather than through equality in numbers and sameness in behavior. This transformational shift in thinking has brought greater economic value to these companies and contributed significantly to the personal and professional growth and happiness of their employees.

This book is about that true meaning and the journey of gender-intelligent organizations today.

As we collected our thoughts for this book, we couldn't help but reflect back on where we were when we had our first "aha!" moment—that gender insight that altered the course of our thinking, changed our outlook for the better, and put us on the path to the practice we're engaged in today.

Barbara's "aha!" moment came while working with an organization that was trying, with all the right intentions, to close its gender gap—but failing. She says:

> It was actually the very first organization I worked with that brought me that gender insight that changed my whole perspective and gave birth to Gender Intelligence.
>
> In all of our client meetings and discussions on closing the gender gap, we naturally thought only about women. We never considered men when the subject of gender would come up. They weren't part of the equation.
>
> It dawned on me that we were focusing on closing the women gap, not the gender gap. My "aha!" moment was that this organization I was working with—or any organization for that matter—was not going to close the gender gap by just focusing on women and putting the burden on women to solve the "woman problem." We had to involve men in a much greater and more meaningful way.

Our practice transformed because of that "aha!" moment. And as we embarked on working with men and women together, we were so pleasantly surprised at how interested many male leaders were and how committed they were to empowering women. We discovered that it wasn't that they were resisting or avoiding making changes, or that they were intentional in their lack of awareness and interest. They, by and large, just didn't know what to do and, for many, didn't even know something had to be done!

Keith's "aha!" moment came at the end of what he thought was a successful leadership workshop. He says:

I've been an organizational consultant for over thirty years, committed to transforming organizations and making them more collaborative and inclusive. For the first twenty, I had never paid particular attention to gender. Instead, my focus was on creating inclusive and collaborative cultures with a focus on leadership in general.

About thirteen years ago, I was facilitating a leadership workshop and after the session, most of the men and several of the women commented that it had been a great experience for them. A number of female participants, however, said it felt "a little too male" for their tastes. I was shocked. I had never received this kind of feedback before. The women who shared those comments said they couldn't quite put a finger on it but that the whole experience just felt too masculine—from the way in which I spoke to the examples I gave, and in the design of the workshop activities themselves.

I am deeply grateful to these women, because through their feedback I started to wonder about what I had been missing. Here I was, a relatively conscious man, committed to everyone being fully themselves and becoming powerful leaders, not so much in the image of what I might be, but in their own image (a key part of the workshop), and here was a group of women giving me feedback to the contrary.

I took it to heart and began a deep journey of self-exploration about the many blind spots that I had as a man. I thought, if I am at least this conscious and committed, and yet still missing some key awareness of my own blind spots, what about the consciousness and commitment of other men? What gender blind spots are preventing them from having this line of sight?

Somewhere around that time, Barbara and I met, and it opened my eyes to a whole world of gender differences that I hadn't been aware of. After that, I was all hands in and totally committed to Gender Intelligence and the work we are now all about.

Barbara set out on this journey twenty-seven years ago, and Keith more recently, to lift the veil on our gender blind spots and misunderstandings and raise the level of appreciation for gender differences in general. Along the way, we have had the privilege and honor to work with some of the top organizations throughout the world, most of which are Fortune 500 companies.

To date, we have worked closely with the leaders of well over one hundred such companies and have, along with them, learned much about what it takes to produce lasting change, and, of course, have made many mistakes along the way as well. This book is an amalgam of that experience, and much more. It is a manifesto designed to challenge some of the prevailing beliefs about gender, differences, leadership, and organizational life— meant to provoke, prod, and catalyze a new and emerging way of being.

We believe that organizations shape the face of the world and that to make our world truly sustainable and create organizations that are highly effective in an ever-changing, uncertain, and highly competitive environment requires the principles and practices expressed in this book. It is intended to produce a revolution of thought and action such that organizations are far more fluid, inclusive, innovative, and effective.

Moreover, our desire was and remains to produce an outcome such that books of this nature are no longer required. We realize that we may not get there for some time to come. But for leaders and their organizations that have the integrity, courage, and commitment to challenge their own thinking and that of others about gender and its role in organizational well-being and effectiveness, the principles embedded in this book will serve as important guideposts along their journey.

In this book, we present how a small but growing number of courageous, leading-edge companies have been able to break through the barriers to women advancing in leadership. They have made the remarkable transformation from compliance to choice, from pressure to preference.

They have discovered that the true measure of gender equality does not reside in a percentage, but in the untapped power of gender-intelligent men and women openly working and succeeding together. And the leaders in these forward-leaning companies have demonstrated the strength of conviction it takes to transform company culture and benefit from the diversity of thought, talent, and skills that both men and women bring to the table. As a result, these companies are far surpassing the financial outcomes of their less effective counterparts, many of which have stalled out because they continue to embrace the paradigms of the past.

This book marks the beginning of that journey. In it, we offer both a perspective and a road map. We chronicle what companies are doing that works and what they are not doing but need to, and what leaders are discovering as they challenge themselves and their organizations to lift to a higher level of being and performance.

Together, we often express our dream with this reflection: What if we understood, appreciated, and valued each other well enough and genuinely enough to the point where men could speak for women and women could speak for men?

Imagine the spirit of collaboration that would exist in businesses and in governments throughout the world. The inclusion of educated and aspiring women would have such an amazing economic impact, especially in countries experiencing huge talent shortages expressly because their traditional cultures undervalue half their populations.

This is the transformational conversation that is taking place today—a new perspective shaped by a greater understanding of our gender differences and the value created when we embrace and engage those differences.

To us, this is not just a dream. We clearly envision a day when our gender blind spots become a thing of the past, when gender-intelligent men and women seek out each other's authentic nature and work and live together in a natural and openly inviting way.

DISCLAIMER

Although throughout our book we identify and describe the differences between men and women, we acknowledge that our gender differences are a result of cognitive and behavioral tendencies, first informed by nature, then influenced by culture. This is not to suggest that men will always think and act one way and women will always think and act another. We speak in terms of inclinations and tendencies.

Part One

A New Conversation

1

Gender Intelligence

There's a different conversation taking place today between men and women in the workplace—a transformational conversation that's altering the landscape of business and how we're addressing gender diversity at work. After decades of ineffective finger-pointing and quotas, a revolutionary and effective approach has come into focus for men and women leaders, one shaped by a greater understanding of our gender differences and the value revealed when we engage those differences instead of trying to ignore them.

This awareness is stirring, growing stronger every day, in North America, Europe, and in organizations around the globe. On an individual level, this new approach is improving communication between men and women. It's resulting in more effective problem-solving, in a dual-sided approach to innovation, decision-making, and in increased satisfaction at work and at home. Company-wide, this revolutionary approach is offering organizations significant strategic and economic advantage over companies that are not yet awake to its profound potential. While other businesses are stuck in conventional wisdom, these organizations are moving forward with confidence into the ever-more-competitive global market, able to leverage fully the efforts of every leader and every member of their teams.

And we need a new approach now more than ever. Consider the amazing social changes that have transpired over the last fifty years compared with where we stand today. In education, we've seen a tsunami of women attaining university and graduate degrees in virtually every country on the planet; in many of those countries, women have been surpassing men since the 1980s.[1] This flood of ambitious women seeking careers and starting businesses of their own doesn't show any signs of receding. More and more women hold important leadership positions in top companies and in governments alike. Yet, after so much time and effort, one would think that women would be near to an equal level with men in career opportunity, compensation, advancement, and attainment of leadership positions. They are not.

The sobering reality is that although women now represent 50 percent of the workforce, from entry positions all the way through middle management, women have done no better than to secure about one out of every five senior management positions and only one in ten CEO or board-level posts.[2] After more than forty years of trying to break the glass ceiling, all we've done is push it up. What have we been doing wrong?

The answer is clear! In the past, we've operated from two fundamental beliefs. The first is that balanced gender representation should be achieved in business, government, and education. To achieve that goal requires viewing both genders as identical on the inside. The reach for equal representation has been a tangible and worthy demonstration of our search for gender equity, to be sure. However, we've found that equalizing the numbers doesn't necessarily result in true gender equality or in creating the gender balance we were seeking. Similarly, many believe that treating everyone the same will eradicate bias, another move toward gender equity. Our research and experienc show that this is hardly the case. What if the solution isn't eliminating the differences between men and women themselves, but instead learning how to recognize, value, and leverage those differences?

Many companies who call on us have come to the realization that the focus on sameness and equality in representation has done little to produce meaningful change in the upper echelons of the organization. They're finding that quotas don't get them to gender diversity, and that gender diversity doesn't automatically make them become gender-intelligent. And even after setting those quotas, they're not making them. After targeted recruiting and hiring of more women, the companies are simultaneously losing them. Yet too many are still holding fast to their beliefs, suspended in an ineffective but politically correct paradigm. The question is, what's causing their denial?

Our Collective Limiting Belief

That women are leaving is evidence of the fact that the organization, especially at the top, is not providing a culture that allows for effective collaboration with their male colleagues and that contributes to the women's success and ultimately the organization's success. The reason why the glass ceiling still exists has more to do with organizations not providing a welcoming environment for women than anything else. The natural way in which women's voices are expressed is not part of the model for success for women at the top—a model based primarily on the way men think, communicate, and act.

The standard explanation as to why women haven't advanced into the top ranks is often rationalized as work-life balance. And while many men cite this as the primary reason why women aren't progressing (and sometimes ultimately quit), it's not entirely their fault for making that assumption. Women perpetuate this myth by citing "personal" as their reason for not throwing their hat into the ring for a higher-level position or when submitting their resignation. To call out the real reason, they fear, might burn important bridges, damage their professional networks, and possibly eliminate the possibility of returning.

Men assuming women simply don't choose to pursue those top positions and women reinforcing that assumption has fostered our collective limiting belief that work-life balance explains the "woman problem" that continues to plague major corporations throughout the world. From our experience working with hundreds of companies attempting to solve these problems, both of these assumptions are incomplete. In fact, they're not even close. Yes, work-life balance is an issue for many women all over the world to varying degrees, dependent on support, means, country, and culture. But our research and experience show that work-life balance explains only a small part of what's really going on. The lion's share is the lack of a blended conversation at the top of the corporation and the inability to utilize the differences between the genders for the organization's collective advantage.

Contrary to popular belief, when women quit, most aren't completely opting out of the business world. Many leave to join up with the competition or start their own businesses, and in record numbers. Many people think that this is so they can have greater work-life balance, but this is rarely the case. Instead, they are seeking to be a part of—or create on their own—working environments that value their ideas and contribution and allow them greater self-expression. Women-owned businesses in the United States have been growing at twice the rate of all privately held firms since the 1990s. And the same seeds of self-determination have taken root in Latin America, Europe, and Asia as well. Worldwide, women now own or operate a third of all private businesses, and this percentage is growing at a faster rate than that of private businesses owned by men.[3]

So when we combine the limiting beliefs of gender sameness and diversity of numbers with the misinterpretation that women leave primarily for work-life balance reasons, we arrive at a place where organizations can't take advantage of the greater gender potential that lies in blending the best of what women and men can uniquely offer. Assumptions abound and a unique and powerful opportunity is lost.

Fortunately, a growing number of leaders and their organizations are forgoing this narrow focus and breaking these tired old patterns of thinking. They are uncovering the value of gender difference, not sameness; they are embracing diversity in thought, a more powerful and productive goal than numbers of men versus numbers of women. They are understanding the powerful business case to be made for this approach as the source of improved problem-solving, better decision-making, and greater productivity. They are realizing, for the first time, that the path to creating healthier, more effective, more balanced organizations is not just through the advancement of women, but by understanding, valuing, and blending the contributions of men and women together. They are growing in their Gender Intelligence.

We are at the crest of a paradigm shift in thinking—a tipping point in our understanding of the nature and direction of gender equality in the twenty-first century—and Gender Intelligence *is* the leading edge of that understanding.

What Is Gender Intelligence?

For decades, IQ was viewed as the sole measure of a person's intelligence. Society placed all its emphasis on educating people to improve their logical reasoning, math, spatial skills, use of analogies, and verbal skills.

What was puzzling, though, was that while IQ correlated with academic performance to some extent, it did not correlate nearly as expected

with professional success. While at the extremes, there was some relationship to success (at lower IQ levels, for example, people don't perform
as well), in the middle and higher levels, it did not predict professional
success at all. Clearly, there was some missing factor. There remained
those men and women with great IQ scores who were not achieving their
goals in life nor advancing in their careers. In some way, they seemed to
be thwarting their potential by thinking and behaving in ways that hin-
dered their chances to succeed.

Around thirty years ago, social scientists figured out what that missing
element might be in the success equation. Emotional Intelligence (EQ) is
a concept formulated by psychologists John D. Mayer and Peter Salovey
during the 1980s and made popular in 1995 with the groundbreaking
book *Emotional Intelligence*, by Daniel Goleman. Emotional Intelligence
describes the ability to perceive, assess, and manage the emotions of
one's self and of others. Although EQ went a long way in expanding our
idea of intelligence by adding in the emotional component, it didn't go
far enough in distinguishing the underlying characteristics by gender, including vital pieces like how we communicate, how we respond to social
cues in our environment, and how we respond to and manage stress.[4]

Enter Gender Intelligence, an idea we find to be an exciting expansion
of the complex conversation around predicting and maximizing potential,
not just in our interpersonal dealings, but at the team and organizational
levels as well. In the following chapters, we hope you will also begin to
see what this more complete and gender-balanced notion of intelligence,
one more revealing and inclusive of the differences between the genders,
can bring to our personal and organizational success.

At its core, Gender Intelligence is an understanding of and appreciation for the natural differences between men and women that goes
beyond the biological and cultural to include variations in brain structure
and chemistry that influence thoughts and actions. Gender Intelligence
is the awareness that gender differences are first informed by nature,
then influenced by family, education, culture, and environment.

Gender Intelligence doesn't come to a person by ignoring or tolerating
gender differences or to an organization by pursuing a quota. Nor does
Gender Intelligence require that men and women give up their authenticity in order to get ahead. A company doesn't become gender-intelligent
by simply enforcing diversity compliance policies, offering flexible work
programs, or creating women-only networks or interest groups.

Instead, Gender Intelligence comes from understanding and appreciating the unique talents and skills that men and women bring to the table and how their natural complement can improve the productivity, innovativeness, and economic growth of the organization. It teaches us that once we're aware of how and why men and women generally think and act as they do, we can begin to understand each other's natural tendencies as well as our own. We can begin to engage the other gender more effectively in the workplace and feel the effects ripple out to touch our personal lives as well.

As men and women come to understand each other's ways of thinking and acting, they step up to a new and powerful level of conversation. They stop tiptoeing around differences and are freed of their frustration. As they understand and appreciate each other's unique contribution, they begin to include each other more confidently and more willingly, and uncover the hidden value in their differences. This is where we begin to see the true transformational nature of Gender Intelligence. Not only are conflicts and miscommunication minimized, but women and men alike engage in a more open, expansive conversation that produces powerful results. Internal teams display enhanced problem-solving and decision-making skills as they fully utilize what each gender brings to the table. As Gender Intelligence infuses throughout the organization, turnover decreases, performance improves, and the company forges better connections within the marketplace.

In the time we've been advocating for Gender Intelligence and supporting Fortune 500 companies in their leadership and cultural transformations, we've witnessed the blind spots that are deeply ingrained in the minds of men and women and in the cultures of organizations alike. These perceptual obstructions delay and even prevent the transformation from gender sameness to gender-intelligent thinking. The good news is that the blind spots are easy to target and are fixable. Just being aware of them can start you on your own path toward Gender Intelligence.

Our Biggest Gender Blind Spots

Through survey results of more than 240,000 quantitative and qualitative statements collected from men and women leaders and managers across the globe over the past twenty-seven years, we've amassed a wealth of information about the differences in the thoughts and actions of men and women. From that data, we've identified a number of blind spots. Gender blind spots are the incorrect assumptions held by men and women that cause "accidents" of miscommunication and misunderstanding and help maintain the status quo in gender relations in companies around the globe. These blind spots are not only preventing men and women from working and succeeding together more effectively, but also tend to frustrate organizations seeking culture change, innovativeness, and financial growth.[5] Let's explore.

BLIND SPOT #1: THE BELIEF THAT EQUALITY MEANS SAMENESS

In conflict with our lived experiences, we've been indoctrinated by anti-bias programs and well-meaning gender equality efforts to believe that men and women should think and act the same way, engage the world and relationships the same way, and approach their careers in the same fashion and for the same reasons. This belief is supported by the deeper conviction that socialization is the primary determinant of our behavior. If it were not for the early and suppressive influence of parents, school, and culture, men and women would engage the world the same way. More than any other blind spot, this is the one that contributes most to our talking past each other and misreading one another's intentions. This is also the blind spot that leads us to make uneducated assumptions that may be completely off the mark about the meaning and motivations behind the behavior of others.

BLIND SPOT #2: THE MALE-DESIGNED ORGANIZATION

It's no coincidence that the model on which almost all businesses have been structured since the Industrial Revolution is defined by machine-like characteristics of speed, efficiency, and clear hierarchy—this model was designed by men for men. If the keys to success are order and efficiency, then what better management style to adopt to ensure that success than the hierarchical military model of command and control? In the modern age, men created an organized, competitive work environment that rewarded speed in decision-making, individual performance, and attainment of measurable goals. The automotive industry, following the industrious example of Henry Ford, is an excellent example of speed in production, efficiency in assembly, and reporting structure from the factory floor to the corporate office.

We've come a long way since the belching smokestacks of the Industrial Age, yet that same work model is still the dominant paradigm. Because it aligns well with the way men naturally think and behave, it makes it difficult for them to consider their workplace and their performance in it from any other perspective. A hardwired propensity in men to systemize motivates, aligns, and empowers them when there is a routine in place and there are rules governing that system.

Because so many in the workplace can't even see an alternative, they maintain the belief that this is the best paradigm—for now and in the future. Male-led companies don't question the blind spot because they simply don't recognize it. Supporting this paradigm is well over two hundred years of practice and refinement, making this male-designed model still considered by many as the most effective and efficient way of conducting business and leading and managing people.

While that may have proven true in the past, we exist now in a rapidly shifting global business environment where we can't afford to leave the talents of half the workforce unrealized. Unfortunately, the initiatives and systems we've put in place to better take advantage of women's talent are not accomplishing their goals. Instead, they make women the "problem" for not having made it to the top on their volition and capability.

BLIND SPOT #3: FIXING WOMEN TO THINK AND ACT LIKE MEN

Popular for decades, now more than ever there is an effort to get women to approach and engage in their careers by acting like men. When we conduct a diagnostic analysis of an organization, in almost all cases we discover that embedded within women's networks, in coaching sessions, even in university courses, are training programs designed to help women fit in instead of designed to bring out their own uniqueness and authenticity. This phenomenon started in the 1980s when a deluge of books and training programs emerged, designed to help women learn to "dress for success," manage their way to the top, and learn the keys to executive success. Almost always, they were being taught how the men play the game in corporate life. To this day, women coming into corporations have few options but to learn to adapt as best they can and not appear different, especially toward the top.

"Fixing" women perpetuates the belief that women's contributions and styles are inferior to those of men. Not only do the women feel disenfranchised and discouraged; because of this blind spot, there continues to be a huge opportunity lost for many organizations given the fundamental shift in business over the past forty years—the influx of women into the workforce and the growing influence of women in the marketplace. The forces behind this change—a global economy, new technologies, the power of the consumer, a focus on knowledge instead of industrial production, and the changing face and demands of a new workforce—are altering our standing beliefs about leadership, organizational structure, and business strategy and call for a new, multilayered, and more nuanced way of doing business that can connect better with the marketplace and operate more fluidly in a global environment. If we can stop fixing women and instead open both genders up to new possibilities and ways of being and doing, we can harness the full potential of all the talent we have at our disposal and compete and succeed in new ways in this changing business environment.

BLIND SPOT #4: ASSUMING THE OFF-PUTTING BEHAVIORS OF MEN ARE INTENTIONAL

Women in today's workplace often feel dismissed for their ideas and excluded from events and opportunities for advancement. They often state they have to work harder than men do just to prove themselves half as good, and often feel doubted for their competence and commitment.

Men, on the other hand, are generally comfortable in today's corporate culture. They assume and expect that women want to engage in work as men typically do—whether in prioritizing issues, solving problems, participating on teams, leading others, or making decisions. While the men we talk to don't feel they're acting intentionally against women, it's also true that in general they are not as aware of how their behavior affects women. Oftentimes, leaders have no idea why their senior women walk out the door. The majority of men are not trying to be dismissive or exclusionary. They're just doing what often feels right for the company and not really thinking about the effect their actions tend to have on women in the workplace. While in reality the men are not cognizant of the extent of the discomfort women feel when made to engage like men, there is still the perception by many women that men are aware of the effect—but simply don't care.

As an example, during meetings, men will be most inclined to zero in on a solution and settle on a quick decision, seemingly ignoring or dismissing questions or alternative ideas commonly raised by women on the team during meetings. They don't ignore because they want to be off-putting. Instead, they feel derailed by anything that isn't front and center, so they press on. The men are doing what comes naturally to them, yet women often feel excluded by men's tendency to strictly adhere to agendas and rush to decisions, and imagine it is intentional, even though it rarely is.

You can see why we consider these assumptions the biggest obstacle to women understanding men and men understanding how they're being received. If we assume the other gender has the same understanding, motivations, and meaning in their behavior that we do and they act in ways that are counterproductive or that inhibit our success, we'll feel taken off track, confused, slighted, dismissed, or angry.

The Confluence of Blind Spots

The presence of these four blind spots produces a set of symptoms that we repeatedly discover whenever we perform an organizational diagnostic, suggesting that there's a much larger phenomenon occurring caused by the confluence of these obstructions. The symptoms include:

- Women "quitting and staying." They're delivering good work but they no longer have the aspiration to advance.
- The creation of networks and training for women that are not necessarily gender-intelligent
- Leadership and management behaviors that are incongruent with the organization's policy and value statements
- Great initiatives embarked upon with a lot of commitment and passion that end up as window dressing
- Meaningful parts of the company—senior leadership or sectors like IT and sales—that remain predominantly occupied by men
- Women in senior management who are seldom in positions with P&L or line responsibility, but rather are in support sectors such as HR, diversity, and communications
- Senior women leaders often not wanting to make gender diversity a top priority, in order to avoid pushback

- More women than men leaving in many key roles
- Senior men seemingly unaware of the above phenomenon or explaining it away as just a symptom of women not being able to "cut it" in a difficult, competitive environment.
- Hiring and promoting practices that tend to unconsciously favor men
- Interviewing and assessing men and women based on sameness

That we see these over and over again prompts us to consider that they are more than just a set of problems. They are symptoms of something deeper. They are part of an underlying paradigm that is hard for leaders to see.

If we as leaders believe that the way we lead is intelligent, just, and wise, then when phenomena such as the above occur, we tend to write them off as anomalies, as irrelevant, or we have explanations that focus on the inability of the individual or group. In this way, a leader's beliefs become self-reinforcing of the current paradigm and in his or her style of leadership.

We believe, however, that the cause of the four blind spots and these consequential symptoms, which we will cover more fully in Chapter 11, is not an anomaly at all. It is the direct result of the presence of a sameness mindset that fails to see the wisdom and value of Gender Intelligence in leadership and organizational cultures. Developing that intelligence is the antidote that cannot be seen from the current paradigm, and it is this very same paradigm that our narrative is intending to break. It begins with recognizing and valuing our differences.

The Science That Underlies Our Differences

Researchers in neuroscience have made great strides in identifying gender differences in human brain anatomy, chemical processes, and functions. In fact, brain studies of more than a million participants in more than thirty countries over the past twenty years have shown conclusively how physiological differences in the male and female brain influence memory, emotion, hearing, and spatial orientation.[6]

The difference between men's and women's behavior has been discussed in relationship terms for some time. Too often the behavioral difference has been the only focus. While it's important to understand and

realize how men and women often communicate, solve problems, prioritize, make decisions, resolve conflicts, handle emotions, and deal with
stress differently, we can't stop there. We have to recognize that the differences have purpose, meaning, and value. The major reason our species
has been so successful for millions of years is directly due to our gender
differences—differences naturally designed to complement, not compete
with, the opposite gender. Instead of driving us apart, those differences
were made to help us work together—once in hunting and gathering and
now in the boardroom.

Too often, we think of socialization as taking primacy over biology.
Although nurture, training, and education shape the male and female
brain in important ways, hormones also play a critical role. Sex hormones
work on the embryonic brain and nervous system, causing the structure
or "wiring" to develop differently in males and females. This process
starts as early as the first trimester of pregnancy, and bears the ultimate
biochemical responsibility for producing our gender-related differences.

The way those differences play out most dramatically between the
sexes is in how they think. According to anthropologist Helen Fisher,
"Women tend to think contextually and holistically. They tend to think in
webs of factors, not straight lines." When women think, they collect more
information from their environment and arrange their thoughts into more
complex patterns. They see more relationships between different elements and weigh more variations before they make their decisions. Men,
on the other hand, "tend to focus on a particular issue, omit extraneous
data, and move in a more step-like fashion towards the goal," Fisher says,
and our experience bears this out.

What we find exciting is not how far apart these two ways of thinking
appear to be, but the possibility inherent in the difference. Instead of
thinking in a male way or in a female way, what if we were able to combine the two when making our most important business decisions? Fisher
says, "They're perfectly good ways of thinking, both of them," but perhaps
more important, *men and women were built to put their heads together,*
not only in their professional lives, but in their personal relations as well.
As the sexes come together to understand their different strengths, each
has the opportunity to gain priceless insight into the other's world; both
have the opportunity to achieve new empathy and rapport."[7]

When men and women understand the biological nature of their
gender differences, assumptions and misunderstanding are lessened and

their lenses broaden. They gain the opportunity for greater appreciation for each other's behavior, and actually learn more about their own, too. Starting with the science lifts us to a new level of conversation and encourages us to include and work with each other more productively.

For example, men are naturally inclined to get the problem solved by narrowing down and implementing solutions as quickly as possible in a most decisive and nonambiguous fashion. On the other hand, women instinctively collaborate, ensuring that all voices are heard and all options explored before making a decision.

The Advantages of Gender Intelligence

In the chapters to come, you will see how proactive and forward-thinking it is for an organization to trade in quotas and start down the road of Gender Intelligence. We're talking about a sea change—from the mindset and focus of the leaders to the corporate culture as a whole. Through our work, we've witnessed the powerful shift that occurs when an organization as a whole begins to behave more productively and effectively as a result of gender-intelligent leadership and systems. The functions, strategies, and processes begin to change to reflect more expansive thinking, which affects almost every single pore of the organization's being, influencing how it markets and sells its services or product, how functions relate to one another, how human resources are managed, how talent is accessed, hired, and leveraged, and how the top leads.

There are a number of highly successful organizations showing the way. They are instilling what we call a *culture of difference-thinking*, fueled by Gender Intelligence. These well-known companies are beacons for talented professionals. They're recruiting and retaining the best and brightest men and women across a number of industries and showing a record of proven success that previous methods were never able to achieve. Here you will learn about the journey taken by each of these organizations. Each had an "aha" moment or discovery that was the catalyst for them to make profound changes and invest in future success.

The Beginning of a New Conversation

This isn't just a book about increasing gender diversity in the workplace—leaders looking to succeed in the current organizational paradigm should look elsewhere for resources and support. This book is about fundamental change. We wrote it for leaders who want to lead in a gender-intelligent paradigm. It is a clarion call for difference thinkers in positions of power who have the ability and willingness to alter forever the culture of their organizations.

Gender Intelligence serves the needs of individuals who, unsatisfied with the status quo, are ready to break out of old patterns of behavior and awaken their organizations to what is possible.

2

The Science Behind
Our Gender Differences

Back in the late 1970s, a researcher sat slumped in his chair, running his hand through the rough stubble on his chin. He was stumped. He'd struggled along with his colleagues, trying to find the answer to a profound puzzle: why did male and female victims of stroke recover from the resulting speech impairment and loss of memory so differently? On average, men had a far more difficult time regaining their ability to talk and recall past events than did women.[8]

Researchers finally did arrive at what was then an isolated scientific breakthrough, but now appears to be so obvious as to cause us to wonder why they couldn't figure it out at the time. This revelation that the brains of men and women are clearly different proved a watershed moment in medical history. It prompted scientists and medical researchers across the globe to delve further into this side of brain science, opening the door to a broader exploration of brain-based gender differences in the decades that followed. Tremendous advances in imaging technology in the 1990s allowed brain research to go even further in what was deemed the "Decade of the Brain," a movement sponsored and funded by the Library of Congress and the National Institute of Mental Health.[9]

During that time, we crossed a critical threshold in our knowledge of human behavior, and the last few decades have brought a stunning evolution in our understanding of the hardwired differences between men's and women's brains and how those differences affect behavior. Before that time, scientists were in the dark, many discouraged from looking for those differences in the first place.

While technology was accelerating our ability to learn more and investigate the biological differences between the genders, the feminist movement was applying the brakes, demanding the opposite response. Rallying cries from women declared "we are equal," and women across the country were advocating for the same treatment as men. Although the movement had positive intent, it also had a suppressive effect on individuals and institutions attempting to conduct research into biological differences. There was a palpable fear of challenging the social call for gender blindness.

Moreover, the almost exclusive use of men as test subjects impeded progress in this area. Based on the standing belief that there were no gender differences aside from physical appearance and reproductive capability, many scientists assumed studying male brains and behavior would sufficiently explain physiological functions in both genders. Their motivation in using only male subjects was twofold. First, if the research being done included some chemical or pharmaceutical treatments, they didn't want to put potentially pregnant women at risk. While visibly pregnant women would not have volunteered to be part of the study, researchers were unwilling to risk the chance of including a test subject unknowingly in the earliest stages of pregnancy. The second reason had everything to do with differences between men and women. In general, women have more hormonal activity going on at any given time in their bodies, especially around their menstrual cycles. Researchers work by isolating variables, and adding in active hormones impeded their selection of independent variables unaffected by external factors. Because men's hormone activity is more constant, they made more reliable subjects.

Emblematic of the insights that many researchers have had recently, one of the leading medical researchers in neuroscience today talked about her own personal and professional evolution in understanding how biological differences matter. In 1990, Dr. Marianne J. Legato, professor of clinical medicine at Columbia University and founder of the Foundation for Gender-Specific Medicine, was asked by the American Heart Association to author a book on women and cardiovascular disease. "To the intense amusement of my colleagues now," she said, laughing, "my answer was 'Why? What's different about women's hearts compared with those of men?'" Legato did the research and was astonished to discover how differently men and women experience coronary artery disease. "Men's hearts are not only larger, they actually have a different protein composition than those of women," Legato says. "It occurred to me that if the hearts of men and women were so very different, perhaps there were differences in other body systems," and she embarked upon a research career that focused on exploring those differences.

Her conclusion? "Although nurture, training, and education importantly shape the male and female brain, there are differences that are hardwired in. And it is a confluence of our genes, whether we are XY or XX, and our hormones that cements that sense of ourselves as male or female into the brain." Legato admitted that she hadn't wanted her research to show what it did. In fact, at first she found proven biological differences between the male and female brain a somewhat troubling discovery. "But in the end there was no denying it," she said. "Gender differences stubbornly emerged like dandelions on a chemically treated lawn."

Research like Dr. Legato's, along with that of a slew of others, coupled with the technological advances in imaging of the last decades has produced an explosion in our knowledge of the differences between the brain structures and functions of men and women as well as deepened our understanding of the influence of hormones on human behavior.

The Science That Underlies Our Differences

Beginning in the early 1990s, neuroscientists across the globe began successfully and convincingly illuminating biological sex differences in brain structure, chemistry, and function. In study after study, findings have shown the variations that occur throughout the brain, informing and influencing the (at times) dramatically different ways men and women communicate, listen, solve problems, make decisions, handle emotions, deal with conflict, and manage stress.

But before we break down the differences in brain structure and chemistry that help dictate gendered behavior in order to more fully understand why men and women act the way we do, we want to put forward a disclaimer: When we speak of gender differences, we are describing a bell curve of gendered *tendencies*. This means there is a distribution of behavioral phenomena along a continuum, with a greater number of people exhibiting tendencies that fall toward the middle or norm. In lay-person's terms, if we organized all men on a continuum from factual to intuitive, more of them would fall toward the factual side of midpoint while the average for women would land closer toward intuitive.

If you place these two bell curves alongside each other, you'll notice a sizable difference between the *average* tendency of men and the *average* tendency of women. (Of course, you will also notice that there are a number of men who are intuitive in their orientation and many women who are factual.)

The typical bell-shaped curve pattern

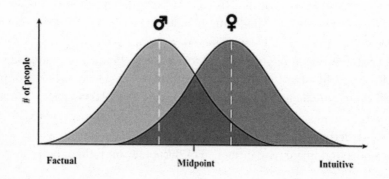

Given the distribution of human dynamics along this curve, it would be an inaccurate overgeneralization to claim that all men are one way and all women are another. After all, there is a lot of overlap on the graph. In fact, research suggests that about 20 percent—one in five—is hardwired more like the opposite gender.[10]

In the narrative below, what we are focusing on are the average tendencies of men and women, and it's what is revealed in those average tendencies that is so striking and meaningful. If it is the natural tendency of one group to be resolutely factual, then trying to shape that gender to behave more intuitively, more like the other, is really forcing people into being something they are not. Some women do make it to the top, to a large extent, because the male model authentically fits their bridge brain. However, a dominant number of women climb the ladder only to find that they don't fit the mold or couldn't if they tried. More than that, if we try to get them to fit the mold, it also means we are not taking advantage of the individual strengths the different approaches offer.

That is why we are interested in the science of gender differences. Rather than trying to force-fit what's not authentic, for men or women, using social and business norms or "shoulds" as a baseline, through science we can understand and focus on what's empirically evident about our differences and our similarities. That's the essence of Gender Intelligence.

Gender Differences in Brain Structure and Function

While there are many parts of the brain that reflect variations by gender, and a growing number emerging as science continues to make meaningful gender-based discoveries, in our work we find it valuable to concentrate on seven main areas of significance. The following areas of the brain are those where gender-based differences are most readily observed and lead to notable and predictable patterns in behavior.

CORPUS CALLOSUM

Let's begin with the rather formally named corpus callosum (Latin for "tough body"), a part of the brain that plays a very significant role in how we process information. As is now commonly known, the brain is divided into two hemispheres: the left brain, which is the source of linear, logical, and serial thinking; and the right brain, the basis of intuitive, holistic, and creative thought. The corpus callosum is a thick bundle of nerves connecting the right and left hemispheres of our brains.

Where men tend to use the different hemispheres of their brain sequentially, women tend to engage in right-brained and left-brained activities simultaneously. It may not surprise you, then, that the corpus callosum is larger on average in women's brains than in men's. It is also shaped differently and contains more nerve fibers that enable women to travel back and forth between the left and right sides of their brains more easily.[11]

Because of this, when a man is using logic to work through a problem, he is more likely to concentrate on one line of reasoning or see one idea through with fewer interruptions. He's also less likely to try to tackle the problem from alternative viewpoints, as that would require a literal shift to a creative mindset, or the right side of his brain. Think of the male brain as a train track, chugging along its linear pathway with a clear pathway and destination.

A woman, on the other hand, tends to engage in logical and creative thinking at the same time, thanks to the size and shape of her corpus callosum. Her logic flow doesn't necessarily impede her creativity. This can cause confusion in the business world. A woman can mentally jump to a parallel line of reasoning and jump back again within the confines of a single conversation or meeting, leaving a man to think, *She keeps changing the subject!* Though it seems off-topic to him, the woman keeps to a linear progression of thought while incorporating information of a more creative or intuitive nature. To her, it's all relevant.

If the male brain is a train track, then the female brain might be intersecting tracks, with switches that allow the train to reverse direction and take a different path, or even resemble a train able to use more than one track at a time. For men, trying to be as expeditious as possible, the insertion of more creative or emotional content into the conversation feels like a distraction. Women often get the response, "Can we just stick to the point, please?" with some anger. The woman responds by rolling her eyes, thinking, *You're totally missing the greater point.* And he is. On the other hand, women, in their multiplicity of functioning, might have trouble locating the central point. Men will find it immediately and latch on, not wanting to let go.

The size and shape of a woman's corpus callosum also enables her to decode the unspoken components of a meeting or exchange—such as body language, tone of voice, and facial expression—while at the same time staying engaged in the content of the meeting or discussion. As a result, women tend to engage in more contextual, weblike thinking than men. They often take in a broader, more inclusive perspective of situations and typically view the disparate elements of a problem or task as interconnected.

ANTERIOR CORTEX

As with the corpus callosum, women typically have a larger anterior cortex than do men, a difference to which many scientists attribute women's superior ability to integrate and arrange memories and emotions into more complex patterns of thought. As a result, women tend to weigh more variables, consider more options, and visualize a wider array of solutions and outcomes to a problem than do their male counterparts. The anterior cortex plays a role in a wide variety of unconscious functions, such as regulating blood pressure and heart rate. It also helps govern rational cognitive functions such as anticipation, decision-making, empathy, and emotion. As a result, women tend to reflect (ruminate) and feel and express concerns more often and in a deeper contextual setting than men.[12]

Brain scan studies indicate that the female brain has larger areas of sensitivity to track gut instincts—specifically through the anterior cortex. For this reason, many scientists have concluded that the famous "women's intuition" is real and actually grounded in biology. By possessing a larger anterior cortex, the female brain is designed to quickly assess the thoughts, beliefs, and intentions of others based on even the smallest hints, intuitive gut feelings, and hunches.

While a larger anterior cortex can help women play the hunch more accurately than men, it can also translate into increased anxiety. The anterior cortex is also known as the "worrywart" center of the brain, and research demonstrates that anxiety is more common in women than in men. So while evolution prompted women to be more cautious and collaborative so that they could protect their young, in today's business world the same caution is often interpreted as a lack of confidence or a reticence to take risks. The fairer evaluation is that those risks simply tend to be more calculated in women than in men, who often feel less apprehension about the outcome of risk-taking behavior.[13] As in all differences, there are trade-offs. While men may more readily take risks, they sometimes jump with blinders on. While women may be more risk averse, their more cautious approach also takes into account a wider set of variables that may be crucial to a given decision.

INSULAR CORTEX

The role of the insular cortex (often called the insula), found within each hemisphere of the brain, is very complex, influencing our emotional response to our surroundings, helping us control our heart beat and blood pressure, affecting basic functions like swallowing and speech, and even governing our very consciousness and sense of self. The insular cortex regulates our experience of pain as well as warmth and coldness, and guides our responses to external stimuli, producing feelings such as disgust or empathy.

The insular cortex is, on average, twice as large in the female brain as in the male brain, helping women translate physical sensations and thoughts in the subconscious mind into conscious thoughts that are in turn often richly colored by memories and emotions. The insular cortex enables women to draw on past memories and learn from them, preventing women from acting hastily and taking unnecessary risks.[14] Working together with the anterior cortex and the corpus callosum, the insular cortex also tends to heighten women's perception and intuition, making women far more sensitive than men to the feelings and mood of people and events around them.

HIPPOCAMPUS

Similar in some functions to the insula, the hippocampus serves as the center for memory and emotion, and is both larger and far more active in women.[15] This tends to explain why women are usually better at expressing emotions as well as at recalling intricate details from the past. The larger and more active hippocampus explains why women benefit so much from talking through their problems; women's brains are wired in such a way that they can access and freely express their emotions, all of which helps women cope and deal with stress.

Possessing a larger hippocampus also enables women to be more effective at processing and coding emotional experiences into their long-term memory. As a result, women tend to have richer, more intense memories of emotional events than do men and are able to recall and link to past events more readily. This is a difference played out across the globe daily. Picture a couple married ten years, sitting together. "Do you remember the time when . . . ," she asks him, recalling a hike they took three years before. He replies he does not and she sighs, interpreting his lack of memory as a sign that he does not love her, or love her enough to care. Or she points out something troubling that happened in the beginning of their marriage and he says, "Why can't you just leave it alone!"

In the business world, that rich connection to past emotional memories can prove useful to women in decision-making. However, that same connection can also manifest in a negative manner by making women more hesitant in their decision-making process. Men, unencumbered by that storehouse of lived emotional experience, tend to move forward more boldly. This can translate into their taking greater risk in crisis situations or in highly competitive environments, such as being first to market where there is no evidence that the product will be successful.

AMYGDALA

One of the most elemental parts of the brain, the amygdala is located in the limbic system and is best known for governing our "flight or fight" response to fear, danger, or stress. The limbic system is the general region of the brain where there is a high degree of hormonal activity. Given that hormones secrete chemicals that affect our emotions, the limbic system is often referred to as the emotional center of our brains.

Influenced by hormones, the amygdala processes fear, triggers aggression and action, and stimulates competitiveness. It alerts us to danger and switches on the rest of the body, preparing us to deal appropriately with the situation. Unlike the last three parts of the brain we have looked at, the amygdala is larger and more active in men's brains than in women's. Moreover, because of hormonal differences, men and women also tend to respond differently to fear signals coming from the amygdala.[16]

When the amygdala fires a fear signal, the "fight or flight" reaction is triggered in both men and women. What we have now learned, however, is that in men, the amygdala has a greater number of testosterone receptors that heighten responses, and direct neural connections to other areas in the brain allow men to respond rapidly to sensory input, focus on external factors, and take immediate action.

As a result of their larger amygdala, men react more quickly than women to stressful stimuli. They tend to stay present and concentrate on the situation at hand rather than recalling past events and making emotional connections to help guide their responses.

PREFRONTAL CORTEX

If it seems that girls mature faster than boys, it is because it is true. The prefrontal cortex—the part of our brains that controls judgment, decision-making, and consequential thinking—is not only larger in women than in men but also develops earlier in girls than in boys.[17]

To use a business metaphor we all understand, the most common psychological term for duties carried out by the prefrontal cortex area is "executive function." Executive function relates to the ability to differentiate among conflicting thoughts and make determinations between good and bad, better and best, and same and different. The prefrontal cortex is also the source of enhanced consequential thinking in women, including the prediction of outcomes and expectations related to a given action.

As the judgment center of the brain, the prefrontal cortex also moderates and controls social behavior by acting as the brake on the more reflexive amygdala. The underlying differences between the structure and size of the amygdala and the prefrontal cortex are one of the reasons young boys tend to be more exploratory, more mischievous, and often, more careless than young girls—a tendency in males that can continue well into their adult lives. As adults, these differences can affect the way different genders respond to conflict, one of the most common modern-day stressors.

Having more perceptive and judicious executive function related to a larger prefrontal cortex, combined with less testosterone and more estrogen flowing through their brains, biologically steers women toward win-win solutions to conflict. The differences are also reflected in the ways women and men approach negotiations or handle customers. Women tend to look for ways to compromise and serve the needs of others, even at their own expense. Men, on the other hand, tend to look for ways to come out on top, sometimes even in competition with their own clients.[18]

CEREBELLUM

Finally, the cerebellum (Latin for "little brain") is a region of the brain that plays an important role in motor control. It may also be involved in cognitive functions such as attention and language and in regulating fear and pleasure responses. The cerebellum doesn't initiate movement, but it contributes to coordination, precision, and accurate timing. It receives input from sensory systems of the spinal cord and from other parts of the brain, and integrates these inputs to fine-tune motor activity.[19]

As we noted earlier, the amygdala is larger in men than in women. It also has direct neural connections to other response areas in the brain—primarily, the cerebellum and its regulation of motor control. Working together, the structure of the amygdala and the cerebellum in men allow them to respond rapidly to sensory input, focus on external factors, and take immediate action with greater physical coordination, confidence, and comfort. In addition to aiding men's reaction time and fluidity, the greater size of the cerebellum in men influences them to communicate more nonverbally than women, with more emphasis on movement and physicality than on words.[20]

Though the actual function of the cerebellum is not significantly different between the genders, its influence and the interplay between this structure and the amygdala can be seen as early as childhood, with boys testing and pushing the limits of their physical abilities earlier and more often than girls.

Hormonal Differences and Their Influence

Just as variations in brain structure help explain our behavioral tendencies, the roles of certain hormones help explain gender differences, especially in how men and women deal with stress. Contrary to popular perception, there are no hormones that are specific to men or specific to women. Men and women produce all the same hormones; we just produce different amounts, and it's the difference in those levels that produces distinct effects in each gender. When you couple the differences in brain structure and function with varying hormonal levels, difference-thinking between women and men becomes even more accentuated, especially in relation to three key hormones: testosterone, oxytocin, and cortisol.

TESTOSTERONE
Testosterone, the principal male sex hormone, is one of the key elements in determining the sexual characteristics in men, including physical strength, body shape, and deeper voice, as well as sexual drive. Women also produce testosterone, though men typically produce twenty to thirty times more than women do. Overall, testosterone gets a bad rap; it is not simply the fuel for aggressive behavior. It also plays an important role in men's drive, competitiveness, creativity, intellect, and in their ability to develop and execute new ideas. More than anything, having the

right level of testosterone is essential to help men cope appropriately with stress.[21]

Normal levels of testosterone are linked to feelings of success in men. When a man experiences difficulty or failure, his testosterone levels will begin to drop and he'll experience lowered spirits or feel depressed until his levels are replenished. This dynamic also underlies the reason men will often seem to ignore a difficult problem; the waiting period gives them time to rebuild their testosterone levels, and gain the mental strength and drive to tackle the issue.

Though women produce testosterone, the hormone does not function in the same stress-reducing manner as for men. For women, oxytocin is the drug of choice.

OXYTOCIN

Also known as the social attachment hormone, oxytocin is produced in great quantities in women during childbirth and in both women and men during orgasm. The hormone affects social recognition and bonding as well as the formation of trust between people.

While oxytocin works to lower stress levels in women, in men too much oxytocin can actually reduce testosterone levels, thereby increasing their stress. Alternately, too much testosterone in women reduces the effectiveness with which oxytocin functions in their bodies.[22]

In women, oxytocin levels can rise during a relaxing conversation and fall in response to feeling ignored or abandoned. Oxytocin also reduces blood pressure, feelings of fear, and levels of cortisol—a hormone produced by the adrenal glands in both men and women.

CORTISOL

Cortisol plays an important function in the body, involved in glucose metabolism, the regulation of blood pressure, blood sugar maintenance, and the functioning of the immune system. While cortisol is a natural and helpful part of the body's response to stress, higher and prolonged levels of cortisol in the bloodstream can have negative effects. Physical effects include an increase in blood pressure, high blood sugar levels, and even more fat around the belly. Too much cortisol can also lead to impaired cognitive performance or an inability to think clearly.[23]

When cortisol rushes through a woman's bloodstream during a stressful situation, oxytocin is released from the brain. The oxytocin counteracts the production of cortisol and promotes relaxing emotions and a nurturing response.

While cortisol is an important and helpful trigger for the body's response to stress, it's equally important that following a stressful event—whether it's an actual scare or a bad day at the office—the body's relaxation response be activated so the body's functions can return to normal. Unfortunately, in our high-stress culture, the body's stress response is activated so often that our metabolism doesn't always have a chance to normalize, resulting in a state of chronic stress and anxiety in both women and men.[24]

In women, oxytocin-producing activities work to lower cortisol levels and reduce stress. But when a woman is not able to engage in satisfying collaborative activities at work, or there's not enough time to attend to her nurturing relationships, her stress and anxiety will increase beyond her ability to produce a relaxation response. That unresolved increase in stress brought on by the rush of cortisol stimulates the production of testosterone in her system and inhibits the secretion of oxytocin, perpetuating the cycle.

Elevated cortisol levels can have a debilitating effect on men as well, depleting their testosterone levels and increasing their blood pressure, anxiety, irritability, and fatigue, as well as causing weight gain. However, studies have shown that women pay the price in modern society. Women's cortisol levels at work tend to be twice as high as men's, and at home, their levels are four times higher—a demonstration of the need for greater work-life harmony.[25]

Continued Research

Today, research on brain differences continues to accelerate in a profound way and help illuminate our differing motivations and behaviors. That men and women are more alike than different has been the consensus view for many years among the researchers who study personality differences between the sexes. But a new study claims this perspective is wrong. The research, conducted by Marco Del Giudice of Italy's University of Turin and Paul Irwing and Tom Booth of England's University of

Manchester, involved ten thousand men and women taking a question-
naire that measured fifteen different personality traits.

According to their analysis, men are far more dominant, reserved, util-
itarian, vigilant, rule-conscious, and emotionally stable, while women are
far more deferential, warm, trusting, sensitive, and emotionally "reactive."
The differences the study shows are staggering when compared with the
consensus view that we are by and large the same. Moreover, there is
surprisingly little overlap between the two genders. Depending on which
measure is used, the study indicates there is only 10–24 percent overlap
in the average personality traits of men versus women (much like the
overlap depicted in the figure on page 20). This overlap reveals the phenomenon of androgyny, which is, from a personality viewpoint, a rather
rare occurrence and perhaps not the ideal that many suggested in the
1960s, during the early phases of the feminist movement at the time.

In a soon-to-be-released report on the largest brain imaging study ever
conducted comparing male and female brains, Dr. Daniel Amen and his
team analyzed imaging scans of 26,000 test subjects. They discovered
that women showed increased blood flow in 112 of the 128 brain regions
they studied, indicating that overall, women's brains are much more
active than men's. However, men's brains showed greater activity in targeted regions associated with visual perception, tracking objects through
space, and form recognition.

Ruben Gur, professor of psychology and director of the Brain Behavior
Laboratory at the University of Pennsylvania, along with his associates,
recently released preliminary findings on research involving young boys
and girls in which the team studied gender differences in the early development of the prefrontal cortex.

Continued breakthroughs in the brain sciences that highlight meaningful differences are cropping up all over the world. They portend a sea
change in our understanding of gender and the brain. More important,
the implications are vast and varied, from how we educate boys and girls
to how we raise sons and daughters to romantic relationships and—most
important for our narrative—how we work together. It is to the last subject that we now turn.

3

Brain Science
at Work

ven in the face of so much scientific evidence amassed over the past
thirty-odd years, there are many who continue to grasp firmly to the
belief that, aside from physical appearance, strength, and reproductive capabilities, men and women are not biologically all that different.

This camp maintains that the gender differences in attitudes and behaviors are purely the result of socialization. They argue that the relega-
tion of women to caregiving and nurturing roles in our male-dominated
society has resulted in these prescriptive behaviors and explains the differences we see. We take issue with this line of thinking not only because we find the science self-evident and persuasive, but also because
we dismiss the idea that difference necessarily means that one gendered
style is necessarily weaker or inferior.

Because value is ascribed to both styles, Gender Intelligence views
gender differences as a source of strength, not weakness. It's an understanding that both nature and nurture play a significant role in a person's
life and an admission that the extent to which our differences are informed by our biology or by family, education, and culture is not a question easily answered. There is no general formula that can be applied to
everyone equally; instead, the balance of biology and social influence is
unique to every individual and situation.

To continue to believe that gender differences all stem from social influence is to deny our basic natures. When we maintain the opinion that men and women are the same on the inside, we make assumptions about how easy it should be for the other gender to think and act the same and we undervalue the differences when they show up.

The key element of being a gender-intelligent manager or leader is understanding how these gender differences manifest so that we do not misinterpret them when they arise in the workplace. The ultimate goal is to use this knowledge to be more effective and successful with each other in our work lives as well as in our personal lives, increasing communication and reducing stress.

Now that we understand the underlying differences in our structural and chemical makeup, let's explore how we can leverage this understanding when we're engaged with the other gender in solving problems, making decisions, and resolving conflicts.

Problem-Solving

Working in a professional environment has no shortage of issues for both men and women. Turf wars with coworkers, difficult clients, and seemingly impossible deadlines present ongoing challenges on a daily basis. Through the course of a normal workday, we work to recognize these problems as they arise, explore and identify their causes, and take action to solve them. While problem-solving is common, deciding what course of action to take often comes down to which voices get heard.

When the pressure is on and stress levels are high, we often find that it's the dominant, male voice and style that leads and controls the conversation. Most men tend to be very comfortable with jumping right in to solve an issue; as we've learned, it's in their wiring to do so. Add in time constraints and pressure to find a solution, and men and women alike default to a model of success based on speed and narrowed focus.

There's strength and value in the male approach, but that style also doesn't allow for other voices and ideas, especially women's. By blending our natural instincts to address something as common as the task of problem-solving, the complement of our differences can significantly improve how we work through issues and find *better*, not just faster, solutions.

Social scientists talk about there being four phases to a typical problem-solving process: problem definition, causal analysis, searching for solutions, and choosing solutions.

Define Problem	Identify Causes	Identify Solutions	Decide
1	2	3	4

In the problem-solving sequence, gender differences often show up first in defining the problem. Men tend to define problems and isolate issues by zeroing in right away. There are certainly advantages in narrowing the problem as quickly as possible; on the other hand, that fast-paced approach is necessarily limiting in scope, which by its very nature often excludes the contribution of women.

Because women tend to see issues in a broader context, they typically identify more opportunities for change and offer a richer field of solutions. There's value in that approach as well, but the broader scope and longer time frame for defining and solving the problem tend to frustrate men.

What matters most is context. When it comes to defining the problem, there are times when limiting and focusing are appropriate, and other times when expanding the field is required to really get to the root of the matter. The wisdom is in knowing when and how to blend both tendencies instead of being hemmed in by the limiting belief that one model of thinking is inherently superior.

During the next two phases, people engage in either *convergent thinking*, which brings an exploration into sharper focus, toward a shared understanding or decision, or *divergent thinking*, where many more possible causes and solutions are considered. We believe borrowing from the differing tendencies of both men and women is crucial in order to arrive at the best possible field of solutions from which a final decision can be made.

In the graph on page 34, you can see how divergent and convergent thinking are relevant for each of the next two phases.

Classic problem-solving process

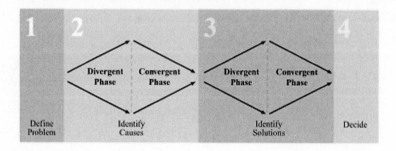

In phase 2, divergent thinking is needed to keep exploring an expanding field of causes, and then convergent thinking is needed to eventually narrow the landscape down to the key issues. The same is true in phase 3.

As we've seen, it's common for women to want to include more possibilities and to explore more options. It is so natural and comfortable that if we only had women in the room, they would often collectively tend toward divergent thinking and it would most likely take a longer time to explore the causes and decide on a solution.

Too much divergence yields lost time

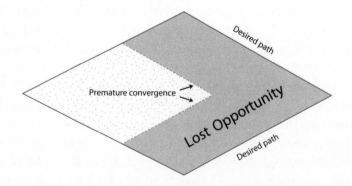

On the other hand, convergent thinking—a style that typically emphasizes speed, accuracy, and focus—is a particular strength of men. Because it centers on coming up with a single, well-established answer to a problem, it leaves no room for ambiguity. This contrasts directly with divergent thinking, where judgment is often suspended while one is sifting through many possible solutions. In their quest for speed and focus, if left alone, men would likely focus too quickly and thereby leave out less obvious options—potentially meaningful ones.

Too rapid convergence yields lost opportunity

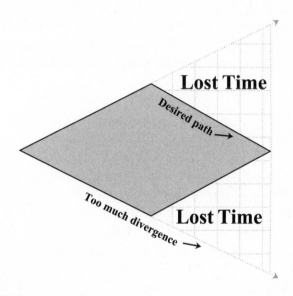

Utilizing only one type of thinking leads to a loss in creativity, potential solutions, and sometimes necessary speed.

The financial markets are a perfect example of the dominant male voice in defining problems and finding solutions. From the beginning, the financial world has been one of male-influenced, aggressive, no-holds-barred competition, with mixed results. All-male teams converging on a problem to find the single best solution has yielded great profits as well as disastrous consequences. Influenced by their high-risk, action-driven approach, they can also make significant mistakes, their single focus blinding them to possible consequence. To our knowledge, at the time of the stock market crash in 2008, none of the leading Wall Street banks had a single woman in a senior executive position reporting to the CEO with profit-and-loss responsibility.

As we saw in the beginning of the chapter, women are different from men in how they trade off risk and opportunity. The fact that women take in and process more information, ask more questions, and worry more about details can sometimes slow down the decision-making process. This tack may seem strategically off to men who value processing information quickly, tend to ask fewer questions, and worry less about details than about moving forward.

By blending both styles of thinking—viewing more solutions and taking more calculated risks—financial markets, we believe, stand a better chance of smoothing out the unsustainable bubbles and precipitous crashes of that economic roller-coaster ride—prolonging the booms and minimizing the busts.

How Gender Affects the Decision-Making Process

Not too long ago, we conducted a Gender Intelligence workshop with a senior leadership team responsible for global innovation and marketing. As part of the session, we asked both men and women in the workshop to describe the biggest difficulties they have working with members of the opposite gender. One of the senior women spoke up first, expressing a deep-felt frustration shared by the other women in the group that got right to the heart of the issue for everyone in the room. "When it comes to making decisions," she said, "they don't think things through. They just react, react, react!"

The top executive in the room, who happened to be male, quickly retorted, "That's our job. We're supposed to be efficient in narrowing down our options in order to make the best decisions."

"No," the woman disagreed, "our job is to be *effective*."

"But that's the most efficient way of being effective! Otherwise, we'll never get to a decision and assign resources. We don't have time to just reflect, reflect, reflect! We have to react quickly."

In the normal workplace environment, this is where the conversation might have ended. It's so ingrained in American culture that efficacy is equal to efficiency, that different ways of doing and being aren't often considered. In this case, the workshop offered a space to talk through the differences. Undeterred, the woman pressed on. "It's not just about think-ing and reacting faster; it's about thinking better and reacting appropri-ately. Let me give you an example. Recently, there were four projects that you guys—and it was just you men in that meeting that day—decided to kill. We had all been developing those programs for weeks. I still have no idea why you decided to shelve them. If we could have kept going I think they could have been successful." At this, the other women on her team nodded vigorously in agreement.

As the workshop progressed, and as we walked through the brain science research we discussed at the beginning of the chapter, the top executive and other men in the room linked back to what their team member had said about reacting too quickly and limiting the field of options. They real-ized they were "very male" in their approach, especially in assessing the four projects they had terminated. The male leader not only had a huge "aha!" moment that afternoon, but expressed an amazing turnaround in his think-ing that demonstrates the power and potential of Gender Intelligence.

"Let's put a test to what we learned today . . . what I learned today," he clarified. "Let's resurrect those four projects and look at them together to see if there was something we missed." They did, and three of those projects ended up being huge successes for the company.

Just as in the above example, men and women often find themselves polarized in the workplace, divided by their differences in decision-making styles. It's a natural and highly valuable inclination on the part of men to narrow down solutions and attempt to implement solutions as quickly as possible. It gets the problem solved. Conversely, it's a powerful instinct on the part of women to collaborate, to see to it that all voices are heard in order to get all the ideas out on the table before making a decision. This process allows space for the more innovative approach or a more creative or longer-term solution.

The challenge is that the male style, though powerful in its own right, doesn't incorporate the balanced perspective women often bring to the table. It's almost as if there's a fear that divergent thinking might hinder progress, or that the best conclusion might not be reached if more options are first considered. On the other hand, the more female style doesn't in-corporate the targeted focus. Decisions can stall out, held back by a fear not everything is being considered and not everyone is being heard when making decisions.

A BLENDED MODEL

In order to create a new model that takes the best from each approach, the classic business problem-solving process must be revamped. The classic model itself is highly linear and thus may prove suboptimal for solving highly complex and uncertain problems. We are buoyed by the many researchers and practitioners of creativity and problem-solving who are finding alternatives to the linear, male-designed approach. Instead, they allow for expanded thinking and ways of seeing, grounded in more of a blend of male and female styles. The Theory U system of problem-solving is one such emerging system. Developed by Otto Scharmer, a thought leader in the field of organizational behavior, and others, it advocates a more balanced problem-solving approach, which involves five phases:[26]

1. **Co-initiating**, during which a common intention is developed;
2. **Co-sensing**, during which participants open their hearts and minds and from this expanded place begin to identify causes and patterns in the causes;
3. **Presencing**, during which participants go into a place of silence to allow deeper, inner knowing and intuition to emerge;
4. **Co-creating**, during which expanded and deeper solutions are explored;
5. **Co-evolving**, during which participants see and take action from a more holistic perspective.

The "U" process

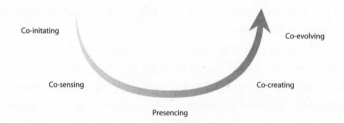

As many emerging problem-solving processes do, Theory U places a high value not just on the active thought process, but also on the "being"

states needed to identify breakthrough solutions to knotty problems. This is the more seemingly passive but highly creative time necessary for truly innovative thinking.

This and other similar methods are paving a way for a new and exciting blended male/female approach that better fits today's global business environment and takes our underlying differences into account.

One of the greatest contemporary examples of the value of bringing together the efficiency and effectiveness of the male and female points of view is found in IKEA, the international home products corporation known as much for affordable furniture with simple lines as for the iconic pictographs that stand in for assembly instructions.

Founded in 1943, IKEA developed a very successful business concept based on teenage founder Ingvar Kamprad's vision of efficiency in warehousing and shipping furniture.

For decades the company sold furniture exclusively from catalogs. After placing their orders, customers would receive flat boxes efficiently filled with unassembled furniture along with detailed instructions on how to assemble their new bookcase or table. That was how IKEA did it for close to fifty years, and it worked.

In 1985, the first U.S. store opened in Philadelphia, Pennsylvania. Female executives at IKEA headquarters in Leiden, Netherlands, wanted to create a unique experience for their new market. Statistics showed that women in the United States made 90 percent of the purchasing decisions for furniture, and American women were not inclined to part with their cash based on nothing more than a picture in a catalog.

The IKEA execs felt that shoppers should be able to experience what the furniture would look like when completely assembled—whether in a living room, kitchen, bedroom, or child's room. IKEA decided to create showrooms in the United States and other countries, creating a "what would it look like if I lived there" perspective. Homey touches were added, including wall art, pillows, and toys. The approach was particularly appealing to women, who were, at the time, and still are, the larger percentage of buyers. Sales skyrocketed and today, because of this change, IKEA is the largest furniture retailer in the world.

As it turns out, men love the showroom idea as well—for different reasons. It's far easier to follow assembly directions and determine the amount of space needed for the furniture item after having seen the fully assembled product in the showroom.

IKEA is the perfect example of packaged efficiency created by men combined with the added outside-the-box experience conceived by women looking to improve on an already great concept. This is Gender Intelligence in action—men and women bridging efficiency and effectiveness to create a better product, resulting in true innovation and increased market share.

Conflict Resolution, the Blame Game, and Finding Resolution

Just as with problem-solving and decision-making, men and women tend to deal with conflict and conflict resolution differently. (If you have a significant other of a different gender, you probably don't need us to tell you that.) Going back to the science of the brain, we now understand that how we deal with conflict is very much instinctual. The stress associated with conflict only enhances each gender's natural, and in many ways, unconscious manner of dealing with conflict as our bodies strive to reduce stress and find balance.

Remembering women's enhanced abilities to ascribe emotional significance and recall past emotional events, we shouldn't be surprised that women's first reaction to conflict is to personalize the situation and ask themselves, "What have I done wrong?" While that is going on internally, they will seem relatively calm and collected in their initial reaction. In the face of conflict, many women hold back their response while they try to make sense of the situation. They do this by gathering information, often in the form of listening attentively to others. Tapping in to the emotional side of their brain and effectively processing and coding emotional experiences, they'll work on their reaction to conflict internally—even if only briefly—before they respond.

While women tend to personalize and turn inward, men typically externalize the issue, instinctively and instantly looking outside to someone or something else at which they can direct blame, irritation, or anger. Minor issues often elicit a physical reaction as an immediate response, from raising their voice to slamming their hand on a table. If an issue is overwhelming, men will often mentally (and initially physically) remove themselves from the issue to think it through on their own. There are several reasons why, including not wanting to react with anger or out of concern their reaction may be too strong. During this time, unlike women, men are unable to process information coming in from others. Instead of listening, they are engaged in an internal thought process. While women might interpret the men's behavior as tuning out or being dismissive or avoidant, in reality the men need time to think it through and will often come back when they are ready to move forward.

If we think about how our bodies are hardwired to respond, we realize that these different reactions are mostly about reducing stress. Women's natural reaction is to internalize and take it personally, that is, they'll *tend* to and *befriend* those close to them, to protect existing relationships and gain greater understanding. Men's natural reaction is to externalize and immediately process or *fight* the issue or engage in *flight* by completely ignoring the problem in the moment and coming back to deal with it later.

The different ways in which women and men react initially to conflict informs and influences the way in which they attempt to resolve the issue. Men tend to get competitive and often take a win-lose position while women instinctively strive for the win-win. Couple that difference with the tendency for women to want to talk through conflict and with men's preference to think through problems on their own in isolation and it's no wonder that conflict in the workplace only widens the divide between genders.

If we broaden our view of what constitutes conflict in the work environment, we see that these tendencies color everything from contract negotiations to engaging with customers. Women tend to look for collaborative solutions and ways to compromise and serve the needs of others, even at their own professional expense.

For women, addressing conflict is primarily about building alliances. That's a key reason women tend to approach a conflict by treating it as an opportunity—a chance to clear the air, to build rapport, and to get closer in the relationship. Women assume, from the start, that the way to solve a conflict is through conciliation. "Winning" is not usually the real point.

Men, on the other hand, tend to address conflict by staking out a position—treating interpersonal conflict in much the same way as a negotiation. Unlike women, men tend to depersonalize and detach themselves from the conflict from the onset and, whether they win or lose, to let go of all the feelings once the conflict is resolved. At times, it amazes women how men can argue vehemently and at times violently with each other, only to continue on as if nothing happened when the argument is done. For women, the relationship would have lasting impacts from a similar altercation.

In blending styles, this latter ability to let go of the charged emotion is an important skill women can learn from men: exercise the muscle that lets it go. Even when the conflict is resolved, whether win-win or win-lose, it tends not to be *really* resolved for women who, prompted by their internal wiring, will replay and ruminate about past conflicts. One of the biggest "aha!" moments for women we work with tends to come from learning to be more rigorous in their practice of what we call "exquisite self-care," in part by learning to let go of conflict once it is resolved, especially in the case of a win-win outcome.

Whether in problem-solving, decision-making, or conflict resolution, what we see in each instance is the value in knowing the limitations of one pattern of thinking. Making the proper choice according to context is the height of business intelligence. True wisdom and leadership lie in knowing what style is called for and in what times.

In the 1970s, IBM launched a memorable television commercial with the theme "Great Minds Think Alike." The ad depicted men in identical blue suits, with white shirts and red ties, all sitting together in a conference room. This advertising campaign was paraded with pride—the success model for organizations, the ad suggested, lay in thinking the same way. Because IBM was a dominant leader in business at the time, many companies looked to emulate IBM's marketplace success.

Of course, fast-forward from that moment and we see that IBM's success hit a plateau in the late 1980s. When Lou Gerstner became CEO in 1993, he pivoted away from those blue suits in mental lockstep and the company's theme was turned on its head: "Great Minds Think *Un*Alike." The changes at IBM mirror the shift in business thinking that was reinforced by the realization that we are indeed hardwired differently.

Nonetheless, as far as we've come, "thinking alike" is still the reflexive mindset of many leaders and organizations today, primarily because the male-dominant work model still characterizes so many of the elements and style of today's workplace environment. It ensures speed in problem-solving and decision-making and tends to downplay subjective experiences and values as well as the nonmeasurable dimensions of emotions, relationships, and individual creativity.

It is no accident that the status quo aligns so well with the way men are hardwired to think—efficiently, sequentially, and with singular focus.

"Great minds think *unalike*" is a meaningful departure from that old standard in order to bring attention to the value of "difference-thinking"—a key feature of the gender-intelligent organization. Uniformity in thought may have been a point of strength in the past, but not so much in the last forty years or so, not in today's complex world, and not in tomorrow's. Thinking unalike is and will be the more successful approach to problem-solving and decision-making.

So, what makes great minds think unalike? Well, it's the nature of men and women to think differently. It has been and will always be the best piece of equipment we have in our human survival toolbox. The key is learning how to make that difference work for us today.

Strength Through Difference

We've realized so much progress through the mechanistic, driven, competitive male mind—there's no doubt about it. However, now the question is, what could the world look like if we took the best of both styles, blending men's and women's unique and highly complementary minds?

By rooting this question firmly in the empirical findings of brain science research, we can begin a truly transformational conversation that ends the blame game for good. Our goal is that men and women alike will begin to recognize, value, and include these differences and begin to listen to one another in a more generous and appreciative way.

To appreciate and value difference creates an indelible shift in our attitudes and behaviors—a remarkable change that we've experienced firsthand. By sharing the science behind our gender differences in our practice over the past twenty-seven years, we have helped countless men and women around the world learn to relate with one another, and not just as business colleagues. This awareness and valuing of our hardwired differences has also helped us improve our patience and understanding as couples, and in our efforts as parents, looking to raise sons and daughters to become authentic men and women.

Understanding that our differences are complementary strengths and not offsetting weaknesses goes a long way to ending misunderstanding and miscommunication. That's the intellectual and emotional transformation we need to embrace and commit to making an enduring part of our leadership of self and others.

4

Breakthrough Insights That Are Transforming Companies

W e had this *exact* conversation ten years ago!" one leader told us, holding his head in both hands. The CEO of one of the largest financial services companies in the world was clearly frustrated. Despite the company trying multiple initiatives in an effort to become more gender diverse, nothing—neither the conversations they were having in the executive conference room that day nor the presence of women in their top ranks—had changed. His emotion was in earnest. He had wanted his company to be more gender diverse back then and was still looking to increase the numbers of women at the executive level. He looked down at the data breakdown on the table before him that showed middle management in some departments at 70 percent women.

In fact, there had been significant change in his company in terms of women's representation in the lower and mid levels over the years. In what we find is a very common story, what hadn't changed was the number of women in the top echelons of the company. Top leadership was not gender diverse. "I don't *get it*," he said, puzzling over the results. "Where's the breakdown?"

Years before, this CEO, like so many other leaders, bought into the prevailing beliefs of equality through sameness and diversity by numbers. Believing his efforts would fight bias, he personally saw to it that company culture became gender-blind. In an effort to prove the company was gender-equal, he also put in motion a system of reward and advancement based on a standard set of abilities, talents, and results. *Everyone will have an equal chance of succeeding,* he had thought. He hired the best of the best women from competing companies and promoted high-potential women from within. Despite all these changes, here we were, called in to help analyze and fix the problem of gender disparity.

While the CEO's spreadsheets could tell him how many female hires he had, our diagnostic was able to paint a much more nuanced picture—one we see almost all the time. We had asked men and women at all levels of the organization a set of questions, including some in the area of personal satisfaction, participation in decision-making, their sense of the inclusivity of the corporate culture, as well as their perception of advancement. The results of the survey stunned the CEO. The answers from the women at the senior level on those specific questions were strikingly different from those of the women in middle management. And they were strikingly different from those of men. Not surprising, as a result, in some critical departments, such as sales and product development, the percent of senior women was actually *lower* compared with ten years before.

Our diagnostic revealed the hidden truth that the experience women were having at higher levels in the company was not as fulfilling as it was for their male peers. Moreover, it showed how so few senior women saw any opportunity for advancement. As a consequence, many of the best and brightest women—including those lured from competitors—were leaving. It was quite a wake-up call for the CEO that morning. All that time and money spent on initiatives, the institution of a meritocracy that treated men and women the same with the best intentions of equality and fairness, and there was little to show for it at the end of the day.

Bowled over by that insight, he wanted to know more. He wanted to know why.

Breakthrough Insights

We were thrilled by this CEO's response as well as those of many others all over the world looking to find out where the breakdown lies. In wanting to get to the root of the problem, his and scores of other companies have arrived on the brink of a critical transformation in their thinking about gender and the deeper meaning of gender equality—embracing Gender Intelligence.

A demonstration of that transformation in thinking took place in the first of our quarterly deep dives into Gender Intelligence held in November 2013 at our Gender Intelligence retreat in Sedona, Arizona. Men and women senior executives from Fortune 500 companies and various organizations in the United States, Canada, Germany, and Scandinavia spoke of their most transformational "aha!" moment—the discovery of how common the challenges are for men and women working together, regardless of country or culture.

As the retreat unfolded, it became apparent to the Scandinavian leaders who attended that although they had made tremendous social strides in terms of gender attitudes toward improving women's roles in business, society, and government, they had not advanced in their Gender Intelligence. With these and many other insights, company leaders generated new ways in which their organizations could grow in their Gender Intelligence and begin uncovering the economic and cultural value of authentic gender diversity.

What is adding momentum to this new conversation on gender are dynamic shifts in thinking—the moments of discovery that we call **breakthrough insights**. Leaders and their organizations are realizing that the imperative behind becoming more gender-diverse extends beyond compliance or "fairness"; the data shows that economically it's the right thing to do to the point of proving crucial to the future of the organization.

These seven are the most stirring breakthrough insights for leaders and their organizations that have emerged from the totality of our work to date. Although each is a powerful recognition in its own right, in our experience all seven (or at least most) need to be experienced and embraced by an organization intent on undergoing a thorough transformation to Gender Intelligence:

1. Transformation begins with leadership.
2. Numbers don't solve the problem.
3. Meritocracies are not enough.
4. There's a science to our difference.
5. It's not just about women.
6. Gender Intelligence accelerates all diversity.
7. Fear of stereotyping blocks progress.

Let's now delve a little into each of these insights by first defining what we mean, then sharing real-world examples of how leaders came upon their most meaningful insight, and showing how their breakthroughs changed the culture of their organizations.

TRANSFORMATION BEGINS WITH LEADERSHIP

Too often, the goal of gender diversity translates into company leadership handing off mandates to HR to ensure compliance with internal or external metrics. HR departments respond with related policies and programs—from targeted recruitment, to pay equity, to work flexibility. And they track progress each year on the percent gains of women in senior management, which they may, though not necessarily, report back to leadership.

When leaders simply hand the responsibility over to HR they are signaling that they don't see the strategic value in gender diversity. To them, it's not related to the core initiatives of the company. In fact, for many it's a nuisance. They don't truly understand the value of gender balance, while they do understand that the perception they don't care can bring with it bad publicity. Toeing the line then becomes just a matter of complying with numeric mandates, which is one of the major reasons why after forty years of new laws, and subsequent lawsuits, quotas, diversity training, and legal expenses, there's been no appreciable change in the level and impact of women in leadership. The glass ceiling remains, with few explanations as to why and even fewer meaningful solutions.

When change rests solely on the shoulders of HR, leaders and middle managers both tend to perceive gender diversity as a mandated exercise, disconnected from the key strategies of the organization, and therefore unproductive. Alternatively, if change is seen through the lens of Gender Intelligence, the company's leadership realizes that true diversity—especially that derived from natural gender differences—is strategic to the future of the business. With that insight, mandates become irrelevant. Leaders stop wringing their hands over percentages and instead shift their focus to the shifts in thinking and action that affect the bottom line, a motivation understood by all.

Gender diversity is clearly a worthy goal, but if it's pursued solely for compliance or for the *appearance* of equality, it's not going to create sustainable change. All too many companies establish gender initiatives to look good or to reduce complaints from employees and other constituencies that they're not doing anything. Diversity programs become window dressing destined to fail because they're not linked to the financial goals of the company and lack the full support of top leadership, from whom everyone else takes their cues.

The outcome is almost always the same—one shared by the CEO who opened this chapter. Gender diversity initiatives may expand the number of women in the organization at the entry and middle management levels, but not so much at the top. There, the glass ceiling remains. Moreover, the company culture will be unlikely to change because the culture is a reflection of senior leadership and the priorities and goals of those individuals. And without a meaningful culture change as a result of these initiatives, the outcomes of the business are not affected in any significant way.

Leaders who understand the business reasons for Gender Intelligence know that more of the same isn't going to have a powerful impact. Putting the responsibility on HR to "solve the problem" may help avoid a lawsuit or some bad press, but rarely will anything sustainable take root. Cultural transformation begins at the top.

To understand how critical it is that leadership understand the value of gender diversity, consider this recent example:

Patricia, a dynamic and passionate professional, served as the senior vice president of global HR for a large communications company headquartered in Europe. In August 2012, Patricia was asked by leadership to attend the quarterly board meeting to present the results of HR's initiatives for bringing more women into senior management, as well as to review her plans and budget for 2013.

Patricia was thrilled to be able to present her work and eager to have the board as a captive audience—she had important numbers to share and specific ideas for how the company could improve going into the next fiscal year. She worked for a full month on her presentation . . . and then never even got a chance to speak. The entire board meeting centered on the company's top three strategic initiatives, all tied to the bottom line, and none of which was linked to HR's talent management efforts. Not only did Patricia not get a chance to present her findings, but the board cut her budget in order to fund other strategic priorities. What went unchanged were the target quotas: the board wanted an increase from the current 18 percent to 30 percent women in senior management by 2018.

The quotas expressed the image the company wanted to project, while the behavior of leadership clearly signaled their priorities.

About a month after the board meeting, Patricia submitted her resignation. Although she cited personal reasons for quitting, she shared with us what really pushed her out. She had been in a no-win situation with no reasonable and effective pathway to success. The greatest and most tragic irony came when she showed us the data that she had wanted to show the board. Women as a percent of senior management was actually declining in the largest and most critical departments of sales and finance, making 30 percent by 2018 not just improbable, but *impossible* without a deep cultural change. In losing Patricia's voice at the table and refusing to link talent management strategically to the future of the company, leadership only made the problem worse.

Companies focused on success need to not only communicate values that include diversity and collaboration, but also make them more than just aspirations in the "Our Values" section of their website. It is the job of leadership, not just HR, to understand the value of Gender Intelligence and see how those values can be operational, strategic, and connected to the bottom line.

NUMBERS DON'T SOLVE THE PROBLEM

There is no arguing that compliance is a powerful force in today's business world. While we can say Gender Intelligence needs to extend beyond the HR department, others may argue we live in a world where regulators and lawmakers create rules, policies, and "safe" boundaries in order to ensure we don't create egregious organizational errors or exclusions. When we, in our organizations, achieve certain numeric objectives it demonstrates that we're doing okay, staying on course, and perhaps somewhat advancing.

Interestingly, by defaulting to numeric goals without seeing the broader context and ramifications of Gender Intelligence, we unconsciously attempt to solve the gender problem in a typically male way. Compliance and a sense of fairness become our primary motivators. The result is that when we can safely and confidently claim that we've hired an appropriate number of women or put together a new diversity initiative, we have little excuse to do more. We feel we have met our obligations, have checked off that box.

Do we see any transformation happening as a result? After years of pumping in women at the entry level and surgically recruiting women to plum executive spots, it's simply not sticking. In fact, the percentage of women in senior management has hardly changed at all since the 1990s.[27] More important, with so much attention on numeric goals, the leadership in so many of these organizations fails to recognize the deeper innovative and economic possibilities inherent in Gender Intelligence.

Consider this: The number-one reason men may leave their companies is for a better opportunity in income or position. But, more than any other factor, women's primary reasons for leaving center on not feeling valued or in having their contributions ignored or dismissed.[28] Too often, they feel poorly treated by their boss, by management in general, and find themselves in a climate that doesn't quite welcome their different gifts. They feel molded into something they are not. Discouragement leads to disengagement, and the many women who are not advancing leave, or they stay in a position where only a fraction of their efforts and ideas are valued.

There is a very clear distinction between complying with social or legal expectations—which is where we believe many corporations operate today—and achieving extraordinarily high-performing organizational states. This is the difference between mediocrity and greatness! Driving for gender balance through numbers alone will not change a culture. Nor will it lead to extraordinary achievement. In many ways, the mindset intent on doing it "by the numbers" is part of the prevailing problem. It is what highly analytic male (and sometimes female) leaders focus on when faced with a massive problem, and as a result they offer a limiting objective driven by a faulty set of beliefs. Yet, regardless of the failure to effect change, the pressure to hire and advance more women only grows. In some cases, governments, not seeing the progress they want, are getting more involved.

Let's take this observation of what is arguably one of the most gender-diverse places on earth. Norway, along with other Nordic countries including Sweden, Iceland, and Finland, has for generations been a leader in advocating women's rights. In 1913, Norway became the second country in the world (Finland being the first) to grant women the right to vote and today is one of the top ten countries in terms of percentage of women in parliament. It once achieved 40 percent and has never fallen below 35 percent since 1985.[29]

Most recently, in 2005, Norway's parliament legislated gender representation on the boards of public companies. Ratified in 2006, the law stipulated that by 2008, at least 40 percent of board members had to be women. Today, Norway *is* at 40 percent and has the highest representation of women on boards in the world. Gender inequity solved, right? Again, numbers don't tell the whole story. Women still represent less than 20 percent of senior management in the companies led by those very same boards—no different in that respect from companies in countries without legislation![30]

Moreover, even though representation does little to change the actual business landscape in terms of gender balance, it does even less to change the culture to become more gender-intelligent. As a result, while the increase in women on company boards created quite a buzz in the press and among those working for gender diversity, it has done little to change the underlying cultural fabric.

The prevailing belief in many organizations is that when their company achieves greater gender balance at the low to middle levels, then everything else will take care of itself. This will naturally expand the talent pool of women, they will rise to the top, and this will ultimately make the company more competitive, or so the belief goes. But changing the numbers doesn't change the conversation. All it changes is the balance of representation of women to men within the *same male paradigm*.

Of course, some women in these organizations do make it to the top, but they are usually the ones who can adapt and survive the male model of business. Other women who don't assimilate well eventually leave, discouraged by a male-influenced culture that doesn't reflect who *they* are and value how *they* prefer to think and act.

The high cost of turnover

Realizing that just hiring more women doesn't solve the problem was Deloitte's breakthrough insight. Before their "aha!" moment, they couldn't explain the cause of the high turnover of women in their North America division, a trend that was costing the company upwards of $240 million a year. The company was losing more women than it was hiring in, and in exit interviews, the departing women didn't offer any specific reasons for the exodus aside from it being personal or family-related. They didn't want to burn bridges by speaking to the real reasons for their leaving or risk being tagged as negative by competing firms. Word gets out quickly in many industries and we often find that exit interviews don't reveal the full truth as to why people leave.

When we conducted post-exit interviews several months later we were able to discover the real reasons why Deloitte's women executives were quitting. Many were more willing to open up to us with the truth because we were an outside firm asking the questions. With their trust in our commitment to confidentiality and the deepest truth, they were now willing to come clean. And what they shared with us was telling—they did not feel valued in what they deemed a very male-influenced environment and many believed they would never make partner.

Deloitte realized that their focus on doing it "by the numbers" was costing them a lot and getting them nowhere. They spent money to get the talent only to lose it because of the business environment.

Once they saw past the numbers, they made more valuable discoveries. They learned that men and women do not think through issues, make decisions, lead teams, and engage clients in the same fashion. Ultimately, they came to the game-changing realization that it's not merely a balance in numbers but the balance in contribution that gives a sense of satisfaction and worth to men and women individually and economic value to the organization as a whole.

Deloitte's "aha!" moment changed the mindset of the organization. They realized the value of difference-thinking to clients and began to view partnership in a new light. With that discovery in mind, they became the first organization in their industry to focus on retaining women and men as partners with less than full-time work commitments. In a little less than two years, the turnover rate of women in the accounting division dropped from 27 to 11 percent.

MERITOCRACIES ARE NOT ENOUGH

One of the first things we do when working with new clients is to ask them to describe gender dynamics in their company. Invariably, we hear leaders and their organizations proclaim their company operates as a meritocracy, saying some version of the following:

> We have a diverse talent management system where everything is based on merit and men and women are treated the same. Everyone has a fair and equal chance. We have one set of competencies for everyone and

we use the same criteria to measure each individual's performance against corporate goals.

The part that is so hard for so many organizational leaders to see is the degree to which those competencies on which advancement is based are male-modeled, often expressed in a male way, and usually evaluated based on how a man would exhibit that proficiency. A woman may have the same level of ability and express the same competency, just not in a familiar way—the male way. Her evaluations, and her advancement, may suffer as a result.

Barbara saw this firsthand recently working with Carla, a senior vice president of finance, who expressed her complete bewilderment at being scored so low on some of the competencies on which she was being measured. When Barbara asked her which one she was measured the lowest on, she said it was on thinking strategically. Frustrated, she countered, "I think strategically all the time!"

Having seen this many times before, Barbara explained to Carla that the problem might be in how she was expressing "thinking strategically," specifically by expressing it differently than the way men typically do. "Try putting the word *strategic* in your sentences more often when you're working with the senior leadership team," Barbara told her. "And reiterate how your initiatives strategically link to the objectives of the organization. I'm not asking you to give up your authenticity to try to fit in, but rather, to reframe your conversation in a way that men can better understand and connect with you."

Months later, Carla was actually outscoring others on "thinking strategically." She still had her own female hardwiring where she saw the larger context of issues, and she still thought strategically her own unique way, but she was able to frame her conversations so the men could hear them and follow her reasoning. She wasn't just dropping the word *strategic*. Instead she was inviting them to see what she was doing *as* strategic. She was not turning into one of the men, but letting them know that this was her way of being strategic. That was a huge "aha!" moment for Carla.

Understanding this same dynamic is a critical breakthrough insight for companies seeking to equalize the gender imbalance in their system of reward and advancement. Company leadership needs to understand how male-dominated thinking may color how women in the organization are scored in their "everybody's equal" system, and consider the subjective expression of those core competencies they are looking for in their talent pipeline.

THERE'S A SCIENCE TO OUR DIFFERENCE

For too long in the business world we've been so enamored with the conventional male mode and so convinced that the real challenge is simply finding the right women that we haven't focused on how to best engage and blend the unique strengths found in the entire talent pool. That latter point is the key differentiator of a gender-intelligent organization and an important breakthrough insight. The real science behind our gender differences is quite compelling. We find that as more business leaders become familiar with the brain science we outlined earlier, rather than trying to unnaturally force women into a male mode, they're seeing the potential value in the differences.

After attending a Gender Intelligence session with the company's senior management, American Express was convinced. Executive leadership wanted to realize the extraordinary potential in reaping the full complement of what each gender has to offer. They soon declared that increasing the company's understanding of the value of gender differences in communication, problem-solving, and decision-making would take precedence at all levels of the organization and across all business units. With this in mind, we began rolling out Gender Intelligence workshops from the top of the company through the mid-management level and then began to explore with managers ways they can apply that learning to key operations, functions, and processes.

This was the beginning of consciousness for the company, with leadership on down grasping the value of hardwiring and the advantage of Gender Intelligence. Within two years, it was commonplace during strategic planning sessions and team meetings throughout the company to hear men and women confirm the balanced thinking that went into their problem-solving and decision-making by continually checking themselves, asking, "Are we being gender-intelligent about this?"

Today, all critical decisions at the executive level at American Express are made with the input of both men and women. Gender Intelligence even informs interactions with customers.

Advancing Gender Intelligence throughout the organization required a deep and deliberate commitment on the part of the leadership at American Express rooted in the science behind our differences and the value in men and women's sometimes distinct approaches. By making this change, the company shifted its focus from identifying and reporting on the barriers to women's advancement to promoting the number of innovative solutions rising out of a team able to take full advantage of its greater gender diversity.

IT'S NOT JUST ABOUT WOMEN

Does this sound like your organization—caught in a women-focused-initiatives frenzy? Many organizations send women off to universities for leadership and management development, put them through sales training programs, assign them male mentors, have them role-play their assertiveness in conflict-resolution workshops . . . the list goes on and on. While the focus on women's advancement has value, if you take a closer look at these initiatives you'll see what else they have in common: they are all instructing women how to behave like men in order to survive and thrive in the world of business.

It goes even deeper than that. Many companies form women's networks and task them with finding solutions to the challenges facing women—putting the responsibility squarely on the shoulders of women to solve the "woman problem."

Having come across dozens of flavors of women-oriented programs over the years that did not bear fruit, we decided to conduct a comparative analysis to discover what works and what doesn't work in attracting, retaining, and advancing women. We surveyed men and women senior managers and leaders from three technology firms, four financial services companies, and two accounting firms and asked them what initially prompted their interest in gender diversity, the types of programs they were running to meet their quotas, and how successful they were in achieving and sustaining their goals.[31]

We began by asking why their focus on gender, and found a pattern in their responses:

- Trouble recruiting women into the organization
- Problems advancing and retaining women at the senior level
- Increased turnover of women compared to men in middle management
- Different gender perspectives in engagement survey results

• Recent fierce competition in the industry for women with talent and experience

We then sought to better understand their implementation. In one-on-one interviews and senior management focus groups, we asked the leaders in each of these nine companies to describe the programs being implemented to address and correct the challenges they targeted above in recruiting women and advancing them in the organization. Again, we found common themes. These were the programs they cited as not working, and our assessment, based on their responses and our own experience, of the reasons why:

PROGRAM	REASONS FOR FAILURE
Women's networks	*Excluded men*

• Provided a venue to complain but not to drive positive change
• Lacked strategy and ended up becoming social networks
• Heightened the sense of separateness from company

Training and coaching for women	*Programs focused on "fixing" the way women think and act*

• Designed to help women fit in a sameness model

Metrics and targeted recruitment	*Focused on reaching numeric goals, not cultural goals*

• Assumed that critical mass is the solution
• Targeted recruitment at the senior level not sticking

Work-life flexibility programs	*Many women did not feel able to take advantage of the policies*

• Worked as a recruitment strategy, but had no impact on advancing women to senior positions

Women's mentors	*Mentors/mentees not trained on how to be gender-intelligent*

• Matched women with women instead of having gender-mixed pairs
• Matches did not have chemistry
• Mentors were not as valuable as gender-mixed sponsors

PROGRAM	REASONS FOR FAILURE
Diversity workshops	*Diversity and compliance workshops created a reverse effect*

- Resulted in producing overly sensitive, politically correct men who practice avoidance as a best solution

These decades-old programs, while producing some modest inroads, have never really worked as well as was hoped. The mindset that creates these programs, with the best of intentions, is not *seeing* the environment that women are coming into. It's a business environment that is male-designed and very comfortable—for men. It's an environment that's easy to defend in that historically it has served as a relatively successful business model.

It naturally follows that companies would think, *Let's hire more women and "fix" them or expect them to assimilate. It's the women that need to adapt, because the system works fine as is.*

The business landscape, however, has changed dramatically in the past two decades. It is far more fluid, unpredictable, and globally connected and competitive than ever before. There have been fundamental shifts not only in the composition of the workforce but also in the customer base that must influence how businesses operate if they are to move successfully into the future.

And there are a number of companies that are beginning to respond effectively. The German software company SAP is attempting to take Gender Intelligence further than anyone else in the technology industry. They have gender diversity goals but are not attempting to attain those goals by focusing on women only and implementing women-centric programs. Men are becoming involved in the conversation because, in the end, it's about women and men working together.

Their breakthrough insight came during a Gender Intelligence pilot workshop in Walldorf, Germany. During this time, senior leadership discovered the element that was missing in their thinking in order to expand globally and sustain their goals for increasing the presence of senior women leaders in the organization. That element was gender-intelligent relationships and teamwork. The company made a commitment to rolling out two hundred Women and Men Leading Together workshops for all managers to participate in globally. The result, according to chief diversity officer Anka Wittenberg, is "tremendous progress. Leaders and managers are returning from the Gender Intelligence sessions and embedding their learning into how they manage people, work in teams, and together win with prospects and clients."

GENDER INTELLIGENCE ACCELERATES ALL DIVERSITY

As a business leader or HR executive, sometimes it seems like no matter what diversity issue you focus on, another disenfranchised group is prompted to ask, "What about us?" Because our workforce and marketplace are increasingly diverse, we are often asked, "Why do you place gender in front of other visible minorities? Why do you lead with gender?"

Our approach to Gender Intelligence doesn't focus on gender to the exclusion of other diversity issues. It does place purpose and significance on *leading* with gender, for we believe and have seen that doing the work of Gender Intelligence can create a powerful domino effect in positively affecting inclusiveness as a whole, which in turn affects all minorities. It forces us to confront differences that reach to the core of who we are as men and women in ways that are universally understood.

What amazes us in our practice is that, regardless of the country in which we're conducting a Gender Intelligence workshop, the blind spots and challenges men and women face in cross-gender relationships are often identical, right down to the experiences. It doesn't matter if we're in Copenhagen or Cairo or Toronto or Pittsburgh—the brain-based differences between men and women emerge during each of our conversations, interviews, and workshops. Of course, culture adds its own layers of influence and learning, but the similarities shared by men and women are universal and undeniable. Our experience tells us that there's something that underlies our gender differences—something more fundamental than culture. Gender is the only type of diversity for which there is proven, scientific evidence of actual differences in our hardwiring. Those differences play out in decision-making processes, communication, and problem-solving so profoundly and universally that companies around the world that are able to take advantage of both styles leverage that into success.

There are other powerful reasons for beginning with Gender Intelligence. While the cultural, racial, and ethnic makeup of the workforce is constantly shifting, the presence of men and women in the workplace has become de rigueur. Second, unlike other diversity issues, mostly rooted in bias and discrimination, we find what gets in the way of Gender Intelligence is often simply bewilderment or a sense of not understanding or being understood. Of course there is gender discrimination in the workplace, but in our workshop conversations around gender difference we find the conversations hold less anger or resentment. Unlike with race, where science has found no differences in reasoning capabilities or thought processes between different racial groups, the brain science differentiating men and women is clear. Perhaps made more secure by the data, the men and women we work with are able to investigate their own assumptions and achieve an expansiveness of thought and an openness of heart toward different styles and approaches that goes beyond overcoming bias.

Let's put it differently. Oftentimes, in investigating isms such as racism or classism, the goal is simply to eradicate bias—to create fairness by overcoming stereotypic belief and even bigotry. In first acknowledging their own bias, people can become defensive. People face an internal hurdle in examining their past and their experiences to see how they shaped their ingrained beliefs, assumptions, and, frankly, fear around people who differ from them, be it in terms of race or sexual orientation or cultural background. That process is valuable, and we would argue that any time you engage in that type of self-evaluation it will positively affect your movement toward Gender Intelligence.

In achieving true Gender Intelligence, you not only look at your past assumptions but also examine your way of being in the world. Knowing the biology in which your behavior is rooted, there is more empirical evidence to help you better understand how and why you act the way you do. You can then move on to examine what it takes to be effective in a given situation, and allow yourself to admit to how narrow or rigid your thought process might be and move toward an inclusiveness of more effective styles. Understanding and owning your very thought process, not just about gender but about everything, is by definition a transformational shift in your state of being that can't help but positively affect how you work through other issues of diversity. Instead of focusing on gender to the exclusion of race or any other differences, we find that leading with gender can open up a powerful conversation and lead to a sustained shift toward inclusivity. In practice, our experience has been that companies that have a better blend of women and men at all managerial levels who think with Gender Intelligence foster an environment where broader cultural diversity efforts can take root and an inclusive culture can grow.

That's what happened at BMO (Bank of Montreal) Financial Group, where valuing gender differences has expanded inclusiveness throughout the organization. Employees participate with each other more openly and with greater confidence. They work together more easily and more effectively, with a greater sense of shared accomplishment.

Initially, the company's goal was to accelerate diversity and inclusiveness throughout their North American operations. The breakthrough insight for BMO came in watching their company progress through the stages of awareness, appreciation, and valuing of gender differences. As they underwent that shift, they noticed a broader culture change, saw inclusiveness in team meetings and town hall sessions, and experienced a broader, more diverse market presence. Within a year of implementing Gender Intelligence workshops and executive one-on-one coaching sessions, the company reported expanding race and ethnicity levels in employee populations as well, a tangible result of the culture change that began with Gender Intelligence.

Like the companies chronicled in this book, organizations all over the globe are waking up to the power and potency of Gender Intelligence in accelerating diversity and positively affecting the bottom line. It does not come without resistance or detractors. One of the biggest challenges we face in our work comes from some heads of diversity who have a broader and sometimes highly politically charged agenda. Perhaps a story will be instructive here.

Barbara was in Chicago presenting to the leadership of a recent merger of two large global banks. She had done great work with the acquiring bank and they were making tremendous progress in advancing their understanding and application of Gender Intelligence enterprise-wide—both internally and externally.

That day, Barbara was presenting to the now joint global team in charge of talent management and diversity. There must have been more than one hundred people in the small auditorium. She started talking about the inclusive nature of a gender-intelligent conversation and the value in difference-thinking when men and women work together in an open and respecting environment.

An African-American male who was sitting at the front of the room immediately stood up for all to see and walked out. Barbara continued her presentation and discussion but asked to speak with the black diversity leader afterward.

I recalled that what he was so upset about was the focus was on balance in genders and not balance in race. He had all the statistics at his fingertips of the number of black men and even black women in the various departments and in senior management. Anything I said was nothing more than irritation in his ears, so I listened and thanked him for meeting with me.

He was not from the bank that we had done so much work with, and when that acquiring bank asked us to do a 360-degree evaluation of the leadership in both banks to ensure a cultural fit, we learned more about the black gentleman who had walked out. It was fascinating to see how high he scored himself and how challenging it was for him to include other forms of diversity, and in particular, gender.

Many people have enormous passion for what they're passionate about. They're intent on righting a wrong and the wrong is the bias that has caused them and their people or group to be unfairly judged and not having gotten the right opportunity. They have a difficult time seeing anything else.

When the leadership of an organization declares their commitment to gender diversity and Gender Intelligence, the HR department or the diversity department within HR may start to feel concerned that the attention on gender will circumvent their efforts at establishing other diversity efforts. So often, what they advocate is that the company does not focus on gender, but subsume gender diversity into their larger diversity strategy. While we can understand their desire (it is often a constant push uphill to get the attention of senior management, let alone their commitment), we do not believe it is wise to fold gender diversity within diversity in general, until and at such time Gender Intelligence takes root. There are two reasons for this:

1. Gender differences are not the same as all other differences. They are biologically based and not just socially based, so there is a unique set of learning that is needed to honor these differences.

2. When done well, it has the potential to positively create such a powerful "great minds think unalike" effect, that it positively affects the rest of diversity. This is the domino effect we spoke about earlier.

So often, in our experience, what is most difficult to convey at times is that Gender Intelligence is *the* most inclusive approach in the area of diversity. When we look at diagnostics by race and ethnic group, for example, the greatest deviations are between the genders, particularly in the African-American and Hispanic cultures. It is, in our observations and supporting data, the pattern that affects so many other patterns of diversity that it deserves its own space in the diversity agenda of an organization, and almost always a prominent one. In the end, Gender Intelligence or lack thereof is not a problem that needs to be corrected through quotas. Instead, it is a strategic opportunity to create an organizational culture that represents the world of today and tomorrow.

FEAR OF STEREOTYPING BLOCKS PROGRESS

"Women are so sensitive."
"Men are too competitive."
"Women aren't as ambitious."
"Men don't care."

Each and every one of the statements above is a gender stereotype, a negative generalized assumption or observation made about men or women. While it's important to recognize and address the stereotypes we hold about one another, in this day and age it seems our fear of saying something wrong is holding us back from entering into any dialogue on difference at all. Instead of helping advance our conversation on gender diversity, the gender-sameness tack we've taken in society is actually blocking our progress.

As we've discussed in the last two chapters, over the last few decades there's been a push to eradicate bias and discrimination by adopting a meritocracy based on a gender-blind mindset. Believing in everyone's capability and right for equal opportunity, we treat everyone the same. And while these fundamental tenets have advanced our world, there's been an unintended negative consequence: We've become too politically correct, too afraid to acknowledge differences—too afraid to speak to those differences that really do exist.

In our practice, we see this play out across the globe. Successful businesspeople, leaders, and educators, out of fear of stereotyping or engaging in discrimination, purposefully ignore and discount the presence of any gender differences and chastise anyone who suggests otherwise. As a result, they actually lose their ability to discuss, explore, and take advantage of the gender differences hardwired into our brains. Are women less ambitious? No. Are they hardwired to take more calculated risk? Yes. Do men really not care about maintaining relationships? No. Are they more likely to let go of a tough conversation with a colleague as they walk out the door? Yes.

Caught between our lived experience of difference and our mandate to ignore it, we find ourselves in an organizational and societal quandary (what do we do about the conflicting messages?) that results in no movement at all. On this flat surface there is little welcome for variations in thought and process. However, we are unable to step up and off the plateau because of our fear of being labeled as prejudiced, hateful, or ignorant. We've arrived at what we call "enlightened denial."

We're enlightened because we're committed at some level to the ideal of gender equality; we honestly believe that we have the right values and the best of intentions. Yet there remains that elephant in the room that many simply refuse to acknowledge—our authentic, hardwired gender differences.

The breakthrough insight for many people who attend our workshops is the realization, especially after reading through the science and participating in the discussions, that they are blocking not only their own learning, but everyone else's around them, especially if they are in positions of power.

We explore gender blind spots in our workshops and we share the latest in brain science research. We then make connections to the thoughts and behaviors of men and women, linking back to those observed differences everyone has experienced and no one has been able to talk about. Almost everyone participating is amazed at what they didn't know. Able to freely discuss and explore difference, they begin to see and get comfortable with their new, more educated and accepting view of the other gender as well as more fully understand the roots of their own behavior. They learn that calling out and appreciating their natural differences can be done in a productive light that has nothing to do with blind stereotyping because value is assigned to both ways of being, rather than one style being placed above the other in a hierarchy. It also involves an expansion of thought and a personal change of behavior.

The breakthrough insight begins with a willingness to question one's fundamental beliefs and discover that men and women really are different, that we're meant to be different, and that there is a natural complement and power in our differences—if we can only find the courage to call it out. Transformation lies in using that courage as a self-challenge to work more productively and effectively with the other gender.

The Progression of Gender Intelligence

Inclusion is key to the concept of Gender Intelligence; our practice is based on the premise that our work is not just about advancing women, but about advancing women and men in unison. We get the best of both worlds when we work together, that's true, but Gender Intelligence is more critical than that. Ultimately, we need each other to sustain success, both in an economic sense and in broader terms. The organizations that are experiencing breakthrough insights are not content with business as usual. Instead, they are courageously questioning their own paradigms and looking for ways to see what they are not seeing now.

The successful organizations in the global Information Age will be those with leaders who see the value in diversity and who have committed to change that goes beyond gender sameness and mandates and quotas. The leading businesses in the new age will be those who look for equality in value and diversity of thought. Gender Intelligence is not for leaders who want to succeed in the current organizational paradigm. It's for leaders like you, leaders who want to lead in the *new* paradigm—to break old patterns of behavior and awaken their organizations to the possibilities of the future.

5

The Journey of Gender-Intelligent Companies

n the fields of chemistry and physics, a chain reaction describes a sequence of events that begins when one powerful element causes additional reactions to take place. The initial catalyst causes a release of energy, touching off more reactions and more energy releases in an expanding chain.

And so it goes in the business world. Many factors can affect a company's bottom line—timing, market conditions, strategy, competition, and operational efficiency come to mind. But there is no factor as influential over the long term as a company's culture. And while there's much that can shape a company's culture—the history of the organization, where it's located or headquartered, even the changing nature of the industry itself—no single element can set off as powerful a reaction inside the company culture as the style and behavior of its leadership. Research shows that as much as a 50 percent variation in company cultures can be attributed to the difference in leadership.[32]

Finally, at the core of all leadership styles is the *leadership mindset*—the attitudes and beliefs that the CEO and senior leaders carry with them, shaping the choices they make, from sweeping initiatives to the way they run a meeting or solicit feedback.

The Leadership Chain

In our work, we like to describe this organizational chain reaction or sequence of "energy releases" as the *Leadership Chain*.[33] As in chemistry, it traces back to a singular, powerful element, in this case the mindset of the leader. A leader's mindset encompasses his or her viewpoints, thinking patterns, and psychological maturity. How a leader sees the world and what a leader believes to be true directly influence his or her style and, in turn, shape the rest of the organization in inimitable ways.

This is especially true in high-stress times, for example when organizations find themselves struggling to make product development deadlines or not responding quickly enough to market changes. There are a number of responses that could come from the top, including what you will now recognize as a very male, amygdala-fired response. These leaders and managers react quickly and negatively, spewing everything from annoyance to anger to frustration. They externalize the issue by blaming the situation on one department, team, or person. They then take full control of the situation and make quick, unilateral decisions. The response can appear surgical and strong, yet this coping style, by its very nature, often makes matters worse.

This leadership style tends to create dependent, reactive cultures instead of self-directing, proactive, confident teams that could help deconstruct the problem and prevent it from happening in the future.

The Leadership Chain

We believe there is a more effective way to lead, including when crises occur and stress is at its peak. The Leadership Chain, from mindset to results, parallels the perspective and subsequent impact of a gender-intelligent leader, one who walks the talk and builds a coalition for change around him or her. The senior team acts to release that first burst of positive energy and creates a multipart chain that begins to shift the company's culture. Leadership's mindset inspires and motivates men and women—at all levels—to higher outcomes and greater results.

In enacting the Leadership Chain, there has to be a change in the behavior of the company's leaders to create change in company culture and, in turn, to elicit the best responses from their teams. Critically, there must also be a change in *attitude* underlying those new behaviors to make them stick. We noticed the difference early on in our practice when we saw hardly any gains for leaders and companies trying to become more gender diverse. Certain behaviors were changing, but the energy wasn't touching off similar reactions throughout the organization. In diagnosing the results, we discovered why many companies, managers, and CEOs, all with the best of intentions, weren't making headway. Many, it turned out, were striving to become gender diverse for incomplete or limited reasons. Only when there was true change in the mindset and style of leadership—change deep and thorough enough to effect cultural change—did Gender Intelligence take root and have the potential to flourish.

The Gender Intelligence Continuum

In response to this lack of progress on the part of some of our clients, we developed the *Gender Intelligence Continuum* to help organizations learn for themselves the resistance inherent in their cultures and visualize the journey their people still needed to take. Using the combined assessments of the company's own leaders and managers, we help the organization determine where they lie on the continuum toward Gender Intelligence.[34]

Over the years, we've found that organizations fall along a spectrum of Gender Intelligence—from denial to realization, from realization to practice, and from practice to personal and economic growth. We've also noticed two important trends. The first is that organizations further along the continuum are showing the way for others who are less advanced. There exists as well a critical point (we'll reveal it later in the book) that organizations must reach if they are to progress further along the continuum. Without attaining that point, these organizations are failing, some considerably, in their efforts. As you look through each of the stages below, take a moment to reflect on where you believe you stand as a leader, where your senior team might be, and where your organization's culture currently resides on our continuum.

The Gender Intelligence Continuum

STAGE	OUTLOOK
0	*"We don't care."*
1	*"We have to do this."*
2	*"It's a good thing to do."*
3	*"We have business reasons."*
4	*"We're in transition."*
5	*"Authentically, a gender-intelligent organization."*

Origins of the Continuum

In 1999, we co-created the Gender Intelligence Continuum with a major computer manufacturer in a combined effort to determine where their company stood on their journey to becoming a gender-intelligent organization. More than two hundred of the company's top leaders participated in the project, offering an extensive and enlightened view into the attitudes and beliefs of top leadership—those setting the tone for the company's leadership.

We began by describing each stage to the leaders, sharing the meaning and importance of each juncture, and revealing the style of leadership and organizational culture often found there. We gave the leaders examples of companies we had worked with at each stage and described how the leadership mindset either prevented those other companies from making progress or encouraged change and growth.

The method for determining where the computer company stood on the continuum boiled down to an old-fashioned dot exercise that also gave us a window into the differing attitudes between the genders. We gave the men green dots and black to the women, then asked them one by one to walk behind a curtain and privately place their dot on the stage they thought described the company. The computer maker discovered that the majority of the dots were placed at stages Zero and One, with very few at stages Two and Three and none beyond that point. It seemed they had a long way to go.

While both men and women mainly placed their dots in the early stages of the continuum, overall the men gave the company higher scores than did the women (a pattern we see repeated in almost all organizations today). And when we asked the men and women why they placed their dots where they did, the men were generally more positive and spoke to the company's potential, offering comments like "This company has the best of intentions to move along the continuum" and "We're making progress." Women, on the other hand, were more negatively and personally affected by the company's current position. "We're not even close," they told us, or "I don't feel it yet." Though a simple scale, the Gender Intelligence Continuum offered an excellent means by which to measure different attitudes and beliefs, lending specificity to future steps and shaping a vision of the ultimate goal.

We've been using the continuum ever since, helping organizations discover where they believe their companies rest on that journey from denial to authenticity. As with the different perspectives from the men and women in this collaboration, we've found it starts a powerful conversation around the assumptions and blind spots that generally prevent companies from making progress.

The goal of all organizations committed to Gender Intelligence is to reach Stage Five, a place where managers and leaders at all levels of the organization believe in and behave with Gender Intelligence in all circumstances: internally and externally facing the customer, in all engagements, from problem-solving to decision-making. Only at Stage Five do companies truly begin to transform their practices, processes, and functions to reflect gender-intelligent behavior and realize the best results.

While Stage Five is attainable, it takes significant work and commitment to get there. Most of us will begin our journey either at the very beginning or somewhere in the middle. In order to illustrate what it really means to perform and flourish at Stage Five, we'll go through and describe the behaviors of companies in each of the preceding stages to help you recognize your own company's actions. We'll explain the leadership mindset and behaviors as well as cultures that prevent or advance progress along the continuum to help you visualize your path toward complete Gender Intelligence.

STAGE ZERO: "WE DON'T CARE"

"Can't we just stay focused here on our primary goal—make money."
"We have a fair system here. They'll make it if they want to."
"This is a bunch of crap. If it won't help the bottom line, I'm not interested."
"Give them a network or something."

These are words that come out of the mouths of leaders at Stage Zero. They are disinterested in the subject and have no intention of leading a company that will become gender-intelligent. They don't see it as part of their critical path. They focus on their other priorities and treat gender diversity as an annoyance and a nonissue, often to their own detriment. Unfortunately, a large percentage of companies worldwide tends to fall into this category. More and more organizations are climbing out of this stage, however, as they come to recognize that gender diversity creates economic opportunity, and for some organizations, mitigates unnecessary risk.

Recently, a Fortune 500 company agreed to pay more than $150 million to settle a gender-discrimination class-action lawsuit brought by female employees. The women claimed discrimination in pay, promotion, and maternity leave policies. Even in the face of this kind of a wake-up call, the CEO insisted there was no systemic discrimination at the company. While he tepidly offered that some female associates had "experiences influenced by managerial behavior inconsistent with company values," he refused to take responsibility for the company culture. Moreover, he didn't recognize that his own leadership style and behavior were at the root, a mindset mimicked by many of his direct reports, and theirs, and so on down the line.

In addition to coming to a monetary settlement with the women who filed the lawsuit, the company agreed to revise its sexual harassment policies and training, strengthen its employee complaint process, and hire an outside specialist to help identify gender pay disparities and alter its performance management process. Unfortunately, these superficial revisions to company policies will unlikely yield sustainable culture change. To respond by stressing more diversity training for men reflects a reactive leadership mindset not ready to commit. As a result of all of these efforts, senior leadership will most likely accomplish little more than nudge the company along the continuum to Stage One.

Not all men are necessarily comfortable in Stage Zero companies. Barbara recently spoke with a bright Gen-Y male executive and senior officer candidate who graduated with honors from the Massachusetts Institute of Technology. He had really valued the diversity of ideas generated by the women in his study group at college and was incensed and demoralized by what he observed once he entered the workforce. He read through the emperor's-new-clothes façade of gender diversity, and even correctly tied discriminatory behavior back to the leadership mindset. "I can't believe how hard it is for talented women in the company to navigate the male roadblocks," he confided, referring to the resistance that surfaced in *every* meeting. "What women experience in this company is such blatant and exclusionary behavior on the part of leadership—from the board through to the CEO and his leadership team."

The young exec also found himself bumping up against the same alpha-male mentality and grew disgusted by the constant jockeying for power. He found that the hyperaggressive culture negatively affected his team's ability to battle their real opponent—the competition. "I couldn't stand the constant power plays that had nothing to do with actual business strategy." Feeling that the games detracted from the company's ability to be effective, he left. He, of course, is not alone in his feelings. Many men echo these same feelings in Stage Zero companies but often feel hesitant to voice their opinion. It would likely fall on deaf ears, and so they, like the women, eventually vote with their feet.

The leadership mindset at Stage Zero is grounded in the belief that there are no meaningful differences between men and women and in wishes that the gender problem would just go away. These leaders believe that the reason women haven't advanced is due to their own shortcomings or lack of commitment. To compensate, leadership at Stage Zero believes that if the company is fair in its hiring, and has in place a system whereby people are promoted and rewarded based only on effort and merit, then there's no gender issue and nothing more that they have to do. The cream of the crop have risen and it's a natural selection process.

Moreover, there are leaders in Stage Zero who don't care that they don't care! They believe that the world of business is intense and competitive and any conversation about gender diversity is nothing more than a distraction from their mission of beating the competition and being the best.

This is partly why there are few women at the top of these organizations. A select few will tough it out, and certainly some make it who fit the male mold quite comfortably, but many others won't accept being forced into a male mold that doesn't value their unique contribution.

What causes a company to move from Stage Zero to Stage One is usually a catastrophic event such as a class-action suit against them, a highly visible sexual harassment suit, or a mass exodus of highly valued women in a short enough span of time to be a wake-up call. These companies eventually heed the call, legally, and move into Stage One.

STAGE ONE: "WE HAVE TO DO THIS"

In our practice, we come across a great deal of negativity in companies struggling in Stage One. These are organizations target-recruiting women just to comply with legal mandates and quotas, with perhaps predictable results. At this stage, there's little to no awareness of the value of diversity or connecting diversity directly to increased productivity and bottom-line results—leadership just isn't convinced.

It follows then that many men in these organizations are angry and see this "focus on women" as reverse discrimination. In some instances, their bonuses are tied to achieving hiring quotas, further fueling their resentment as their fate rests on bringing in more women they may not believe can do as good a job as the male candidates they're unable to hire by mandate. While Stage Zero companies are in denial, those in Stage One are almost purely reactive and defensive.

In a one-on-one coaching session, a senior woman executive told us the quotas tainted her success with feelings of "helping someone check off a box." Though on the surface new policies in her company may have helped her get the promotion, she was worried about the long-term consequences and the effect the same policies were having on her colleagues who felt she was getting an unfair leg up. "I hear some of the conversations that the men are having, and I sense their resistance." Since the institution of the quotas, she felt "I'm going to get scrutinized even *more* now! I didn't want to advance this way. I don't define this as personal success." This coveted senior woman exec, a visible signal of the company's achievement of gender equity, was ready to quit. She said her female colleagues felt the same way.

She may have put her finger on something real in sensing the growing resentment among the men in her organization. Men in companies at Stage One often do feel snubbed. They see more women than men hired into the organization and may resent the amount of money and resources focused on the advancement of women. And they can't help but notice the targeted recruitment of women into the higher levels; some-times they are put in charge of it. Rather than equalizing the playing field, the company may experience an unintended backlash that can re-verse any intended progress. One of the senior woman's male colleagues said, "I've been with the company for ten years and have a strong track record. I don't mind straight-up competing for that open position, but for leadership to go outside the company and pay top dollar just to have a woman on the team is not what I would call fair competition or good business sense." While he said he didn't wish her ill, he also didn't feel motivated to support or mentor her and predicted she would indeed have a hard time fitting in with the rest of the executive team—all men. As with the women, the male executive said his colleagues had started look-ing around for other opportunities, feeling they were at a distinct disad-vantage where they were. There is no better example to us of a lose-lose situation. Stand-alone quotas often cause discord instead of improving communication, fueling resentment in some and demoralizing others by making their success seem inauthentic or undeserved.

We recently flew to Miami to conduct a preliminary organizational diagnosis with the chairman of a large Swiss electronics company. The chairman had brought along his top management, including his CEO and the entire senior management team of eight men and two women. As the sun shone fiercely outside, inside the conference room there was a new mindset dawning. We were exhilarated when, during that morn-ing session, we could sense a growing awareness among the team and hear a new tone in their dialogue. They were zooming along, exploring what would be involved to move from Stage Zero to a Three, and were in the midst of discussing what Stage Three would look like and what they would need to do to make it to that level, when the CEO jumped in.

It was clear that the CEO just wasn't getting it. Instead of encourag-ing the discussion or listening to the others, he kept changing the sub-ject back to complaining and blaming the Swiss government for "forcing these quotas on me." We observed him carefully, knowing full well the power his early-stage mindset could have over the rest of the group.

The head of HR then took her turn presenting a well-thought-out ex-planation of recent focus groups and one-on-one sessions with the senior women in the company. The results were sobering. Many senior women felt excluded and dismissed. More than that, their discouragement had come to a head—the percentage of women in the top two tiers who were thinking of leaving stunned many in the room, especially the chairman, the shock evident on his face. As the group sat silently, absorbing the news, the CEO jumped in and dismissed her presentation out of hand. "I don't think you have enough data," he blurted out defensively. "We should ask the women more questions or other questions to reveal the *real* truth."

Through it all, the chairman sat quietly, even during the rant by the CEO. He saved his one and only comment for the end of the meeting: "Gender diversity has to be a top priority for us. Our consumer base is more than sixty-five percent women. It makes total business sense for us to increase the voice of women in senior, decision-making roles."

Throughout our diagnostics and workshops, it's encouraging how many leaders recognize their blind spots and have immediate insights into their behavior and that of the people around them. In a fairly short period of time, they begin their journey to see diversity through a whole new lens—a world of possibility that is either encouraged by the top leader, or deflected and dismissed.

Many male leaders in Stage One believe, deep down, that the focus on diversity and numbers is an irritation—a distraction from the real strategic initiatives of the business. And while they'd like to hold out on making any changes at all, they reluctantly acknowledge that it's something that has to be dealt with. They then pass the problem on to HR to ensure compliance and do what's minimally required and nothing more, which is one of the primary reasons organizations don't progress from Stage One—they're not acknowledging and owning the issue.

Because they don't recognize the power of diversity, many Stage One leaders undervalue the women on their teams. Their direct reports then mirror that behavior with the women on their teams. You can see that the Swiss company's HR's report on women leaving at the top two levels was accurate enough. What usually prompts a company to move to Stage Two is a change of leadership (a new CEO coming in who has an agenda relative to gender diversity), an event on the part of the current CEO that changes his or her life significantly, a class-action lawsuit, or a mass exodus of women at the senior level.

STAGE TWO: "IT'S A GOOD THING TO DO"
Moving on from the anger and resentment that characterize Stage One, this stage is all about good people with the best of intentions trying to do

good things. In fact, many companies in Stage Two put a great deal of thought and effort into gender diversity. Stage Two is populated with organizations of people who want to be socially responsible and do the right thing when it comes to gender equality. They focus on gender diversity because of a sense of obligation and fairness.

While some leaders are still reactive and defensive at this stage, others approach gender balance from the standpoint of genuine compassion for women. They want them to succeed. Leaders at this stage tend to see it as the right thing to do, but only in that light. They still aren't considering the economic value of gender diversity, outside of perhaps showing their organizations and themselves as socially progressive, which from a public relations standpoint has residual value. They point to their statistics to prove that they're making progress.

Nonetheless, in Stage Two, leadership has not thought through the implications completely. They envision diversity mostly in terms of enlarging the talent pool or perhaps reducing turnover, both of which are valuable, but are only part of the issue. For these leaders, there is nothing that connects it to a more foundational business case related to how we do business and how we work with one another, removing a powerful motivator for foundational culture shift. To Stage Two companies, gender equality is a not a strategic but a social imperative. Because of that limited scope, the diversity efforts of companies at Stage Two are often not sustainable.

We know of a charismatic CEO of a major retail company who talked a very good game. To be fair, he genuinely cared about the advancement of women. And it wasn't a purely academic topic for him—at least not in the usual way. His two daughters were graduating from a prestigious university, one daughter in technology—a field that embodies the male-driven paradigm. He wanted to be seen and have his company recognized as "doing the right and fair thing for gender equality."

During town hall meetings and in interviews with the press, he would let drop the check he signed last spring for $2 million for the women's initiative and emphasized frequently that diversity and inclusiveness comprised a core part of the company's values.

And he didn't stop there. He initiated a partnership between his organization and a top college to create a women's leadership development program for the company's female senior managers and directors to attend. He encouraged that regional women's network meetings be held every quarter and he personally attended all six sessions in North America (a fact we knew because the communications department well publicized his attendance).

Unfortunately, the public face of the company and the CEO didn't match at all his behavior at the office and in his dealings with leadership. It would be fair to say there was a complete disconnect between what one would consider a leadership model of inclusivity and his own personal style. His team reported that he was often painfully direct, singularly focused on his agenda, uninterested in collaboration, and unilateral in his decision-making.

As a result, few people were very comfortable working with him, especially the women on his staff. Instead, they feared him to the point that any issues related to his own conduct and character they considered out of bounds. The scant number of women in the upper levels was the most telling symptom of his lack of Gender Intelligence, but not the only one. The biggest problem was in all the money applied to gender diversity with so little movement. With all the women's initiatives in play, the company had only three women at the top of the organization, and through one-on-one coaching, we discovered that one of the three was dusting off her resume.

The worst part was that the CEO couldn't see the huge chasm between his intention and his behavior. He was completely blind to the effect his leadership was having on the company's ability to retain senior-level women and on its consequent inability to expand into the women's apparel market.

In practice, it is his leadership mindset—not his press releases—that continues to set the tone. He recently scored big by hiring the female head of marketing away from his number-one competitor, upping her considerable salary and perks in order to get her creative talent and skill in marketing to women. He even sent her to attend the company's leadership training program. According to most, she lived up to her resume and brought great ideas for growth, and the company's advertising agency loved working with her. The CEO, however, had difficulty straying from his strategic plan and dismissed nearly all of her ideas. She lasted less than twelve months.

Leaders at this stage are trying to do the right thing and perhaps even manage to modestly improve gender diversity. They seem to care about advancing women and their values seem to be in the right place. Their efforts are misplaced, though, with many also acting out of a sense of guilt. They sign checks, speak about feminist values, and make appearances to assuage their feelings of omission. Others do it to "support women" out of a sense of compassion, which is interpreted by many women as condescending and patronizing rather than supportive—especially in the case when the leader's behaviors don't line up with his (or her) values.

On the positive side, we see movement away from the denial in Stage Zero and the resistance in Stage One, but leaders at Stage Two still approach gender diversity with a somewhat incomplete mindset. Few if any have yet to make the connection to economic value. The ones that do often get a wake-up call from a competitor who seizes an advantage in the industry by hiring a number of highly sought-after female executives, or they get exposed to the growing body of research on the relationship between Gender Intelligence and the bottom line and heed the call.

STAGE THREE: "WE HAVE BUSINESS REASONS"

The strategic connection lacking in Stage Two begins to come into play in Stage Three, with companies starting to view gender balance as a tactical imperative and to want women in positions of power because it makes good business sense. A company may reason, for example, that if their products are purchased in large part by women, then the organization should have a meaningful representation of women running key business units or heading up departments that help connect to the marketplace.

That it makes good business sense even well beyond the market potential is *the* breakthrough insight for companies in Stage Three: the business case for gender diversity. Leaders in this stage are beginning to realize that Gender Intelligence produces a better financial outcome. They can see the results in the marketplace as gender-blended teams start to create more innovative ideas, operate more effectively, and produce greater profitability. This stage, more than any other, marks the breakthrough point that is crucial for sustainability. Without it, the efforts in prior stages don't have a lasting effect. With it, there is a meaningful chance, especially if understood in gender-intelligent terms and not just in terms of diversity of representation.

Though their efforts are still often initiative-based, there are the beginning signs of Gender Intelligence in Stage Three organizations. This might look like intense targeted recruitment of women and an intentional focus on filling the leadership pipeline, but there is still a general lack of women in senior leadership, for reasons as yet unknown to the company.

The research is compelling—companies that are inclusive of both women and men at all management levels are simply more productive. Acknowledging the diversity advantage and making a concerted effort to recruit, retain, and advance women in conjunction with men help improve company culture and boost the bottom line. In practice, Gender Intelligence benefits organizations in six distinct and profound ways:

1. Improved Decision-Making and Increased Innovation

Behavioral studies consistently show that more balanced gender-blended teams are more likely to make better decisions, produce more innovative solutions, and achieve substantially greater results than homogeneous teams.

The level of collaboration in teams is directly related to the balance of men and women. Balance in teams encourages innovation, not because one gender is more clever or better, but because gender blending adds a richer collection of viewpoints and perspectives to the decision-making process. Teams containing a better balance of men and women demonstrate greater emotional perception, collective intelligence, and encouragement of ideas.[35]

2. Responsiveness to Customers and Markets

Responsiveness to customers and markets is the one advantage that is powerful when customized to the company's industry. Gender-blended teams in design, development, marketing, and sales ensure their products and services satisfy the most diverse markets.

Today in the United States, women spend more than $5 trillion annually (half the U.S. gross domestic product) and account for 83 percent of all consumer spending decisions.[36] Globally, women control over $20 trillion in spending, twice the GDP of China and India combined.[37]

The more a company mirrors its customers demographically, the better positioned it is to sense and respond to evolving market needs.

3. Balanced Leadership

The Impact Research Center recently compiled sixty-two studies on gender differences in leadership. Here is the summary of the leadership traits most often expressed by men and women:[38]

Gender and Leadership Traits: Summary of 62 Studies

MEN'S TENDENCIES	WOMEN'S TENDENCIES
Form structures	Form relationships
Competes	Collaborates
Sequential thinking	Multitask thinking
Ritualized action	Cross connections
Separate emotions	Show direct empathy
Promote risk-taking	Scrutinize risk-taking
Solve quickly	Help coworkers more
Demonstrate authority	Demonstrate relationship
Immediate action	Reflection before action

If you view each of the nine behavioral traits as a continuum with men's and women's tendency for that trait on opposite ends, then the complement of that trait would rest somewhere balanced between the two genders. If you consider then that equilibrium across all nine leadership traits is valuable to the economic growth of an organization, it follows that you would ideally strive for gender balance on the leadership team.

4. Minimized Risks and Costs

Gender discrimination cases have risen by 400 percent in the United States in the last decade, with the vast majority related to motherhood. A similar dynamic is taking place in many countries, though it is not as prevalent as in the United States.[39]

Apart from direct costs including legal fees and potential fines, gender discrimination suits bring significant indirect costs to the company, such as bad publicity, loss of market share, and damage to the brand.

Discrimination is part of a company's risk assessment. Companies that are good employers for women add to their credibility with key stakeholders (employees, investors, consumer groups, regulators). They not only minimize their risk, but also build brand credibility and goodwill.

Companies that are bad employers for women risk a crisis of confidence for their brand name and their survival in an increasingly competitive global economy.

5. Tapping into a Broader and More Complete Talent Pool

Companies that tap into this powerful talent pool and effectively apply Gender Intelligence in the hiring, promotion, and utilization of both men and women have a huge talent advantage over their less gender-intelligent counterparts.

These five advantages all contribute to and result in the sixth and most important advantage of a gender-intelligent organization:

6. Superior Financial Performance

Study after study shows that companies with more gender-diverse top management teams financially outperform companies with less diverse leadership. The most long-term study to date involving 215 Fortune 500 companies over a nineteen-year period showed strong correlations between a better balance of men and women in leadership positions and high profitability, including a 34 percent higher profit margin, 18 percent higher asset value, and 69 percent greater stockholder equity.[40]

The bottom line is that companies that practice Gender Intelligence and sustain a culture conducive to gender diversity and inclusiveness grow in their global competitiveness. They secure and retain the best talent, make better strategic decisions, produce more relevant products and services, and, as a result, achieve superior financial results, details of which we'll provide later on in the book.

Years ago, Dove soap, a division of Unilever, had a huge "aha!" moment that changed the course of their marketing and advertising forever. They shifted away from the industry's traditional portrayal of idealized female beauty and moved toward showing, and connecting with, real women. Perhaps unsurprisingly, it was real women who showed them the way.

We were front and center as this shift happened, beginning with our moderating a series of focus groups with women consumers. A parade of women who bore little resemblance to the models featured in Dove's ads filed into the building that morning: Some with cinnamon-colored skin and others fair and freckled. Hair that ranged from black to bottle blond to gray, and kinky to stick-straight. Some women were slimmer, others decidedly more rounded in the hip and thigh.

Divided up, they were ushered group by group into a room and given their task of offering feedback on Dove's newest ad campaign. While Dove company leaders and members of their ad agency sat behind a two-way mirror, the women scrutinized the messaging and images before them, all taken from the company's current campaign, and let it fly. Those sitting behind the mirror looked on in horror as they listened to the reactions from the would-be customers they were trying to appeal to:

- "These women's figures are Photoshopped."
- "This isn't what an average woman looks like."
- "I don't know any mothers who look like that."
- "How will these skinny models affect my daughter's self-esteem?"

They spoke, and they were heard. Their collective insights that day began a huge paradigm shift within the company. The Dove Campaign for Real Beauty launched immediately afterward, becoming a global effort and a catalyst for change in the industry by widening the definition and discussion of beauty. Leadership launched the campaign to support Dove's mission to "make women feel more beautiful every day by challenging the contemporary, stereotypic view of beauty and inspiring women to take great care of themselves."[41]

In an industry where the standard of beauty is the six-foot, size-zero, sixteen-year-old supermodel, Dove distinguishes itself by using models who range from size six to fourteen, abandoning the conventional method of portraying only "perfect" idealized women that creates unrealistic role models for young girls and alienates a host of potential consumers. Instead, the company aims to honor and respond to what they heard in that room that day—the fact that beauty comes in all shapes, colors, ages, and sizes. Since Dove began its Real Beauty campaign, they've gained a greater market share. And the company has been attracting the most talented women in the industry—from product development to marketing and sales.

Those in leadership in Stage Three begin to see that women and men working in unity make for a powerful strategic combination. They realize that the blending of diversity of thought in problem-solving and decision-making can change the work environment for the better, drive retention and productivity, and, most important, deliver results. They work to message the strategic impact of gender-balanced teams throughout the organization.

Closing the leadership gap and leveraging gender-diverse talent become a priority for businesses in Stage Three, for what drives the leadership mindset in these companies is the intention to remain competitive in the global marketplace. Companies at this stage have woken up to the fact that having women in positions of power makes strategic sense. As a result, they move into Stage Four and take significant action. Whether they sustain that action and do it wisely is what determines whether they finally make it to Stage Five.

STAGE FOUR: "WE'RE IN TRANSITION"

The picture is beginning to coalesce for the companies in Stage Four who have a clear business plan for gender balance and are on the path to becoming genuinely inclusive employers. They have various initiatives in the works and are wholly committed to gender diversity. Although aggressive at recruiting women and increasing the percentage of women in middle and senior management, like so many companies they're often unable to sustain the percentages of women at the top.

Though they're very advanced along the continuum, this can be a confusing time for the leadership in these organizations. They've made the connection of gender diversity to greater innovation, competitive advantage, and bottom-line results, yet they still find themselves at a transformational crossroads and the continued reversal of gains. Often, not always, they also begin to suffer from initiative fatigue and find their efforts starting to stall. This causes many to question their progress.

Though they try their best to create and maintain gender balance, too often they fall into the trap of viewing it only in terms of numbers, not as diversity of thought. While they are more attuned to women's voices, they may still believe that treating everyone the same is the key to success, rather than wholly embracing gender differences and utilizing the powerful balance that comes from those differences.

As a result, many companies in Stage Four experience battle fatigue and begin slipping backward. This is often linked to their business case becoming outdated and lowering the pressure or to their failure to link gender diversity to the company's top strategic priorities. The transition to Stage Four can be a positive thing, which is the case with many of the companies we work with. The transition can also prove a frustrating experience for leaders who understand the economic value in diversity but still find it challenging to change the culture of their companies.

"Eight years ago you asked us about women in leadership here," one senior vice president of diversity told us, "yet we still haven't changed the dynamic in the executive team." She worked in a major consumer goods company that had worked hard on diversity initiatives. "There are actually *more* women than men in middle management, but our talent management and retention programs aren't working," she complained, despite the company having poured money into programs that focused on gender diversity. For a consumer goods company, they were also falling behind in critical departments that could not afford missed connections with female consumers. "The percent of women in our sales departments has declined two years in a row now, and women still represent only eighteen percent of our senior leadership team."

Organizations that understand the economic value but don't transition well to Stage Four often still harbor a Stage One or Stage Two mindset. Leadership still frames the initiatives as "fixing" the woman problem and still default to a uniformity of behavior for men and women, primarily guided by male-designed functions, processes, and systems. It's no wonder that many of these companies describe their progress as two steps forward and one step back.

Then there are those companies that are making the transition and reaping results. Companies like American Express, BMO, Deloitte Canada, eBay, and IBM are intent on learning and are getting better and making greater strides. The key difference is that they're approaching gender diversity appropriately, as not only a business strategy but also a deep culture change. We can't make this point strong enough: culture change is the hallmark of organizations at this stage. They are creating learning opportunities for managers and leaders on how to become more gender-intelligent and modeling the right mindset at the top.

Below are some of the practices that Stage Four organizations discovered to have a significant, positive effect on shifting company cultures and, as a result, creating gender-intelligent organizations:

PRACTICE	REASONS FOR SUCCESS
Women's networks are part of a strong task force	• Network focused on action • Appoints key **men and women** to chapter leadership instead of taking volunteers • Chapter head is a high-profile developmental assignment
Culture change	• Operates on many levels; permeates everything the company does
Visible leadership commitment	• Supports culture change • Empowers leaders to learn what they need so they can walk the talk
Reporting metrics and accountability for results	• Tracks representation, retention, attrition, and leadership behaviors • Ranks leadership behaviors equally with all other metrics • Captures management attention • Empowers managers to walk the talk
Sponsorship of women	• Senior men sponsor high-potential women • Training provides opportunity to learn about effective sponsorship
Succession planning	• Removes potential blind spots based on assessing people on sameness • Creates a gender-mixed and diverse slate of candidates
New talent management	• Redesign includes different leadership competencies and the strengths of gender and cultural differences

When successful, the mindset of Stage Four CEOs reflects Gender Intelligence and incorporates those principles into a clear vision for the future direction of the company. Many leaders in this stage are so committed to change, they often express concern over whether the company can sustain that commitment once they're gone. They experience what we call "the two-to-three-year syndrome." They know they can drive Gender Intelligence and plan for growth through change in the near term, but they also know that they are not going to be the head of the company forever.

The CEO can be as passionate as possible about instilling Gender Intelligence, but it does no good if the focus and prioritization go away when the leader leaves. In order to create sustainability, Gender Intelligence must be infused into the DNA of the culture of the organization and steps must be taken to ensure that all its functions, processes, and systems reflect a gender-intelligent design. Committing to change at the leadership level and building gender-intelligent principles into the company DNA is the only way an organization can attain the Holy Grail, Stage Five, and become an employer of choice in their industry for both men and women alike.

STAGE FIVE: "WE ARE AUTHENTICALLY A GENDER-INTELLIGENT COMPANY"

Admittedly, very few companies make it to Stage Five, but for those that do, we've witnessed an unparalleled excitement and energy as these organizations come to see the whole concept of gender equality in a totally new way. There is a sense of relief and anticipation that accompanies the realization that it *is* possible to create win-win relationships between men and women.

These companies have broken the code of sameness and chosen to view gender unity from a strength-through-differences standpoint, eschewing the false god of equality in numbers. These organizations recognize that women and men bring different and equally valuable perspectives to the table and know they need each other's perspective to sustain growth and success.

In Stage Five, along with changing leadership mindset and its infusion into company culture, there must also be systemic change. Stage Five companies complete their transformation by adjusting their policies, procedures, and marketplace practices to reflect Gender Intelligence and inclusive behavior.

Though it takes hard work to get there, the outcome is truly transformational. We've seen companies become more innovative, more fluid, more inclusive, and more expansive in their use of talent. We've watched them become more effective at solving problems and in making decisions. The entire organization performs better with improved bottom-line results.

Jane Allen, partner and chief diversity officer for Deloitte Canada, enthused, "We don't have the turf wars anymore and the 'men's den' is *gone*. Female partners no longer fight with male partners over procedures and turfs." Allen has watched silos come down because Gender Intelligence "changed the tone and nature in the sharing of information." She says you can feel the inclusivity in every team meeting. Not only have attitudes and communication shifted; all the divisive behavior is in the past. What Allen calls "the exodus of women" has been reduced by half, saving Deloitte tens of millions each year in turnover costs. Because of Gender Intelligence, Allen says, "we are a different company today and still growing."

As with every level, transformation begins with leadership. Especially at Stage Five, no company can attain and maintain at this level without the mindset of the leaders and managers first establishing a commitment to change and a vision of what Gender Intelligence looks like in practice in their organization. Leaders of Stage Five organizations are true believers in Gender Intelligence and exhibit common core qualities and characteristics in their leadership that shape the culture and course of their organizations:

- They don't act on assumptions, but instead, test them.
- They understand how to leverage the strengths men and women bring to the table.
- They actively encourage collaboration and solicit different perspectives in problem-solving and decision-making.
- They're aware of their impact on others and have the ability to self-correct.
- They treat Gender Intelligence as a high priority, always seeking to learn more and encouraging others to do the same.
- They promote gender-mixed input in all situations.

It is worth highlighting that Stage Five leaders create corporate cultures where diversity of thought is encouraged throughout the organization. Men and women alike see the value in engaging authentically and honestly with each other and their collaborative efforts are valued exchanges of ideas. As a result, diversity of thought and of input leads to better product and market decisions that help companies grow and innovate.

"We Think We're a Five!"

There are a number of organizations that don't fit any of these stages. The leaders in these companies are stuck in a *deep* form of denial. Because they have a fair number of women in middle management or a woman or two in their executive ranks or on their board or offer special mentorship programs to women, they believe they have achieved gender equality. They really don't think any additional effort is required on their part, and you can hear that attitude expressed by leaders and managers at all levels:

- "We're always fair in our hiring."
- "We treat everyone the same."
- "We went through unconscious bias training."
- "We have no problems here. Take a look at Brenda—she's on the executive team."
- "We have many initiatives that support women."

In fact, you will often hear senior leaders in these organizations boast about their progress during all-company meetings. Many are even lauded by HR publications and research organizations as hallmark progressive examples because one or two of their officers are women, or they offer the most generous work flexibility programs. All this tends to do is further strengthen their denial and perception of progress.

Despite their great internal and external PR, these companies are far from Stage Five, because they lack awareness. Often, they're just playing it by the numbers, filling the pipeline with women and expecting that time will take care of the rest and create a gender balance without any further intervention on the part of their leadership. They are focusing on gender diversity in terms of representation alone and on the numerical evidence that they are diverse and without bias. What the leadership in companies at this stage fails to grasp is that the true measure of gender diversity isn't found in the numbers.

A Chain Reaction Throughout the Organization

We know many CEOs who are fluidly gender-intelligent and walk the talk. Their style of leadership is not only trusted and respected but is emulated by their direct reports. Wherever your company lands now on the continuum, the fact remains that a company's leader embodies the initial energy needed to create a gender-intelligent chain reaction throughout the organization. The mindset of the leader and style of leadership set the tone; they can discourage and silence or they can inspire and guide others. A gender-intelligent leader has the power to change cultures and move companies along the continuum—from denial, to realization, to practice.

Reproducing these results over time in differing conditions is what separates great companies from good ones. But it's great managers and leaders who make the ultimate difference and who have the power and responsibility to create company cultures that value difference-thinking.

Part Two

Why Gender Intelligence
Is Next in the Evolution

6

Past, Present, and Future

n Part One, we introduced you to a new conversation that's taking place on gender. We shared with you a burgeoning movement that's already transforming organizations as well as the professional and personal lives of men and women across the globe—a new paradigm in thinking called Gender Intelligence.

This movement toward Gender Intelligence didn't come out of the blue. Instead, it's the result of varied historical shifts and trends that brought us to this point. Women's evolving roles in the work world, tremendous advances in brain science research, and the explosion of career opportunities in the Information Age have all contributed to the current state of gender diversity in the workforce and affected how we think about it.

Sifting through time, we begin to notice how each shift and trend gave rise to the next, incrementally advancing women in the workforce. And we get a sense of an important modern convergence in social change, scientific advances, and an evolving economy all pointing to Gender Intelligence as the next and necessary step in the progression of our understanding and valuing of gender differences.

In this chapter, therefore, we take a brief pause in our narrative to explore how this understanding of the brain and gender differences has emerged, and its important implications for organizations. We'll briefly examine modern history to trace the evolution from the economic necessity that first brought women into the workplace to new generations of women who work for money and a love of what they do. Looking at the past through a gender-intelligent lens is illuminating; it shows us that though the face of business—and society—is radically different today, the business model of the workplace, designed by men for men generations ago, remains basically intact. We believe it's time that this remaining artifact of days gone by gets its own modern makeover.

A Matter of Necessity

Though the "workplace" itself has dramatically changed and evolved over the last hundred years, women have always been there. On the farms and in the fields of our early agrarian economy, women worked alongside men, shoulder to shoulder, from spring planting to fall harvest. Entire families toiled, driven by their own subsistence needs as well as to earn more income for the household. In these early communities everyone contributed their share, not just to the family but also to their neighbors or to towns and villages as well. Everyday tasks were divided fairly rigidly along traditional gendered lines. The blurring of those lines is a more modern construct.

Though we think of it as a relatively recent phenomenon, women have always worked outside the home in many countries in the Western world. Even before the Industrial Revolution, women filled domestic service jobs and served as seamstresses, apothecaries, barbers, and midwives. Many women, especially widows, also worked in businesses started or owned by their husbands or started new businesses after their husband's death in order to support their families.

As the Industrial Revolution transformed the Western world, by the middle of the nineteenth century, young men—many just boys—left their family farms to go to work in factories. Economic necessity also compelled women to buck social norms and find paid work. Factory labor provided independent wages for many women, especially young, single women who left their rural homes in order to earn money to send back to their parents and also to seek a better standard of living for themselves. Ten percent of women in the Western world held jobs outside of home in the mid-1800s, a number that rose to 15 percent as the twentieth century dawned.[42]

While the norm was a sole (male) breadwinner for each family, in reality, then as now, many families couldn't make ends meet on what the man brought home alone, pushing ever more women into the workforce.

Looking back, we can draw clear parallels between the situational needs of nineteenth-century families and the economic strain families still experience today.

Of course, having both men and women go off to work didn't make the daily chores any lighter or any less necessary. It often fell to the women, who worked outside the home, to shoulder the double burden of earning a living wage and still taking the primary role in child care, cooking, and cleaning. In some countries, multigenerational households were commonplace and helped alleviate the burden to some degree. Grandparents were able to help look after the children and prepare the meals while women went to work.

As the nineteenth century progressed, the division of jobs by gender began to accelerate as management roles were filled almost exclusively by men. This division went beyond the boardroom. Men were chosen to operate the most expensive and sophisticated machinery, elevating their status in the company and earning them more pay compared to women, even in textile mills.

The Model for Success

While the division of jobs by gender began in earnest during the Industrial Revolution, the male workplace model was also established, a model that holds firm to this day. In the more regulated world of factories and industry, planning efficiency and economies of scale became the most important features of business success. Created by men primarily for men, the industrialized business world was highly structured, hierarchical, and competitive. Fueled by male-brained leadership, the workplace culture rewarded speed in decision-making, efficiency of execution, individual performance, and goal attainment. For close to two hundred years, this male model of thinking and acting seemed like a natural fit for the new business environment.

Few men questioned the model, and though some women might have offered an alternative, given the economic necessity to work, challenging the overwhelmingly male business culture wasn't a luxury most women could afford. Relatively speaking, there were so few women in the workplace that the ones employed rarely questioned the rules of engagement.

Women did what they needed to do in order to fit in and succeed in their workplaces, assimilating to the one mode of behavior, one way to

think, and one way to perform—as quickly and as efficiently as possible. Out of necessity, they learned to work within that structure, with
daily labor often more a test of endurance than a fulfilling job experience.
What mattered most, to both men and women, was getting that paycheck
come the end of the week.

A Show of Competence

Though some women worked outside the home throughout history, it took
a major catalyst in the form of World War II for women to make sizable
inroads into the workforce. As troops shipped out from Allied and Axis
countries alike, women flooded into the workforce in order to backfill the
huge vacuum created by men going off to war, a movement symbolized in
the United States by Rosie the Riveter, a cultural icon representing the
legions of housewives who emerged from the kitchen to enter the factory.
This was a breakthrough moment. The war effort made women working
outside the home a national imperative for many countries. It provided a
compelling argument for men reluctant to embrace women in these new,
traditionally "male" roles. Women took on more physical tasks and were
also required to take on more meaningful roles, including management.
In doing so, something significant happened—they demonstrated enormous competence in their new capacities.

Once the troops returned home to civilian life, they reclaimed the jobs
they had left and many women left the workforce to raise families. Yes,
during the prosperity of the 1950s, many women continued to work outside the home, albeit mostly in secretarial and social services roles. What
wouldn't change was the new light in which societies around the globe
viewed the roles and capabilities of women. While roles did revert back
somewhat following the war, the world had caught a glimpse of the ability of women to adapt and succeed at doing what was previously thought
only men could do.

From Manual Work to Knowledge Work

In the postwar 1950s, yet another dynamic came into play, altering the
model for success in business and creating more opportunities for career

women alongside men. Industrial jobs requiring greater physical strength and endurance, such as working on an assembly line or in construction, started to give way to more jobs requiring significant amounts of creativity and intelligence, specifically in the collection, organization, and use of information.

In the 1950s, writer and business consultant Peter Drucker coined the term "knowledge worker" to describe professionals such as programmers, systems analysts, technical writers, academic professionals, and researchers. The term also included people outside of information technology who worked in the fields of medicine, science, and law.

Drucker emphasized that the future of economic growth had to come from knowledge-based work rather than a focus on manufacturing. That important shift would create heretofore unmatched opportunity for women. While a secretarial job at a bank, as example, would still be filled by a woman, Drucker envisioned a world where the vice president of that same bank might be of either gender.[43] In knowledge work, no longer were physical abilities crucial.

The growth in information management meant more opportunity for women to not only pursue careers in industries that were once predominately male, but also to perform the same tasks expecting the same pay. Today, the higher up the ladder we ascend in knowledge work, the more likely it is that there is little gender-related role differentiation needed between men and women—in principle they are capable of and are doing the same kinds of jobs. What hasn't followed, however, is that an equal number of men and women hold top positions, a fact we'll explore in more depth later on.

Why Fix What Isn't Broken

From the bustling factories of the mid-nineteenth century to the orderly office buildings that would largely come to replace them, the nature of work itself underwent tremendous change from the industrial era to the start of the Information Age. But despite the changing nature and demographics of work, up until recently what remained firmly entrenched was the male-designed and male-managed business model. The processes and procedures were deeply rooted and able to survive the shift from industrial to knowledge economies. Even while job functions became more information-based and less manual and repetitive, planning, managing, goal clarity, and efficiency of execution remained central to the standard business model for success. Moreover, the model seemed to continue to yield results. Throughout the 1960s and 1970s, the world would see more economic growth. Its success meant that not only was there no other business paradigm to consider; there wasn't motivation or interest in changing the game . . . until women made it so.

Expecting Equality

With increased opportunity, women's expectations also changed. They were no longer happy with the status quo and became increasingly dissatisfied with the inability to land the jobs they wanted and to achieve economic and social equality with men. Equality—in the form of equal access to the same jobs, opportunities, and compensation as men— became the new goal. Women strived to be treated the same as men— nothing more, nothing less.

By the early 1970s, the women's movement started to take firm root, with North America and Europe leading the way. Early feminists focused on encouraging young women to pursue college degrees, believing that if women were able to achieve a critical mass in higher education, then gender equality would follow. The prevailing belief was that it would just be a matter of time before these young women would naturally ascend into positions of power and influence in business, education, and government. History had other plans.

And all it took was ten years! By the early 1980s, women surpassed men in attaining undergraduate and postgraduate degrees in both North America and Europe. And this trend was not limited to only Western societies. Since 1990, women have represented the majority of college graduates in most every country around the globe and in most every field, even making inroads into those disciplines such as science and engineering, previously nearly exclusive bastions of men.[44] Even in Qatar, a country with a very traditional male-centered culture, fully 70 percent of college graduates are women.[45]

Consider the totality of seismic shifts that happened in a matter of mere decades. The world shifted from women working for economic necessity to women attaining and surpassing men in higher education degrees to women asking for equal treatment in the business world. They weren't challenging the rules of engagement or asking for special treatment. They just wanted an equal shot.

We see now the genesis of gender diversity in the workplace focusing on eradicating inequity, making the workplace fair for men and women by reducing hiring and promotion biases. Born from the feminist movement, this focus on equality through sameness proliferated, taken up by researchers, consultants, and policy makers. Beginning in the 1970s, this focus began to play an important role in the gender diversity conversation and remains central even today.

While the goals were laudable, with the wave of women demanding and expecting equality *within* the existing business paradigm, few if any stopped to consider or appreciate the value that might be found in *changing* the paradigm. Few men or women stopped to consider that the ultimate solution might lie in blending the different ways men and women think. Those who did have been lone voices crying in the wilderness, almost seen as a distraction from mainstream business.

And so, just the opposite has happened. Gender became the elephant in the room as organizations enacted gender-blind policies to demonstrate they were bias-free. Leaders and managers were admonished for even mentioning gender differences. "Unbiased" training and other similar diversity programs sprang up and flourished, advancing some important lessons about how to reduce unconscious bias. An unintended and unfortunate side effect was that it also prevented a richer, more nuanced conversation around men's and women's differences and how they might both play a part in the business world.

It follows that in a world bent on treating and thinking of men and women equally there is no room for the exploration of their natural differences, even if the exploration is based on valuing the differences between them rather than placing one sex above the other. Though there existed social evidence that men and women are not the same, there was little evidence in medical science to support the idea. Any talk of hardwired gender differences, especially around how they played out in the workplace, went underground.

The Same Model for Success?

Of course, there are many things men and women share and ways in which we are alike. We all aspire to success and to set and achieve goals in our lives—it's human nature. But even if our goals—such as bringing a product to market, leading a team, or becoming CEO—are the same, the natural talents and skills each gender brings to the project or the role will tend to be different—*valuably* different.

And so the fundamental way business was conducted stayed static. As we've seen, most men were comfortable with the rules, policies, and procedures of the workplace. It suited them. And although they felt some discomfort, most women coming into the workplace generally accepted the premise that they had to behave like men to get the job—then behave like men to get the job done. While there are women-led companies that offer an exception, these businesses are often small to medium-sized, while the larger corporations remain mired in the male model, fueled by quarterly expectations of Wall Street and keeping their eye on the prize for their stockholders: financial results.

The 1980s saw a spate of books published on how women could make it in a man's world. While even women's casual fashion highlights included shoulder pads and men's style suits, business books coached women on how to dress properly, speak like an executive, behave in meetings, and play office politics just like the boys to give them the boost they needed in order to get ahead. According to prevailing beliefs, more women didn't make it to the top in part because men were unwilling to support them but also because women just weren't a good fit.

What was the solution? Fix the women so that they work equally well, meaning, make the women work in the same way as their male colleagues. It hasn't changed. As we write this book, ever more articles, books, and discussions encourage women to take charge of their pro- fessions as men do. While it's certainly worthwhile to continue to help women to grow and develop in their capabilities, this strategy—then and now—doesn't ultimately change the conversation. It doesn't do anything to create conditions where uniquely masculine and feminine strengths can be blended and utilized to their best effect, and because of that, it doesn't solve the problem.

Knowledge work accelerated the women's movement across the globe, opening doors for careers alongside men in virtually every industry. New technologies allowed decentralized computing, the opening of global markets, and what has now become commonplace—communicating and working every day with people on the other side of the planet.

As the landscape shifted and new opportunities arose, women rose to fill the professional gaps, becoming ever more prevalent in entry-level and mid-management positions. In order to accommodate this growing influx of women and their talent, women demanded and organizations defined ways of making it easier for women to balance their responsibilities at home with their growing demands at work. Work-life balance became the new catchphrase as work flexibility became a key component enabling women to "have it all"—work at demanding and fulfilling careers, but with time for their families and time for themselves.

Knowledge-based work, remote technology, and an emphasis on work-life balance began to have an effect. The command-and-control model began to give way to a more organic, and female, workplace culture. Organizations dotted the business landscape with less hierarchy; more fluid, self-managing teams; and greater emphasis on collaboration across silos and functions.

This shifted how the workplace felt on some levels. Speed, laser focus, and centralized decision-making were no longer the only attributes viewed as contributing to organizational success. Except, that is, at the top, especially in large companies, where the successful leader, executive, vice president, or CEO continued to fit the male mold. Top leaders and managers wanted a quick summary, not the whole story. Reports spoke in bullet points to their bosses in order to get to the bottom line more quickly. Leadership was still equated with male-patterned decision-making, problem-solving, and communication styles. Conversations and meetings might get heated, but that didn't matter—only quarterly results.

While the male-dominated business environment made some room for increased collaboration and a less linear style in middle management on down, the tendency for men and women to think and act differently in the workplace was still not viewed as a competitive advantage. And, as we saw in example after example along the Gender Intelligence Continuum, many leaders, managers, and their organizations still don't see it today.

Seeking Authenticity

In years past, people assimilated to fit into the organizational and leadership culture at work and assumed a new way of doing things. For many women and men it felt unnatural, inauthentic, but hey, it was a paycheck.

In decades past, the main goals for many professionals were not about finding meaning in their work. Instead, the goals were much more practical than ideological: find a job, pay the bills, sacrifice for the children, and retire. There was a certain safety and security in being the "company man," even if you were a woman.

However, the head-down, hard-driving, industrial model for success proves a poor fit for many women and for many men today, especially for younger workers. Long ago we began with subsistence. Fast-forward and paid work was a means to better our personal lives outside the workplace—it allowed us to buy a new car, take a summer vacation, or send the kids to college. Today's workers, some enmeshed 24-7 with work through smartphones and global offices and remote servers, want their professional selves to be more congruous and authentic to their lives as a whole. In gender terms, many women are growing increasingly weary of having to put on a mask or play a role in order to fit in and succeed. They're tired of being forced to think and communicate in ways that are unnatural to them, and tired of putting their hearts into their work while not being valued. They are tired of being held back for not fitting a particular mold. "In meetings, we've learned that it's often best not to express divergent feelings, not to stray off the agenda, and not to ask too many questions," said one woman executive, talking of the daily struggle to fit in. "Too many questions and all of a sudden you're not considered a team player." It's worth noting that all of the generational research out there seems to say that meaningful work and team collaboration are rising to the top for Gen-Ys choosing their careers.

In our diagnostics, we have found that even women who have assimilated into the male paradigm share a uniform opinion of not feeling valued related to their sense of contribution, self-expression, and participation.

In fact, our diagnostics show that the higher women move in the hierarchy of an organization, the more suppressed they feel. They watch the men who find success adopt a goal-oriented, action-driven mindset that speeds through decision-making, leading to immediate action. For many of the women we talk to, this linear, limited mindset, played out day in and day out in meetings, is like water torture. But because of organizational culture, they feel they don't have other alternatives. You're not seen as a team player by saying, "Why won't that work?" or "Have you considered another option?" or "Hold on a minute, not so fast."

However, the women we talk to are less and less inclined to put aside their natural strengths and gifts in order to assume a subordinate role to men's nature—and that's a major shift. More and more women now expect a new kind of equality—not one of sameness, but of *value*.

Anne Mulcahy, former CEO of Xerox, serves as a positive example of a gender-intelligent woman who broke through as an authentic female leader of the future. Asked to speak at the Women's Leadership Board at Harvard's Kennedy School of Government in 2010, Mulcahy stressed the theme of authenticity, offering a picture of corporate life lived much more on her own terms:

> I could feel the pull toward the male paradigm of conducting business every day and I sometimes have to fight it to ensure we have greater collaboration of ideas. I want us to put more thought behind our strategic initiatives and corporate-wide decisions and work to have all voices heard.
>
> I'm also being asked to be on boards, but I don't want to fall prey to the "First Woman Syndrome," where my ideas and suggestions will have a difficult time breaking through. That doesn't create the kind of gender-blended dialogue and diversity of thinking I prefer to be a part of. So I tell them, "When you have thirty percent representation by women on your board, call me."

Work-Life Harmony

In the diagnostics we conduct today, we are seeing another trend emerging. It's not just women who are shifting their values and priorities; many men are seeking greater authenticity as well. We find this expressed in our data that shows there is little to no difference between women and men in their expressed desire for work-life flexibility. Women naturally think in broader terms, and as a whole they have brought a more expanded view of life and work-life balance to the conversation around workplace culture, and their male colleagues are benefiting. Women and men just entering the workforce watched their parents struggle in trying to balance two competing lives—work life and personal life—and witnessed firsthand the effect it had on both the parents and their kids.

Today, a growing percentage of men say they want more time with their children, a desire quite pronounced in the youngest generation of Gen-Y parents, who experienced their boomer mothers and fathers put-

ting in sixty- to seventy-hour weeks. As children, they looked in vain for
their parents' faces at soccer games and opened birthday presents without
mom or dad because a parent was traveling or holed up at the office on
a next-day deadline. A growing number don't want to create that kind of
disconnection with family and to do so would be an incongruity in their
own lives; they don't want to miss what their parents missed.

Today, however, there is greater opportunity for women and men to
create and cultivate authenticity, to make their own choices and live their
values at work and at home. And although this is an emerging trend in
the Western world, the men and women we speak to around the globe
also speak to their work as the expression of something deeper than their
desire for a paycheck. Men and women alike want to feel fulfilled and
also feel that what they love to do contributes to society.

From necessity to ambition to authenticity, we begin to see why history
has been leading us to this time and place where Gender Intelligence
can take root and thrive. But shifting from home to the marketplace, we
find another trend is heating up this dialogue and exposing damaging
incongruities and missed opportunities for companies that don't embrace
Gender Intelligence as our future.

The Voice of the Marketplace

We said this before in making the business case for Gender Intelligence
but it bears repeating: Worldwide today, women control more than $20
trillion in consumer spending, representing two-thirds of total global
spending. Their $18 trillion in combined total yearly earnings is more
than twice as large as China's and India's gross domestic product combined.[46]

In the United States alone, women spend more than $5 trillion annu-
ally (half the country's GDP) and account for 83 percent of all consumer
spending decisions, including:[47]

- 93% of OTC pharmaceuticals
- 93% of groceries
- 92% of vacations
- 91% of new homes
- 89% of bank accounts

- 80% of health care
- 66% of personal computers
- 65% of new cars

When it comes to marketing and advertising, we know that women process information and make purchasing decisions differently than men. Yet despite the fact that 83 percent of consumer purchasing decisions are made by women, surveys indicate that products and services are missing their mark:

- 59% of women feel misunderstood by food marketers
- 66% feel misunderstood by health-care marketers
- 74% feel misunderstood by automotive marketers
- 84% feel misunderstood by investment marketers

Many of the same companies that have put greater emphasis on understanding the diverse needs and wants of varying ethnic groups in the marketplace have ignored doing the same with regard to how women make buying decisions or envisioning the products women really want. The conventional wisdom that men make the money, choose the goods, and write the checks couldn't be more wrong, yet companies have been painfully slow to wake up to the new consumer reality.

Once consumer satisfaction studies were split by gender, the dissatisfaction women had in dealing with banks and other institutions starkly emerged, and now a growing number of companies have begun to pay attention. Companies that employ a gender-blended workforce and that are gender-intelligent are better able to identify with and understand the demographics of the marketplace they serve and can leverage the diversity of thought to provide more and better options for target consumers.

In order to thrive, organizations need mixed teams of men and women at all management levels if they are to produce goods and services that satisfy the buying needs and expectations of both men and women. The more a company mirrors its markets demographically, the better positioned it is to sense and respond to evolving market needs. Sponsors and power brokers in key positions control departmental budgets and have the ability to kill or champion different initiatives, making diversity at the top all that more critical.

Yet as clear and compelling as the numbers may be, there are a number of industries where those traditional gender blind spots we reviewed in the first chapter come into play. These businesses are only taking from traditional models of business success and in the process are obstructing some obvious opportunities for future growth.

A 2010 study by the Boston Consulting Group found that women across the globe were more dissatisfied with the financial services industry than with any other product or service that affected their daily lives. When working with financial advisors, women reported being treated with disrespect and condescension because of their gender.

As it stands, an estimated 70 percent of married women fire their male advisors once their husband dies, and 90 percent of those hire a female advisor afterward.[48] So it's not a matter of these women not needing or wanting a financial advisor—these widows just don't want that person to be male. Something is going on here.

It turns out to be quite simple. Wealth management—like most financial services—is largely male-dominated. And while couples may be served by a traditional approach, once a woman is on her own she isn't satisfied or mollified by standard performance reporting or the occasional nine holes of golf. Women like to feel that their financial advisor is taking the time to educate them about the financial planning process and understand their personal needs.

They do not want someone who will assume her goals are the same as those directed by her late husband. "Let me just continue to take care of your investments," they are told, hand patted. "I know your finances and I know your goals. We'll just continue along the same path as your husband had taken."

Most women don't cotton to being treated like a silent partner. Like men, women want to be educated, understand fee structures, and have advisors who are trying to help them comprehend their full financial picture. Instead of a sales pitch, they want to be taught about products in language they understand so they can have a sense of agency and control.

These financial services firms will continue to ignore women's needs at their peril. Over the next decade, baby boomer women the world over will control two-thirds of consumer spending *and* be the beneficiaries of the largest transference of wealth in history. Many older women will come into a double inheritance—from both the parents they helped care for and a husband they outlived. And they'll be looking for a professional who respects them, can speak their language, and understands their needs.

Though women influence slightly over 80 percent of new car purchases and 60 percent of new cars are directly purchased by women, only 7 percent of dealership employees are women.[49]

There's a real disconnect here. Surveys show that women feel way more comfortable making a high-stress purchase like an automobile from another woman; even *men* would rather buy cars from women. And it turns out, they also find women less pushy, more informed, and more truthful.

When buying a car, women go prepared. They may go online and comparison-shop before they visit a dealership or gather info from friends or coworkers. They do their homework first and go in expecting to have a transparent sales process, one most dealerships fail to offer. In learning about the car's features, women also tend to share experiences and talk in stories and they prefer to receive that kind of warm sales experience. What they often get are bulleted items rattled off a features list. And women, especially those who prepare beforehand, don't like the *way* cars are sold to them. Often, they feel intimidated by the negotiating process and find negotiating itself to be just another form of "arguing."[50]

It stands to reason that if women buy or influence the purchase of the majority of new cars and they crave a more female-oriented experience, women salespeople would find great success selling cars. Yet women encounter familiar hurdles when they go to work on an auto sales floor. They're often not welcomed by the predominantly male sales force, left out of sales "huddles" and excluded from informal events.

These are just two of countless examples of a changing marketplace and opportunities for companies to respond to that change. While women have always been in the marketplace, they now bring an evolving and powerful sophistication, awareness, and expectation as the consumer. This is true for other diverse groups as well who are now demanding that companies respond to their purchasing power. And while sophisticated consumerism is not necessarily a gender issue, the awareness around gender differences has accelerated as marketers realize the influence and buying power of women.

The Emerging Model for Success

Singular focus, quick decision-making, and speed to market got the business world to where it stands today. In many ways, the male model has proven tremendously successful. However, by reflecting back on the historic gender shifts and trends through a gender-intelligent lens, we can acknowledge the progress that has been made but wonder how much more successful we could have been.

In the last twenty years, our world has made more progress on gender equality than in the last two hundred. This progress has been the direct result of the three dominant strategies for gender diversity: eliminating workplace inequities, helping women more fully participate in a man's world by adopting male styles of leadership and management, and making it easier for women to balance work and personal life.

Not all organizations and industries have evolved and developed equally. The perspective of time helps us measure growth and change and allows us to determine where an organization lies today—in the past, the present, or the future.

TIME FRAME	GENDER DYNAMIC	SOLUTION
Distant Past	Women relegated to specific and usually service or administrative roles	Provide specific training for women such as secretarial school
Recent Past and Present	Influx of women in all roles	Emphasis on equality, work-life balance, teach women to be like men
Emerging Future	Valuing of authenticity and welcoming of gender differences	Gender Intelligence

Knowing the hurdles we still face in achieving gender balance, we can see where the past strategies have fallen short. Work-life balance programs, for example, while useful, do not begin to address the real issues of why women have not broken the glass ceiling. The emphasis on equality has been an important ingredient in making the workplace more just, but when equality is equated with sameness, the power and potential of gender differences get lost. And teaching women to think, act, problem-solve, and lead like men devalues and discourages women while limiting the vast potential of the masculine and feminine blend in leadership that is crucial for success in tomorrow's workplace.

Gender-intelligent leaders understand this well, and with the background understanding of the science of gender differences and their implications, they act and lead very differently than their unaware counterparts.

7

The Gender-Intelligent Leader

When we first met Bjorn, the CEO of a Danish biotech company, we instantly got his appeal. Boyish-looking and charming, Bjorn is not only charismatic, he's a goodhearted leader who's admired and respected throughout the organization. As we came to know him he told us he was raised by a strong feminist mother who reinforced in him the importance of treating women well. We could see that Bjorn was well-meaning, and had been nurtured to recognize that women are equal to men and should have the same opportunities.

He practiced his enlightened view of women and equality while in college and collaborated well with the few women in his engineering classes while he pursued his PhD. Bright and motivated, Bjorn graduated in his early twenties from one of Europe's top institutions and today, about ten years later, Bjorn is the youngest CEO in his field, leading a successful company with offices and research facilities scattered throughout Scandinavia. Not only that, but his company reflects those same values of gender equality, diversity, and inclusion.

All of the men in the organization see Bjorn as a role model and work hard to emulate his management and leadership style. They love the fact that he's a hard-charging risk taker. They admire his self-certainty, and his confidence in making quick decisions—even when tremendous sums of money are riding on the outcome. The bolder he gets, the more they're in awe.

Bjorn's female employees have more mixed feelings about their leader. In general, they love his enthusiasm, they align with his values, and they believe that he genuinely wants to understand and really cares. We heard more than one woman say with warmth, "He's got two daughters. How can he *not* understand?"

But those women full of good feeling are those who admire Bjorn from a distance, at least two levels down the hierarchy. His female direct reports tell a different story. They find him off-putting and hard to engage with in real, meaningful dialogue. When they raise an issue, he's already moved on to the next thing.

The women executives in his company chafe at his hard-charging, results-only style. As we huddled together in focus groups and in one-on-ones, all the senior women in the company told us there was no true exploration of ideas during meetings, the goal of which, as Bjorn defined it, was "to surface critical issues and resolve them—as many as possible with little discussion." Speed was of the essence. As far as his belief in treating men and women equally well, "you're okay as long as you keep up with him, play on his playing field, and play by his rules." They said he thought he was being fair, but didn't at all realize, or make space to learn, how the women engaged differently in strategic thinking and decision-making.

When we gathered in an austere room in Copenhagen, the chair and board members were there, along with Bjorn and his COO. Together, as we looked at their current-state analysis we'd conducted on why the company hadn't made progress on advancing women, we saw the Bjorn his women executives had described. Unhappy with the data, Bjorn went on the attack, challenging the data and survey results with a domineering swagger. We observed that he didn't listen or stop to consider other opinions. Instead, he reacted defensively by speaking to his intentions, completely unaware of his behavior and its impact on the others at that meeting and the women on his team. "I treat everyone equally," he insisted, shutting down discussion. "That's always been my intent and I practice it every day." He was so clear in his intent, and blind to his behavior, that the data *must* be wrong.

Bjorn is so convinced that his business model for success is the best and only model that he can't comprehend an alternative approach. He can't even see that he's leaving no space for someone to suggest one. More important, he was completely unaware of the effect his own behavior was having and the impact on his leadership team. On the one hand, he claims to want a collaborative organization, yet he consistently shut down dialogue with those who wouldn't compete in his verbal sparring. While the women executives were honest with us, Bjorn's rapid-fire arrogance sent a clear message: "Don't give me feedback." The silence works to keep him in the dark about the Leadership Chain he is creating with his bombastic behavior.

As we've seen in previous chapters, he's not alone. There are many leaders—both men and women—many with goodhearted intentions to do the right thing, who struggle with the same gender blind spots and assumptions that hamper their chances for personal success as well as the sustained success of their companies.

Bjorn represents a dominant percentage of the leadership population, those who have pro-gender equality values and really talk the talk, yet remain mostly gender-unaware themselves. Because they're looking at the world through their prisms of sameness, they can't see the incongruence between their intentions and their behaviors. As with many such leaders, this happened to be Bjorn's greatest blind spot.

Bjorn actually believes his organization is a Five on the Gender Intelligence Continuum, when in reality, it's stuck in Stage One. What he doesn't realize is that his belief is more intention than practice. In reality, it's his hardwiring that's running the show. Playing a part too is his upbringing. He was raised to believe that gender differences do not exist. The only way he knows to play fair is to treat women the same as men.

What's so interesting about Bjorn's story is that it exposes a number of myths in the narrative around gender equality. Here we have a Danish CEO, raised by a professional working mother who has been heavily involved in the women's movement in Denmark since the 1960s. The Nordic countries in which Bjorn grew up and traveled frequently pioneered gender equality more than forty years ago. And that area of Europe is still leading the world today in legislation for gender equality, and, by a huge margin, in work-flexibility programs.

Yet in a turn of events that should by now sound familiar, the percent of women in senior management is little better in the Nordic countries of Finland, Denmark, Iceland, Norway, and Sweden than in other regions of the world that offer far less in the way of structured advancement of women into senior management.[51]

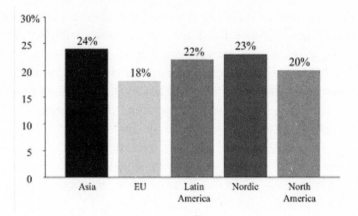

Percent of women in senior management in key regions

Bjorn's relative youth destroys another myth, that it's just the older generation of men who don't get it and that all younger men are more aware, more tuned in, and more inclusive of women. Remember, Bjorn is in his thirties, the youngest CEO in his industry, and we know many young male leaders in most every industry, particularly in technology, who think and act like him.

Of course, by now we can recognize that Bjorn's male behavioral patterns were hardwired at birth, informing and influencing male-oriented thoughts and actions throughout his childhood and teenage years and well into his adult life. Bjorn's style and approach stemmed from this hardwiring, which despite a feminist mother still gets reinforced through the competitive male rituals boys experience growing up, which then translates into high-action orientation in adulthood. The combination is what serves to influence behavior and sets a leader's style. In the case with Bjorn, his intention is to be gender-intelligent, but his nature and some nurture tend to conflict with his intentions. Cloak it all in the myth that sameness creates gender equality, and Bjorn is convinced he's doing the right thing. He is difficult to dissuade because he can't see the problem.

What is it that's keeping Bjorn and other leaders from making the shift to Gender Intelligence? If they have such good intentions, why can't they see the disconnect? We've found that three mental models work to prevent him and others from breaking through. They expect everyone else to act like they do; they're building meritocracies based on a sameness mindset; and they're not recognizing how their behaviors don't align with their intentions.

Recognizing these roadblocks that are keeping even well-intentioned leaders from moving forward led us to identify the correlated fixes that leaders might employ. A growing number of gender-intelligent leaders make their transformation by undergoing three fundamental shifts in leadership that yield real results. They're changing their perception of others, embracing new models for success, and becoming more self-reflective and congruous between intention and behavior.

Three Fundamental Shifts for Becoming a Gender-Intelligent Leader

As the saying goes, "You can't get there from here." So, too, you can't become a gender-intelligent leader without first making shifts in perception, practice, and integrity. In this chapter we'll explain each of the following in more depth:

1. *From Sameness Mindset to Difference Mindset*—Leaders must let go of the belief that men and women are the same and embrace the value in difference-thinking.
2. *From a Gender-Blind Meritocracy to a Gender-Intelligent Meritocracy*—Leaders must shift to creating meritocracies that embrace different models for success rather than sameness.
3. *From Incongruence Between Intention and Behavior to Congruence*—Leaders have to shift from the core belief that "my behavior always flows from my intention" and learn to identify and correct incongruence between the two.

What's key here, too, is that when we envision leadership—and this is a global phenomenon—we still think *male*. This happens with men and women, who each suffer from these leadership assumptions and blind spots. Male leaders are those primarily asked to shift their fundamental beliefs because the business environment was designed with them in mind. But many women have taken on the traits of men and embraced the male model for success in order to survive at the top. As a result, these third-sex women have developed similar blind spots.

In other instances, women hold fast to a female-centered leadership model and reject males on their team who engage in male-oriented behavior that doesn't fit the female model for success. Men who dominate discussions, who prefer to work alone, or who aren't easily able to juggle more than one or two projects at a time will find little empathy with these women, who may misconstrue their style as aggressive, brash, or centered on individual, rather than team, success.

Bjorn's mother had tried to create a feminist son, socialized in a culture of equality, in order to advance the rights of women. Unfortunately, the sameness mindset has almost sterilized his thinking to the point that he can little recognize any form of difference when it comes to gender because he incorrectly assumes that to do so in any case is to employ bias. In Bjorn, and in many other leaders we see, this has created what we call enlightened denial—a resistance to talk through or even consider gender differences for fear of appearing politically incorrect and prejudiced.

As we first covered in Part One, "sameness" is the belief that, if not for the early and suppressive influence of parents, teachers, and culture, men and women would engage the world the same way. It's a nurture-over-nature argument that asserts men and women think and act the same way, engage the world and relationships the same way, and lead and aspire in the same ways, for the same reasons. We have known for a while now that this is simply not true. People who operate from this belief then act as if there are no gender differences; they don't speak to them and are trained to ignore them when they appear.

Gender sameness just isn't working as a strategy, resulting in leadership disconnects like Bjorn's and increasing resentment on the part of women, too. We watched a fascinating and compelling display of this fact at a recent gender diversity panel discussion in Asia featuring two powerful women on the dais: one a senior vice president of global HR for one of the largest technology companies in the world and one a senior officer of a Fortune 500 company and a leading contemporary voice in the feminist movement. There were more than three hundred people in attendance, predominately women managers and leaders from the hosting company itself, but the audience also included other company leaders in Asia as well as members of the Asian media. Everyone in the room was on tenterhooks, waiting for the pearls of wisdom these two accomplished women could offer on how women might break the glass ceiling and achieve comparable success.

The featured speaker from the feminist movement was talking about how to compete and succeed in a male world of business. Her solution was simple, if not revolutionary. "If you want to play with the big boys," she told the audience, "you have to take charge like men do, speak up, and let your voice be heard." In her eyes, any limitations on women's advancement were tied back to the women themselves. "If you're not making it, it's because *you're* not being assertive enough." Life is tough, she seemed to say. It follows that in a competitive world, women need to rise to the challenge. Do it better, do it faster, prove you're better at their game than they are, and you'll win respect.

While this was probably a familiar refrain for many of the older women in the audience, one that some of them surely bought into, a twenty-four-year-old engineer from Tokyo wasn't having it. This slight woman sitting near the front of the room raised her hand. When called on, she firmly said she didn't agree. The room went silent, all eyes on this Gen-Y woman who had ridden the coattails of feminism and dared to disagree with some of the most prominent female business leaders in the world. "I see these two ways of living my life right in front of me now," she said to the women onstage. "The old one, your way, telling me I have to be outspoken and forceful, and I think what you're saying is 'play it like a man in order to succeed.' Then there's my way, the way I really feel, which is to take a stand and say, 'I'm not going to do it that way. I graduated from MIT, top of my class, and I'm going to do it on my terms.'" She'd done as the woman suggested in her college years, she told the audience, and had succeeded by any metric. But the success wasn't on her terms. She was more than capable of playing the game; she just didn't want to. She wanted to be her authentic self and still find success. "I can do what they do," she said, countering, "but it's not the only way, or necessarily the best way." In her own company, she went on to say, she was made to participate in engineering sessions that lasted twenty-four hours at a stretch. "No one showers, or eats. We just work."

Recently, the young woman had caught a glimpse of how it could be. Attending a similar session at another company, the boot camp had been replaced with a very different experience that valued self-care: they had showers, frequent breaks, and even carefully prepared meals. "We even had yoga!" she said. The difference in style made a huge difference in output. "We were very creative," the engineer concluded. "The militaristic, tough way is not the only way to do it."

What's notable about this story is not just that there are options; the story also raises the question, why do we institute boot camp conditions at work in the first place? The answer may be traced back to the time-honored male rituals of testing one's worth. Young male initiations, like fraternity hazing, are a common example, but the same mentality often extends far beyond college. Recently, Keith had a conversation with a male physician friend who reflected on his days as an intern. For two years he worked extraordinary hours, to the point of complete physical and mental exhaustion. Keith asked his friend, what is the purpose of working young doctors so hard that it is not only unhealthy for the interns, but also puts patients at risk because the doctors are so fatigued? His friend had no explanation except that the internship seemed like a proving ground and there was a legacy that perpetuated the system—his advisors had to face it, and theirs before them, and so on. Gender Intelligence offers us a chance to break from these potentially unhealthy traditions and create new systems based on balance.

The healthy applause that followed the young female engineer's statement sent a clear signal that the majority of the women in the audience aligned with her perspective. And hers is just one of countless examples of how the sameness mindset doesn't get the best out of everyone. It overlooks the natural tendencies of women and because of that undervalues what women can offer; it doesn't draw out the best they have to give.

The yoga, the showers, and the thoughtful food (even food at all!) encourage more innovative ideas from women and men and tend to create a more energized environment. The second company's approach feels more self-honoring, which in turn encourages participants to work together more powerfully.

The second approach acknowledges that it's not just about competing faster, but better. When work and workplace culture feel self-honoring, teams don't experience as much burnout. While perhaps not more efficient in terms of every minute being spent on active problem-solving, in the end that approach proves far more effective, eliciting more creative, innovative, and collaborative results.

That female engineer from Tokyo had a different kind of confidence, and a certainty of her own unique strengths that made her one of a powerful group of women and men exhibiting gender-intelligent leadership as they seek personal authenticity and forge ahead.

We met a similar leader recently at a chamber of commerce event where Barbara presented. She was an impeccably dressed Indian woman sheathed in a suit of Chanel armor who was moved to speak after Barbara described how women are often forced to act like men in the workplace. In recognizing herself, she said, "I get the third-sex thing completely. I never looked at it that way. I always thought I had no choice—and maybe I didn't! I even had an executive coach who drilled me to be more like men." In her early forties, the woman was a partner in a Washington, D.C., law firm.

She had "made it." But the victory felt hollow. "I don't feel authentic and this façade becomes stressful because it's not real." What concerned her then was a question many of you may be asking yourselves. If a successful woman is ready to make a move to Gender Intelligence, what will that look like to her superiors, her colleagues, or her direct reports? "How do I undo acting like a man?" she earnestly asked Barbara. "Will I lose my credibility if I bring my authentic self to work, you know, the way I am at home? Will they still think of me as a leader?"

We found this woman's dilemma so poignant, and yet hers is a difficult question to answer and for each individual there is a unique path. Many women can only become their authentic selves by leaving the firm that forced them to change in order to succeed. Some look to other organizations with gender-intelligent company cultures and leaders who set the tone. Many strike out on their own, starting businesses that reflect their values.

If you fit the male model of success, whether you're a man or a woman, you probably feel no pressure to change. But for the many women who only mimic that model, their work selves feel forced and unnatural. Almost without exception, in every organization where we conduct a diagnostic of the organization and its culture, we find the same thing: women toward the top don't feel valued or encouraged to behave in ways that are a more natural fit—no collaboration, no slowing down the pace, no time or encouragement to fully explore different ideas or directions. The message to them is clear: "Conform or pursue a career elsewhere."

For all of us, there's a comfort in sameness and, accordingly, many male leaders hire and promote in their image. Add to that the common and enduring belief that effective leadership behavior looks and acts male and it's no surprise that women don't make it to the top nearly as often as men.

Clearly, to expect women to act in inauthentic ways—more like men—and be the only ones to change creates inherent unfairness that women notice. This is partially why there are so few women at the top of these organizations. Some tough it out, but many just don't accept being forced into a male mold that doesn't value them. They get tired of having to pretend to be something they are not. They feel discouraged that their authentic selves are seen as less than—not leadership material. They may accept it initially, or out of economic necessity, but they don't last long. Or they stay—in body, but not in mind.

Meritocracies Lack Gender Intelligence

We've revealed the inherent unfairness in the sameness model—women and men are completely the same, it says; *both should act like men*, reads the fine print. Leaders who completely buy into the sameness model make every effort to appear unbiased in their day-to-day actions and apply this sameness frame of mind to their expectations around performance. They build a meritocracy of evaluation, promotion, and compensation based on that mindset. They also personally see to it that the culture of their company is gender-blind in order to prove they're equal-opportunity leaders who "*care about women and other minorities.*"

We hear this all the time. During the interviews we conduct as part of our organizational diagnostic, we get *so* many male leaders who look at the continuum and stand up to proudly declare, "Our organization is a Five!" Treating men and women the same and establishing a meritocracy allows them the comfortable assumption that they've already arrived.

The blind spot is in not seeing the built-in inequalities of many organizational meritocracies. Women will often get to the same results using a different path than men. And companies promote not just on results, but on what they believe an employee will do while ascending the ladder of leadership. They also formulate these beliefs based on the behavior they see a promotion candidate exhibit. Seeking comfort in sameness and defaulting to the male paradigm of leadership, organizations look for specific types of behavior from their leaders—behaviors that match most closely with the nature of men.

Without question, promotion based on achievement and ability is the right philosophy. In addition to ensuring an organization stays true to its growth plan and attains its annual objectives, a meritocracy helps shape a truly diverse, engaged, and inclusive workforce. It can also help male leaders overcome the perception of gender bias in sponsoring and promoting only those who remind them of themselves.

Yet many organizational meritocracies are gender-blind and the problem is that the purportedly objective criteria on which someone in the workplace is judged stem from this male model. The objective behaviors that leaders say they want candidates to exhibit are more naturally aligned with male thinking. Objectively, more men will fulfill the criteria than women choosing to be their authentic selves in the workplace. But in this case, objective does not necessarily mean *fair*.

One of the places we see this scenario play out frequently is in high-tech, an industry with a paucity of women in top positions. In high-tech companies, the software engineers and developers who are most often valued—and who therefore climb the ranks—are extremely fast in their communication style, incredibly analytical, and have an ability to tear down any idea or anyone who demonstrates a flaw in their thinking. And not just in high-tech companies. We have worked with many companies that have some semblance of balance of representation at lower levels (not fifty-fifty but plenty of women nonetheless) in the IT department, but as you go up the ladder, the women thin out, sometimes drastically. In one large organization we have worked with, there is only one female software architect among forty-three males! While there are plenty of women in other roles, she is the only software architect, a developer who leads the whole software design.

Many women, even those with equal intelligence and an incredible ability to think through complex problems, will often hold back in environments like these. Worst case, they avoid the aggressive, conflict-ridden environment entirely. The men don't see the problem. That's just business—it's how they relate to one another. As a result, many capable women have difficulty climbing the organizational ladder. And the few who do fit in and survive simply adopt and reinforce the existing model of behavior.

Imagine for a moment that the roles are reversed. Pretend that the prevailing business model was developed by women for women all those generations ago. Now imagine men being invited to participate in a meritocracy based on the metrics of a traditional female model and evaluated and judged based on how women think and behave. Men would feel forced to play a part and feel undervalued. Not allowed to trade on instinct, they would feel as if they were working with their hands tied behind their backs.

That feeling of not quite being in one's element and its effect came to Keith recently. Here is what he experienced, in his own words:

Years ago, I was invited to cofacilitate, with Barbara, a workshop on leadership, the participants of which were solely women. It was part of a larger effort on the part of the client to help women deepen their abilities to lead. We decided it was additive for the client to have me join Barbara, both because of my body of work in leadership and also to bring a man's perspective to the process. For six days, I worked alongside Barbara and thirty participants—all women—and the experience was extraordinary. It was the first time I had worked exclusively with such a large number of women at one time and I found myself, time and time again, needing to alter my natural style in order to meet the needs of the group as a whole.

Like many men, I have a train-track mind. I love an agenda and feel most comfortable and even satisfied when we get through an agenda on time. Typical of most men, my goal-oriented, stepwise-thinking mind loves to establish agreements, set targets, and stay on task and I feel a real sense of accomplishment when I can do this in my work. This didn't seem to be at all what the women in the workshop wanted. Multiple times, conversations would veer off and take a different path than planned. The amount of social engagement they required as part of the process was, for them, natural. I, however, experienced this as a derailment of monumental proportions of my train-track mind.

So often, I wanted to point out, "This is not part of the agenda," or observe, "This is taking us off track." But some little voice inside of me told me to hold off and just let it unfold. Thankfully, I did hold back. Had I intervened as often as I felt the urge to intervene and get the discussion back on track, I would have become a bloody annoyance, to say the least, and would have interrupted the more fluid experience that worked so effectively for the participants. More importantly, I would have been trying to impose my own style onto their field of experience, and would have likely been rejected, my credibility even suffering in the process.

Instead, I practiced patience and deep curiosity. In my own mind, I thought of this group of women as coming from a completely different culture and sought to better understand its fascinating norms. Able to still my own propensities, here is what I saw as I held back and stayed with the flow of the group:

1. What at first appeared as "de-railers" to me were simply part of the larger exploration for the women, a necessary part of the process. Seemingly disconnected side comments and conversations (you know, the kind where a thought triggers another thought which triggers another thought and so on) ultimately comprised parts of the larger quilt-work of thought.

2. Social conversations were part of the glue that kept the group together. There was a beauty to it, and there emerged—quite naturally—a sort of jazzlike dialogue and exchange that created a harmonic resonance.

3. Instead of serving as interrupters, the expressions of personal issues were part of the natural flow, and the needs were addressed organically. They were an integrated part of the whole.

4. It rarely happened that one participant would directly confront another, but when it did happen, it looked different than the system I'm used to of offering direct feedback or being confronted myself on my own behavior. Instead, participants made suggestions, offered input, and invited inquiry. Within this context, the women communicated a lot to one another and learned from one another as well.

5. The women were unabashed in establishing a sort of natural support system. Women took care of each other and of the whole, with little fanfare, and yet with great heart.

6. Women expressed their feelings very naturally, and when they did, there was a sense of ease about it and caring from the group. There was little drama; the women seemed to naturally know what to do in response.

This was a tribe, very different than the tribe I was used to or the one in which I grew up. I was raised in a male tribe, where agendas were set, where we tightly controlled outcomes, and where the alpha male got his way. Hierarchies were natural in my tribe, and focus and direct communications the norm.

In my uninitiated mind, I found the behavior of this different tribe all quite draining at first. It did not produce direct and immediate outcomes. It did not match the way I understood learning to happen. And it certainly didn't follow the design of the workshop. Every bit of me wanted to shout, "Stop it!" or "Stay focused, d*&^% it!" Thankfully, wisdom got the better of me. Rather than try to control the process and the outcome, I kept my frustration rather quiet, and I kept observing. Instead of expecting the women to act like I would (and thus finding them failing at their task), by valuing the difference between us I grew fascinated by the cultural norms that emerged before me. I watched and listened. I thus began to honor this process, so foreign to my male mind.

As the event unfolded, I could see the participants learn. It certainly wasn't at my pace or in the way I was used to, but it happened nonetheless. At the conclusion, I could not clearly identify many moments of direct learning (at least the predefined learning that we had designed to take place). To my surprise, the participants reported that it was a rich and welcome learning experience. It was as though magically the learning happened in the white spaces between conversations. What seemed blank to me was rich with meaning, even the spaces part of the patchwork whole.

Of course, what occurred above is not the norm in most organizations, but it gave me a glimpse of what it must be like for the women who are often in the minority. Their discomfort in not feeling a natural synchronicity with the group's behavior would equal mine, but in their case, the discomfort would be constant. I might add, thankfully. While I learned a huge amount about female culture, I don't know that I could take it as a constant. It was just too foreign for me.

Unlike me, uninitiated in the ways of female culture when I first encountered this experience, women in business, especially at the highest levels, know the rules of male culture quite well. They've had to learn these in order to adapt. But no matter how well they know the rules and how often they practice them, for most women the rules will never feel natural. I had to hold back and quiet my inner voice for six days. Many women in leadership do this for a lifetime.

The stark differences Keith experienced in that workshop form the basis for why meritocracies based on gender sameness don't work. Below are examples of the different orientations and strengths that men and women instinctively bring with them to work every day. (For a more full expression of this model, see "Same Words, Different Language.") Even in well-meaning organizations, many meritocracies primarily, if not exclusively, reward behavior found in the male column alone:

	Men's Model	Women's Model
Prioritizes	Deals with ideas and issues sequentially	Juggles many ideas and issues at once
Solve problems	Converges on the issue to zero in on a solution	Diverges from the issue to exploring many solutions
Make decisions	Isolates issues for quick decisions	Visits the entire context of an issue first
Work in teams	Values, focuses on, and works for the results	Values and works for the journey as well as the results
Lead others	Transactional, hierarchical, competitive, convergent	Interactive, participative, collaborative, divergent

Both women and men lead, supervise, and manage others quite effectively, but in different ways, ways that are often misunderstood and undervalued by the other gender. But the differences remain profound; males and females are hardwired, not just socialized, to lead one another differently. Our organizations today are imbalanced as the natural talents and skills of women are not being utilized. In order for a meritocracy to work effectively, the metrics must be based on more than how men prioritize issues, solve problems, make decisions, work in teams, and lead others. Difference must be valued.

As a doctoral student at Harvard, coauthor Keith got in on the ground floor of the corporate culture movement. His doctoral advisor was none other than Terry Deal, author of the bestseller *Corporate Cultures,* which made that whole concept famous. As a result, Keith has done an extraordinary amount of culture change work in companies around the globe for thirty years. Beginning in the early 1980s, in Keith's experience he found that most all culture change work begins with a vision in the form of a new set of values. Unfortunately, what often follows is that leaders want to showcase their new values on posters and splash them across their website, reshaping the branding of the company.

It doesn't work to showcase values that you have not yet put in practice.

Employees experience the disconnect, rolling their eyes at the company they see on the website, thinking, *This isn't true. We don't live by these values. In fact, you, the leadership, don't live by these values.* The effort to display values on mugs, posters, and marketing materials does little to produce internal change; oftentimes all it does is bring into sharp relief how much the company isn't living them! In our work, it is at this point that one telling difference between male and female leaders begins to emerge.

Male leaders often don't want to talk about that disconnect. They're uncomfortable with the observation that they're not walking the talk, so much so that it's being put out on the table for discussion. The most courageous of leaders face the music, but in our experience, most male leaders do not. Most female leaders, by contrast, tend to welcome the dialogue more so than men. Declaring that adopting new values requires in-depth self-examination, women are more often up for the challenge. As this has happened time and again, we've come to feel that it's almost as if the male leaders, once they declare their intentions and have placed their values on display, feel that it's now up to the organization to live those values and the issue no longer requires their own attention. The declaration is the end point for their involvement, whereas for many female leaders, it's the beginning.

These leaders' perspective undoubtedly reflects the fact that a self-reflective perspective in a hard-driving work environment is not highly valued among most men. What women view as important examination they call "navel-gazing," "off strategy," and "unproductive." The process just doesn't get to the results stage fast enough.

In an alpha-male culture, where male tendencies are amplified to an extreme, "reflection" is considered wimpy and weak, as is asking everyone to offer his or her opinion. Programs designed to create more gender awareness often fail because many men go through the motions, never really believing that the diversity program or effort is needed, and maybe even thinking it's a hindrance to progress on more important organizational goals.

What It Takes to Get There

What does it take for leaders like Bjorn to make the shift and work past these three barriers to Gender Intelligence? How can they come to understand that their actions don't speak to their intentions?

It requires a hard look inward and a willingness to be honestly self-reflective. Oftentimes, it takes an epiphany or "aha!" moment to spur the change, disrupting the leader's thinking enough to reveal the obstacles before them. One of the reasons many high-level leaders like Bjorn are not very self-reflective is that they are so successful, they believe their success strategy is the right strategy. While growing up, they developed ways of thinking and acting that worked to help them get ahead. They believe unconsciously that if it worked so well, it must be the best way. So when problems occur in the organization, they quite quickly look outward, rarely if ever considering it might be their own behavior. If the culture is off, it is often seen as the consequence of the inability of others to follow their leader. "It couldn't be my leadership, could it? It's worked so well in the past, it must be them."

His "Aha!" Moment

It's extremely encouraging to watch these moments happen, like the "aha!" moment we witnessed during a Gender Intelligence workshop for sales executives. All 110 vice presidents of sales from the Americas were in attendance and they seemed quite engaged and quite vocal, thinking aloud about the challenges men and women often have in working with each other.

One male sales executive, Mitch, stood up to take his turn. He was pointing out some differences he'd noticed that women execs exhibit when working with clients, when he was interrupted by his colleague, Edward. Increasingly agitated, Edward cut him off. "You're generalizing here. You shouldn't do that. It's demeaning to women! It seems almost like you're making up these differences. I know lots of men who ask a lot of questions and lots of women who prefer to work alone. And all clients really want to see is the bottom line—what it will do for their company and how much it will cost."

Mitch sat down, silenced. No one else said anything, either to defend or to challenge Edward's assertions. He sat, sullen, and didn't participate at all for the next hour, until he saw the brain science portion of the workshop. He connected what he learned to his personal life, sharing with the table how differently he and his wife communicated at home and how frustrated each got with the other. The women at his table all tended to agree in their self-observation. One woman said, "I do that, I multitask better than most of the men on my team." Another interjected, "I really am interested in results, but I feel relationships are just as important." And a third noted, "Women do tend to show more emotion than men, but it doesn't mean we can't handle the pressure."

That was Edward's "aha!" moment. You could see by the way his body and demeanor shifted. He discovered that, indeed, there are some meaningful differences, and saw women themselves expressing them without any ill will. He also saw that prior to this moment, his assumptions had not been accurate or valid.

Her "Aha!" Moment

A female HR executive for a national bank pulled Barbara aside after a session, eager to share what she had learned from the presentation. She'd been interviewing candidates inside the company for an open position recently vacated by a woman legendary at the company. One woman and two men were on the short list.

"I just couldn't see either of the two male candidates adequately filling Margaret's shoes," she said. During the interview, "they both talked too much about themselves and all about being results-driven. I was asking them questions that had a really broad scope but both their answers were so narrow. I almost got the impression halfway through their sessions that they didn't want to be interviewed at all!"

She admitted to Barbara that she hadn't known before that it's a tendency for men to think sequentially and often not hear anything else when they're locked in a thought. "My husband would do that occasionally but I thought it was him just ignoring me!" she said, half laughing. "I realize now that it's part of male hardwiring and that I was misinterpreting the difference. Now I'm wondering if that mindset is just what that position could use for the next couple of years."

In our workshops and in workplaces alike, more and more leaders are making the transformational shift to Gender Intelligence. Convinced by a growing awareness and the body of brain-based research, they are moving past their limiting perceptions of gender and their one-size-fits-all measure of performance and success. They're becoming more self-reflective and finding truer alignment between their intentions and their behavior and style of leadership.

Gender Intelligence requires leaders to reach past their perception that men and women are the same. That focus on sameness has perpetuated a narrow view of what leadership looks like and reinforced a dominant male style. While that style was once perhaps crucial to success, it is rapidly becoming too narrow for today's business world.

As the denial of gender difference vanishes from a growing number of leaders, so too does their fear of being perceived as biased in their thinking. Talking knowledgeably to the differences and valuing the contributions of both men and women allow a climate in which this conversation can take place without fear. That climate goes a long way toward ending misunderstanding and miscommunication and opens the door to finding better solutions, reaching better thought-out decisions, and forging deeper connections with the marketplace.

These leaders are learning to listen differently. They've come to own their own assumptions about what good leadership looks like and realize that their current frame of reference may be a limiting paradigm. They make changes to better align their behaviors with their expressed intentions.

Through a gender-intelligent lens, leaders see that capabilities should not all be drawn from the male model, nor from the female model exclusively. The workforce today is composed of men and women, so the model for success should be a blend of both models, counted not in the number of bodies, but in the contribution of different ideas.

These leaders are confronting their beliefs and developing a greater inside-out congruency between their intentions and their actions. Once they understand gender differences, they naturally come to value the differences and actually seek them out. Once they truly believe in the value, they can't help but show congruency between what they say and the new level of engagement they have with the women and men in their organizations.

When we put it all together, these emerge as the behavioral patterns of a gender-intelligent leader. There is some overlap in these conducts, but they are meant to build on one another, one strengthening the next. A truly gender-intelligent leader will have a full understanding of each of these six behaviors and be open to self-reflection and breakthrough change.

The Six Behaviors of a Gender-Intelligent Leader

1. Understands how to take advantage of the strengths men and women bring
There are really two parts to this first, and most important, behavior: this leader is both aware of gender differences and able to recognize and seek out opportunities that blend the unique strengths that men and women bring.

Many leaders believe they understand gender differences and show it by placing women in certain roles and men in others, effectively creating gender silos. This only tends to reinforce stereotyping. There is value that women bring to the conversation that is often different from what men tend to bring. A gender-intelligent leader knows the potential that lies in combining these differences to produce a richer outcome for everyone involved, including the organization.

In any communication, problem-solving course of action, or decision-making process, gender-intelligent leaders will also be aware of their *own* strengths and weaknesses. And instead of considering someone who may be different as a potential problem or a derailer, these leaders will see that individual in a different light and appreciate their additive value. They welcome the difference and learn from it. As a result, they enhance interactions, expand the field of potential solutions, and bring forth the best decisions.

2. Treats Gender Intelligence as a high priority
When leaders have embraced the first behavior of finding advantage in difference, they make Gender Intelligence a high priority. They educate team members on Gender Intelligence and encourage teams to learn more. Gender-intelligent leaders actively invite feedback. They recognize that they too have limitations and invite others' perspectives on their actions. They also look for the policies and procedures in their organizations that demonstrate blind spots in Gender Intelligence and take action to remove those obstacles.

3. Actively promotes the presence of both men and women in all situations
When Gender Intelligence is treated as a high priority, gender-intelligent leaders intentionally strive to have both men and women present in all business situations. We're not talking about the fifty-fifty balance that's the endgame of quota-based initiatives; the number doesn't matter. What

matters is the presence and welcomed intermingling of the male and female mind in communication, problem-solving, and decision-making.

There are situations where departments or divisions within an organization will have far more women than men or far more men than women—sometimes as much as 90 percent in either direction. Gender-intelligent leaders recognize the benefit of having a diversity of thought around critical solutions and decisions. In situations where there's a preponderance of one gender or another, leaders will go outside the team to encourage gender-balanced input.

4. Actively encourages collaboration and different perspectives in meetings

Gender-intelligent leaders who seek to blend the presence and contribution of men and women in all situations naturally align with collaborative behavior. Leaders of this mindset encourage collaboration in all meetings and on all teams. They welcome individuals to share and offer their ideas and perspectives equally. Everybody's voice is valued and considered. They inculcate a collaborative culture that stresses, not competition, but instead the propensity to share, collect, and take action on the input of others. It's not just a value. They recognize that collaboration is often the best way to mine the gold that exists among the differing views and voices.

It's important to note that collaboration is not about consensus. Consider the following model, which is a continuum of inclusiveness from one extreme, where the leader doesn't include others at all in the decision process, to the other end of the spectrum, where there is 100 percent inclusiveness.

The Continuum of Inclusiveness

Leader makes decisions without input	Leader makes tentative decisions, then asks for feedback	Leader asks for input, then makes decisions	Team makes decisions

Less Inclusive   More Inclusive

Gender-intelligent leaders tend to be collaborative at any point along this continuum and find that often, the different perspectives found in each instance enrich the entire decision-making process. There's always an openness and a spirit of valuing others' viewpoints.

5. Does not act on assumptions, but instead tests them

Because we all tend to live in a sea of assumptions, learning not to act on them is key. Gender-intelligent leaders treat each moment as a unique moment and each person as a unique contributor. One of the most powerful things gender-intelligent leaders do is proactively test their assumptions.

We often misinterpret each other or generalize one situation onto the entire gender. For instance, just because one woman declines a promotion that involves relocation because of her family doesn't mean all women with families would not want to relocate. The key is treating each individual and situation as an exclusive experience. In this fashion, gender-intelligent leaders constantly challenge their cultural beliefs and assumptions.

6. Is aware of his or her impact on others

This behavior exemplifies the "art of leadership." Leaders who have this ability are masterful in their capacity to reflect and self-correct. This behavior also happens to be one of male leaders' biggest challenges, though some women have trouble with it as well. Men are so results-driven that they're often looking at the goal through a forty-foot straw. With that focus and determined aim, they don't often see the impact they're having on others around them. They don't see the relational part as much as women do.

Gender-intelligent leaders demonstrate maturity by frequently asking themselves, "How is my behavior affecting the people around me?" They always ask this question in the context of any form of difference, whether it's gender, culture, personality, attitude, or generational maturity.

Creating a Culture of Gender Intelligence

The mindset of the gender-intelligent leader and his or her resulting style of leadership can deeply inspire and guide others to build a culture that embraces and practices Gender Intelligence. These leaders have the power to move organizations along the continuum—from denial, to realization, to practice.

More and more leaders are making this transformation. They're moving away from sameness and embracing the value of difference-thinking; they're creating meritocracies that observe different models for success; and they're becoming more self-reflective, and as a result, creating greater congruence between their intention and their behavior.

They are recognizing, more and more, the wisdom of the Leadership Chain. They're realizing that their conduct and behavior have an enormous impact on the quality of the culture and the results. And if they want to improve the results of the organization, they need to create a culture that's expansive and fluid, and honors men and women and their differing skills and talents.

Gender-intelligent leaders realize that the culture is shaped directly by their mindset and behaviors. They grasp that by becoming more gender-intelligent and embodying these six behaviors, they will produce a much more powerful culture and generate greater results.

These six behaviors are not a paint-by-numbers set of traits. Attaining Gender Intelligence requires a more holistic approach—to be more inquisitive of the thoughts, assumptions, and beliefs that cause the incongruent behavior in the first place, then to shift that mindset to one that's more expansive and inclusive. That, in itself, is the ultimate goal.

Part Three

How Gender Intelligence Affects the Organization

8

Functions, Processes, and Systems

On the Path to Stage Five

When a global company was acquired by a larger pharmaceutical firm, we were called in to help facilitate the merging of the cultures. Seeking information first, the companies conducted focus groups with the leadership teams from each company, composed of both men and women. In these sessions, the women openly shared very different experiences than those detailed by the men. The chief diversity officer, whom we had met earlier that year at a Gender Intelligence Summit, called us in and asked us to look at the data and interpret what was happening.

Naturally, many of the comments in the focus groups were about the recent acquisition and surfacing signs of a culture clash. Most telling, however, were the multitude of comments made by women specifically reacting to the strong male mode of operating that was dominant in their company, a fact that didn't seem set to change by the merger of the two organizations.

In our assessment of the focus group findings, we picked up the familiar systemic root causes behind women feeling more discouraged around inclusion and contribution, being valued by the company, and opportunities for advancement than men. To fail in these areas, we know by experience, is to risk losing strategic female talent.

We met with the CEO of the acquired company along with his executive team and shared our assessment. We covered the gender issues and the leadership blind spots that surfaced from the focus groups and their employee survey data, offering a convincing case for change. After presenting our findings, we suggested that the gender issues needed to be treated systemically, which would also go a long way toward advancing the blending of the companies' two cultures. Here again we saw a moment of intention being incongruous with leadership behavior. While he was seemingly committed to gender diversity, the CEO's reaction was quite revealing. He was looking for a quick fix. "This is going to be an overwhelming undertaking if you're talking about treating this system-wide!"

That's often the case when the leaders of an organization are faced with instituting change systemically through their organization. They immediately assume it's going to be a huge and costly activity that would take focus and resources away from the more pressing strategic and economic initiatives of the organization, and they don't see it as a top priority. Leaders who don't see the strategic business advantage of more fully utilizing and blending the talents of both men and women at all levels in the corporation also balk.

The CEO felt he had to do *something*, though. He knew that the gender issues evident in the focus groups weren't good for business, nor would ignoring them help the merger succeed. He turned to the head of diversity and asked, "What's one concrete, specific thing we can get moving on right now?"

Online training, the chief diversity officer offered. And thus an incredible opportunity to promote a successful merger and move the new blended company up the continuum was lost.

The CEO and chief diversity officer were thinking in bandage solutions. Most transformational change efforts—when they're not strategic—get relegated to a training solution. While it's true that people do need to change their behavior as part of a cultural metamorphosis, what causes that behavior goes far beyond their individual learning and knowledge. The functions, systems, and processes that form the backbone of an organization, shaped by leadership, create and reinforce the behavior. Their importance cannot be underestimated; they touch every activity in the organization. Yet they often go underutilized, resistant to change because "that's just how things are done around here."

This represented a failed opportunity because training alone could not create the transformational change in this merged company, for two reasons: It might prove a useful beginning, but ultimately would not be broad and deep enough to create the organizational transformation that Gender Intelligence requires. Second, the mandate was delegated to a function, in effect, three levels down from the CEO. In the end, the commitment wasn't there at the top to infuse Gender Intelligence into the organization.

Organizations on the path to Stage Five see the paradigm shift to Gender Intelligence strategically and systemically and infuse it into all the moving parts of the organization. Companies including American Express, Deloitte, and IBM have made it to the advanced side of the continuum. How? By leaders and managers at every level constantly questioning their thought processes and assumptions and infusing Gender Intelligence into all the activities within their organizations.

Yet even after all their hard work, none of these companies would yet place themselves at Stage Five. Most would say they are "Fours on the way to becoming Fives." They know what being at Stage Five represents and requires. They discovered early on that becoming a gender-intelligent organization is not an isolated initiative but a cultural transformation that will affect the very fabric of the organization and its elements within.

Interestingly, each of these breakthrough organizations began its journey in much the same way. Presented with the same opportunity as the CEO above, leadership made a choice to open their eyes to the obstacles to gender inclusiveness, seeking to understand those they weren't seeing or even expecting. Gender imbalance was cumulatively detracting from the economic value of their companies. They were losing or wasting talent because of high turnover and insufficient productivity, and consequently achieving limited marketplace results.

As a next step, CEOs and their executive teams—and even at times, their boards of directors—attended a Gender Intelligence workshop. There a wave of "aha!" moments washed over the leaders as they came to understand gender differences and the complementary value found in those differences. But these leaders thought in broader terms. They pieced together the implications of Gender Intelligence and its potentially cascading positive effect throughout the organization and into the market.

The leaders continued their journey by requesting that their direct re-

ports attend a Gender Intelligence workshop. And the workshop participants, in turn, saw the implications at their level within the organization
and the potentially positive outcomes for their departments, teams, specific projects, and programs.

And as the understanding of men and women continued deep into the
organization and spread, leaders and managers started to make individual
gender-intelligent decisions for their own business units. Departments and
teams began adopting and owning gender-intelligent behavior. Today, in
any one of these Stage Five companies, you'll hear one employee turn to
another in a meeting and ask, "Are we being gender-intelligent about this?"

Just as the intake of nutrients is carried by functions and systems
throughout the human body, enabling peak function, at Stage Five,
Gender Intelligence is absorbed into the culture and spreads throughout the company. Below we'll detail some examples of the enrichments
organizations are making to their key functions, processes, and systems
through Gender Intelligence that are garnering success.

Gender-Intelligent Functions

Functions refer to the major activities that take place within an organization. In this chapter, we'll focus on the key functions of marketing,
research and development, sales, and customer service since those areas
appear to be most influenced by gender differences and stand to contribute the greatest economic return when Gender Intelligence is applied.

IN MARKETING

There is no denying that gender influences a person's buying decisions—
whether he or she is making a multimillion-dollar purchase for a global
enterprise, hiring a financial advisor, buying a new car, planning a family
vacation, or buying laundry detergent at the store.

Research clearly shows that men and women observe, prioritize,
and process information differently, and they make their decisions
accordingly—including what, where, when, or *if* to buy. To expand and
sustain an organization's success in marketing and selling their product—to an increasingly diverse marketplace—there needs to be an understanding and appreciation for the different ways in which male and

female consumers and clients listen, communicate, solve problems, assess value, and make purchasing decisions.

Deloitte

The prevalence of men in top positions has been a strong influencer at Deloitte, one of the largest professional services firms. The company's leadership felt that it explained why for years Deloitte had mostly male partners—because most of their clients were men. Before Gender Intelligence, the assumption at Deloitte was similar to that of everyone else in the consulting services industry in thinking that men are more successful providing consulting to men. It just stood to reason: men think alike!

While it's true that men tend to communicate in similar patterns, Deloitte's "aha!" moment came in realizing that male (and female) leaders in companies don't necessarily choose their consultant by gender, thinking, *I only want a man consulting to me.* Decision makers are looking for consultants who listen, are understanding, encourage dialogue, and are resourceful. When they took the time to investigate the issue, Deloitte discovered how and why women partners could be quite effective and, in some instances, even *more* effective than their male colleagues in advising and addressing the needs of Deloitte's clientele.

Dove

As we described in Chapter 5, in an industry where female beauty is often depicted in small-sized dresses, Dove has taken a different marketing approach.

You'll remember that their "aha!" moment came when conducting focus groups where women consumers of beauty products, grouped by age, were shown Dove advertising and then asked to comment. Listening to their comments the company realized that, regardless of age, their advertising wasn't speaking to *any* of the women. Across the board, the women in the groups said the ads didn't appeal to them because the models didn't reflect the consumers' self-perceptions, and because the messages they conveyed didn't reflect the attitudes of the women in the focus groups.

Shortly afterward, Dove abandoned traditional portrayals of "perfect" women in order to push their products. They distinguished themselves by using multigenerational models who ranged from size six to fourteen, honoring the reality that beauty comes in all shapes, ages, sizes, and colors.

Since Dove launched the Real Beauty campaign, it has gained a greater market share of the cosmetics industry and the respect of women everywhere in the world. Moreover, the company is able to draw the best talent from universities and a variety of industries alike—women who want to play a part in offering a richer and more expanded view of healthy beauty.

Both Deloitte and Dove, as well as many others, are seeing their markets for the first time through a gender-intelligent lens. They're developing revamped marketing plans and programs, realizing that the traditional marketing methods may now be missing the mark. Gender Intelligence is also helping them recognize new markets and opportunities, giving them a huge advantage over their competition as they rush to court these new consumers.

IN RESEARCH AND DEVELOPMENT

The more a company understands what motivates its male and female customers, the better positioned it is to sense and respond to changing market needs.

While companies conduct research on diverse markets and consumer groups they want to target, the first research should be at a higher level, done to understand what influences the attitudes of the buying public. Having Gender Intelligence motivates R&D teams to understand how brain science and culture affect the different attitudes, beliefs, and motivations of men and women. Products and services can then be designed based on those needs and expectations.

When Carlos Ghosn first took over as CEO of Nissan Motor Company in 1999, the company was on the verge of bankruptcy and drastic measures were called for to save it. Ghosn took immediate and radically corrective measures at Nissan that challenged Japanese business etiquette, but produced results. Interestingly, though, it wasn't his closing of plants, cutting thousands of jobs, and spinning off the Nissan Aerospace division that offended Japanese cultural traditionalists.[52]

Research revealed that the clear majority of Nissan automobiles were either bought by women or bought because women heavily influenced the purchase decision. Women were Nissan's target market, yet there were *no* women in engineering, marketing, or sales at the company. Ghosn saw this as a huge gender blind spot. Nissan was underserving the needs and expectations of women purchasers by not involving women in the design phase, marketing, and selling of Nissan cars. He saw an opportunity for a marketplace breakthrough and accelerated growth by advancing women within Nissan.

Ghosn's first order of business was to create a shift in the mindsets of all Nissan employees, men and women alike. The CEO made attendance of Gender Intelligence workshops mandatory for all employees in order to build greater awareness between men and women and infuse Gender Intelligence in their actions and decisions. Employees learned how their differences could be used to improve the design and functionality of Nissan cars, create marketing campaigns to speak to women's needs and interests, and enhance selling strategies to better accommodate women's preferences for lower-pressure, high-transparency negotiation. Greater numbers of women were recruited and advanced within design, manufacturing, marketing, and sales.

As a result, Nissan realized a dramatic increase in sales and profitability. It became the first company in Asia to win the Catalyst Award in 2008 for gender diversity initiatives, which further served to attract the best women in engineering, marketing, and sales to the company.

Whether you work in health care or high tech, if you run a global enterprise today chances are you run it on SAP software. In reaching out to new clients, the chief information officer and chief technology officer have remained the key points of contact for the SAP sales force since the 1970s. And given that the overwhelming majority of CIOs and CTOs during that time have been men, SAP's product design, marketing strategies, and communications have been developed primarily for a male audience.

What missed opportunities were occurring as a result? This was a big "aha!" moment for SAP—a major shift in their thinking. They had always seen their key clients in major organizations as men. But while the majority of software decision makers in global corporations may be male, the users of the systems designed by SAP are men *and* women, and in some departments, they're *primarily* women.

In order to sustain corporate growth, the company wanted to be of greater value to the end users in the large organizations that SAP serves, as well as to penetrate smaller businesses. SAP then discovered that more than half of the huge market segment of small companies they were targeting with new software solutions and marketing efforts were owned and operated by women, requiring a more diverse approach in product design, marketing, and sales. SAP began applying Gender Intelligence to their product design and marketing efforts, appealing to the greater percentage of women users and buyers.

IN SALES

If the male model for success has remained a dominant fixture in business, that may be nowhere more evident than in the field of sales. In the alpha-male sales culture, it is understood that extroverted, aggressive hunters make the best salespeople. And while in certain industries and marketplace circumstances that's true, in most situations that approach yields great short-term revenue but sacrifices the establishment of long-term client-trusting relationships.

Men and women bring comparable strengths and goals to the selling process. They both express drive, ambition, and a strong desire to close. Talk to anyone in sales and you'll *feel* their energy. Yet men and women tend to bring their own unique set of natural talents and expectations to the selling and buying process, along with learned skills.

On the selling side, there are significant differences between men and women in where they place value and emphasis while in the "selling mode." Men tend to be transactional and results-driven while women are more inclined to focus on the development and retention of the client. They want the gain, but they also want to sustain the results over time.

On the buying side, as you would expect, men and women both make purchases as solutions to personal or organizational needs, but men are more comfortable making that purchase as a dispassionate transactional process. For men, it's all about the *result* of the product and not the *experience* of the product. They want to know—is it worth its price?

Women, on the other hand, tend to buy based on a blend of experiences with the company and its representatives and the value of the product or service. It's most often not a dispassionate transaction. Instead, women will buy based on the totality of their experience: the product or service itself, how it is advertised, how it is sold, its presentation, and how they are treated at each step along the sales cycle. As a result, women don't *buy* brands; they tend to *join* brands, especially if they've had a positive experience. When they do, women become the most loyal of customers, a significant coup. It is therefore hard to comprehend why companies would maintain an all or mostly male sales force, even when their products are purchased primarily by women.

In 2000, IBM's sales force was 48 percent women. By 2002, the proportion had fallen to a jaw-dropping 18 percent. For years, the sales and technical divisions at IBM posted the best track records for recruiting women, yet both divisions also faced the greatest challenges in retaining them, and they didn't understand why.

CEO Lou Gerstner recognized the high cost of turnover and hemorrhaging of female talent at IBM as critical issues that had to be resolved for the health of the company. He put in place a gender diversity task force to uncover the reasons for the sudden drop in women in sales in addition to the inadequate representation of women executives at the top.

During the course of the diagnostics and workshops, the misinterpretations and assumptions that divided women and men were teased out and proved patently false. Leadership had assumed women were ending or putting their careers on hold for personal reasons. The worse news for IBM—they were going to the competition. A significant percentage of women also left to start their own companies.

Eighteen months following the Gender Intelligence workshops, IBM's sales force increased the percentage of women in the sales division from 18 to 40 percent, and a task force composed of women in sales brought in an additional $850 million. For IBM, expanding their sales force to include more women turned out to be a crucial shift for the company and their presence in an increasingly diverse marketplace.

IN CUSTOMER SERVICE

One of the most telling pieces of information emerging from our years of Gender Intelligence diagnostics is that when women experience either a positive or a negative experience, they will share that experience with up to thirty-two people, including strangers. Men, on the other hand, will tell, on average, about three people about their experience, and even then, only people they know.[53] You can see how this behavior is of tremendous import to companies marketing to women. Since women are more inclined than men to develop a relationship with the product and brand, their recalling and sharing their experiences with others can have sweeping effects on product sales, driving them up or causing them to plummet. It would stand to reason, then, that the way in which companies and their customer service departments respond to their customers is crucial.

Gender-Intelligent Processes

In addition to the functions of an organization, there are the company procedures or the ways in which employees engage with one another as they conduct business throughout the day. How men and women interact—the way in which they communicate, their tone of voice, how they listen, and their level of directness—really speaks to the quality of the interrelationships and the culture of the organization.

Of all our interactions, brain-based gender differences are most apparent when we deal with conflict, solve problems, and make decisions. Although there are many opportunities for gender interaction in the day-to-day processes of an organization, these three areas improve significantly and meaningfully when companies employ Gender Intelligence.

CONFLICT RESOLUTION

When conflicts arise at work, we often unconsciously expect the other gender to react to the problem or issue in the same way. Whether your instinct is to call someone out directly, to blame yourself, to talk it through, or to stew in private, your response is the one that makes sense to you. But in reality, dealing with conflict is very much instinctual, especially given the associated stress and how each gender's built-in stress response kicks in. As we learned in Chapter 2, the logic centers shut down while the more primal amygdala fires, cortisol surging through our brains.

You'll remember, too, how the stress response looks different for each gender. Women's first reaction to conflict is to personalize it. They internalize and wonder, *What did I do?* Women will often stay quiet while they try to make sense of the situation. They listen first—even if only briefly—in order to dive deeper looking for a solution and a way to build and strengthen the relationship. Women see conflict as a breakdown destructive to relationships. That's one reason women treat it as an opportunity, a chance to clear the air and even build rapport, creating closeness in the relationship. Women are inclined to talk issues through and search for mutual solutions before taking immediate action.

While women will tend to personalize and retreat inside themselves, men turn the blame outward. They instinctively look outside to someone or something else and direct blame, irritation, or anger at that external force (or person). Men also tend to treat conflict in a more isolated and detached manner. Separating themselves from the issue helps men view the situation as an objective observer and more easily find a solution or, if the conflict is particularly intense, ignore the problem for the moment and come back to deal with it later.

Pit men's competitiveness against the women's instinctive reach for the win-win, then couple that difference with the woman who wants to talk it through while the man is already out the door seeking to avoid conversation, and you have the perfect breeding environment for discord and misunderstandings between the genders.

How the Genders Approach Conflict Resolution

WOMEN'S TENDENCIES	MEN'S TENDENCIES
Take it personally	Assign blame
Talk it through together	Think it through alone
Seek understanding	Seek solutions

Without Gender Intelligence, opposite genders either tend to get locked in battle or in their efforts to resolve conflict actually exacerbate it. We are often at our worst in our interactions when we're dealing with conflict, a time when we most need to be at our best. When men and women use two approaches to the conflict, their patterns become a stressor rather than a salve. The female's tendency to talk it through may not fit the timing for the male, or the man's direct approach may feel corrosive.

By applying Gender Intelligence to conflict resolution, men and women better understand why the other gender acts and reacts as it does. Men grow to realize that women being conciliatory or willing to give up ground to solve the conflict doesn't necessarily mean they're giving up or giving in. They're most likely looking for a win-win in order to preserve the relationship.

Gender-intelligent women grow to realize that when men take a stand or walk away from an issue, it doesn't necessarily mean they don't care. Gender-intelligent men, although inclined to take quick action on issues through a narrow path of solutions, are open to new ideas if these improve effectiveness and efficiency. A cooldown period allows men opportunity to think an issue through. Gender-intelligent women understand that giving men time and space allows them the ability to gain a better perspective.

In such meaningful actions, the conflict already starts to take on a more positive shape. Each player in the conflict drama becomes aware of the other's natural tendency and negotiates the middle ground. Moreover, in discussing the conflict itself and working it through, each party communicates about and navigates the conflict with a commitment to self-discovery, and mutual discovery, rather than making each other wrong. The focus is on win-win, and learning through the conflict, rather than win-lose.

PROBLEM-SOLVING

In business, successful problem-solving is one of the key competencies, yet when there are issues to resolve it is also the time when gender differences first arise. Men are in their comfort zone when a team is able to quickly isolate issues and zero in. Their advantage lies in speed and focus, with their approach sometimes limiting in scope, both in terms of what ideas they consider and in the people from whom they receive input.

Women's strength lies in their tendency to set issues in a broader context, identifying more opportunities and offering a richer field of solutions. Broadening the scope by its very nature lengthens the time it takes to define the problem, which tends to frustrate the men involved in the process.

When it comes to problem definition, there are times when narrowing the scope is appropriate and speed is of the essence, and other times when expanding the field is required to fully characterize a complex problem. The wisdom is in knowing when and how to blend both tendencies and not be limited by the belief that one model of thinking—yours—is better than the other.

In working through the Leadership Chain, we showed how women have a penchant for divergent thinking, the exploration of an expanding field of causes leading to the eventual selection of key issues. On the other hand, the particular strength of men is convergent thinking, whereby narrowing the field of possible solutions is the first priority, with speed, accuracy, and focus receiving primacy. You will note it is also in direct contrast to divergent thinking; once again men and women exhibit strikingly different, yet complementary, approaches.

How the Genders Approach Problem-Solving

WOMEN'S TENDENCIES	MEN'S TENDENCIES
Expand the context	*Isolate the issue*
Be expansive in the number of causes	*Pare down the number of causes*
Explore multiple options	*Narrow the field of options*
A more enduring solution	*A fast solution*

If we tasked a group of women to solve a problem they would leave no stone unturned in searching for solutions, but would take their time to arrive at an answer. Want a quick response? Call in the men, but know that they may leave out options in their haste—potentially meaningful ones. Gender Intelligence blends these two attitudes and produces a wider and, in many instances, better range of solutions from which to decide on a relatively efficient course of action.

For example, with Gender Intelligence, both parties in problem-solving utilize the strengths of the other and navigate through the problem-solving process in a way that brings wisdom. Wisdom implies, in part, the ability to know the strengths and limitations of one's own tendencies. A gender-intelligent male, knowing he has a tendency to want to get to action quickly, will temporarily keep that need at bay, knowing there is wisdom in expanding views before solving the problem too quickly. A gender-intelligent woman, knowing her tendency toward ever-increasing expansion, will weigh that need against the constraints of time, and sometimes even ride the coattails of the man's need for action. Together, they will discuss openly one another's assumptions and tendencies and find wisdom in the balance.

DECISION-MAKING

The decision-making process is more comprehensive and brings into sharper focus the differences between men and women. You'll remember that problem-solving and decision-making are directly correlated in that women use weblike thinking to understand how a problem, solution, or decision has an impact on other individuals, or other parts of the organization. Using past experiences as their guide, they are able to envision who should be brought into the decision-making process. Women tend to come from a bigger "we."

At the extremes, men tend to make decisions too quickly and women not quickly enough. In a business context, neither is desirable. Worse are the assumptions that our differences in decision-making lead us to. Gender Intelligence saves us from our assumptions. A gender-intelligent man will not assume a woman is fearful and not a team player for not wanting to jump to decisions, and a gender-intelligent woman will not assume men are addicted to adrenaline and intentional in their indifference to risk. They will both just be more mindful of the other and, as a result, make better decisions. Men will find value in slowing down and women will look for greater efficiency as Gender Intelligence informs better decisions.

How the Genders Approach Decision-Making

WOMEN'S TENDENCIES	MEN'S TENDENCIES
Think through more fully	Think and act quickly
Intuitive	Fact-based
Multidimensional thinking	Stepwise thinking
Consider the consequences	Focus on the goal

Women often make decisions based on intuition. They feel it in their gut. Maybe they sense that there will be a problem with a recent hire or anticipate an emerging client problem, all based on the mood and tone of the last client meeting. Of course, in business, it helps to back up your assertions with facts and data, but intuition can guide leaders and teams toward the data they need to identify a problem and decide on a course of action.

Diana and her business partner, Jack, were engrossed in an all-day planning session when Jack said, "I should introduce you to the guy who's running my whole training division. He's fantastic—you'll love him. Maybe

I can get him on the phone for a few minutes now, just for introductions and to plan a follow-up call."

Jack dialed his training director, Alex, and for the next fifteen minutes, Diana and Alex chatted and got to know one another a little and Diana shared what she had in mind. Within the first couple of minutes of the call, Diana already had a bad feeling. There was something in Alex's voice and perhaps even in the way he structured his words that just didn't sit right with her. She would have described him as "slimy," even though she couldn't point to any one particular thing he said to make her feel that way. Instead, it was just the overall sense she had. She was put off; she didn't want to have anything to do with Alex. But instead of trusting her intuition, she put it aside. How could Jack, whom she respected so much, have someone like this in the organization if he wasn't good?

Over the course of the next two months, Diana put her feelings aside and tried hard to get to know Alex. But that nagging feeling would not go away. She finally shared with Jack her distrust of Alex. He listened openly, but in the end, Jack said that he thought Alex was a good guy and that she should give him a chance. This time she let intuition rule and she had her assistant research Alex online. She was appalled, but frankly unsurprised, to learn that Alex was swimming in legal problems, with two pending lawsuits against him.

In raising this with Jack, she discovered that Jack already knew about Alex's legal issues. He felt it didn't affect Alex's relationship with the company. Besides, Jack considered Alex a powerhouse of a director who managed the trainers brilliantly and generated a lot of money for the firm. Diana felt otherwise, and was deeply concerned that Alex's legal issues would spill over into her joint endeavor with Jack. She didn't want any exposure to that potential liability and, holding solid to her convictions, she said she was unwilling to work with Alex. If Jack wanted to work with her, he'd have to let Alex go. In the course of doing so, Jack discovered even more about Alex, causing him to realize that all along he had been seduced by Alex's charm and had let his focus on revenue trump his own integrity.

In this example, you can see that both Diana and Jack weighed information differently. It could have been that Diana's intuition was off base, stemming from past experiences not relevant to the present situation. Had she dismissed her own sense, however, or had Jack not had the wisdom to listen, a disaster might have occurred. Instead, blended thinking ruled the day.

Remember the Pushmi-pullyu in *Doctor Dolittle*—the two-headed llama-like creature that tended to want to go in two directions at one time? This is what decision-making is like without Gender Intelligence. Without it, men and women tend to pull away from one another. The man's tendency toward fact-finding seems to sidestep or even ignore the value of the woman's intuition. The woman's tendency toward multidimensional thinking slows down the man, who in his desire for speed, will ignore important input into the decision-making process. Each becomes judged negatively and even dismissed emotionally.

With Gender Intelligence, however, each will appreciate the assets the other brings and blend the two tendencies into a far greater unified whole. Research on the subject of decision-making typically calls for different approaches in different situations. Gender-intelligent people tend to expand their flexibility through seeing the value in the other's approach, and bring wisdom to the decision-making process as a result.

Too often, in companies that are dominated by one gender or the other at the top, the culture takes a shape consistent with the tendencies of the gender dominantly in command. In most cases, that is male, and therefore the organization takes on the shape of the man's thinking. In such conditions, often women will feel on the fringe or disregarded for the gifts they uniquely bring. The opposite is also true. In a company we worked with in the fashion industry, dominated by female executives, the singular male who headed up marketing often felt dismissed and disregarded for his tendency to be so black-and-white about things. He in turn was constantly frustrated with what he considered overworking an issue. Other men in the organization often felt the same, and even complained about the company's own opposite version of the glass ceiling.

We believe that one of the reasons there is a clear and direct correlation between companies that have greater gender balance at the top and better financial results is that, in conflict resolution, problem-solving, or decision-making, through Gender Intelligence we begin to see the value in recognizing the self-limiting patterns of thought and in expanding those patterns to be much more inclusive. We seek to include other perspectives in order to arrive at the best decisions—not just those that are most obvious and expedient. Making the proper choice is the height of business intelligence. The wisdom is in knowing the best means to get there.

Gender-Intelligent Systems

The third and final area in which organizations are infusing Gender Intelligence while seeking sustainable change is in systems related to communication, technology, and HR, areas that affect every department and level. Today's complex organizations can have hundreds of systems. We'll focus only on those that are most positively affected by gender-intelligent thought and design.

The preponderance of these systems reside in HR and include hiring, performance management, compensation, and leadership. Together these systems shape the way in which organizational leaders are cultivated. Gender-intelligent leaders align the efforts of HR departments and connect them to the strategic initiatives of the organization. As a result, gender-intelligent HR departments become incredibly valuable for the business units they serve.

HIRING

In working with companies on gender diversity, we often hear organizations say, "We just can't find qualified women." When we hear that, what we usually discover is that they are hiring based on a male definition of what a successful candidate would look like, directing them to a very specific and often narrow field of candidates. Often when organizations are looking for candidates, their profile expresses very specific terms and frames of reference. They might search for business consultants only from within MBA programs or look for IT people only from within computer science programs at top universities.

Many CIOs want to hire more women for their IT departments, but struggle to find qualified female applicants for the roles they need to fill. They keep searching in the same pool of candidates—namely, computer science programs, which are still populated predominantly by men.

They fail to recognize that many software developers didn't come from that pool. Mark Zuckerberg and Bill Gates became software development leaders and visionaries without ever having graduated with a degree in computer science.

Ironically, while the world of information technology has changed dramatically over the past twenty years, sometimes appearing to shift day by day, many firms have not changed their hiring practices at all, the result

being a failure to keep pace with the skill set now desired in top candidates. According to chief technology officers and IT managers, IT departments are becoming less about building technology and more about
providing services and building better relationships within the company
and with end users. As an example, the growth in social media today
depends more on understanding and communicating the value of the
human interface than on writing code for a new application.

In a recent annual study, chief information officers were asked where
they thought women had the most positive impact in IT, and their responses showed that it's not in women's technical skill so much as in
their ability to build alliances with business sponsors, strengthen team
and morale, and bring divergent ideas to the discipline of programming.[54]

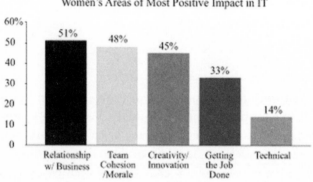

Women's Areas of Most Positive Impact in IT

None of the areas where women are perceived to have the most positive impact in IT necessarily requires a degree in computer science, yet
HR's first course of action selects only for degrees in technology, ignoring
the more diverse needs of the company.

The CIO of a global online retailer recently attended a Gender Intelligence workshop with thirty men and women leaders and senior managers from his company's various IT departments. Of the thirty, there
were only five women in the room, prompting the question "Why are
there so few women in IT?"

The CIO and several of the attendees replied almost in unison, "There
aren't that many getting degrees in computer science."

Yet when one of the women countered, "How many of you here in the room don't have a degree in computer science?" all but one of the women's hands went up as well as several of the men's. With the growth of social media and the focus of programming shifting to the end-user experience as the differentiator, people are being drawn into IT from other disciplines, including women-heavy areas such as literature, art, and history.

Bringing Gender Intelligence to hiring opens the field of possibilities, encouraging companies to think outside the box in hiring and to look for more than candidates who fit a traditional and potentially dated image. The myth that there "aren't enough women" immediately explodes as gender-intelligent HR departments work with business sponsors to understand the qualities needed in the best men and women candidates in order to ensure business success now and in the future.

COMPENSATION

In the United States, 2013 marked the fiftieth anniversary of the Equal Pay Act, a law intended to ensure equality in pay for women. Unfortunately, after five decades, women still earn an average of 77 cents for every dollar earned by a man in this country. For African-American and Hispanic women it's even lower: 64 and 54 cents, respectively. And this disparity is even more pronounced in countries around the world.

Across industrialized countries today, men's median full-time earnings are 18 percent higher than those of women, with the biggest gender gap seen in South Korea and Japan, where men earn wages more than 30 percent higher than women for the same job.[55]

What's behind the startling disparity? It's not a matter of the type of work women choose. Research shows that it's not just in certain fields that women make less, but across the board. One of the main reasons turns out to be that women tend not to negotiate salary in the same fashion or as often and directly as men. Because they think of it as a confrontation, it seems unwise to enter into a confrontation with one's employer just as that relationship is beginning. Men, on the other hand, often see it as a natural part of finding and securing a job. They see it as a check box on their employment list rather than as any sort of confrontation. Research shows that when offered a job, only 7 percent of women will negotiate their incoming salary, while more than 55 percent of men will take that extra step by asking for as much compensation as they can get.[56]

A gender-intelligent organization looks at its compensation practices and makes efforts to close gaps, especially in instances where there are discrepancies in similar positions and job functions. It realizes the cost in turnover due to women who don't feel appreciated for doing the same work. Gender-intelligent companies realize that equal pay for equal work ensures the company retains the best and brightest women, and also attracts the most high-potential candidates from universities and competing organizations.

PERFORMANCE MANAGEMENT

In trying to accomplish their business objectives, women tend to build relationships first, then work to improve those relationships in the course of goal attainment. Sharing and relating with others is a source of tremendous fulfillment for women; it validates their efforts and gives their work meaning.

Men tend to approach work and engage others in a different way. Their inclination is to find the shortest distance between two points and move along that course as effectively as possible, first determining what is right and necessary and establishing an order of importance. They then work through the list, doing so as efficiently as possible both in terms of time and in the amount of resources they use.

Performance management systems are traditionally based on where men place value—on the results. And quarterly, semiannual, and annual performance reviews often measure progress on projects and programs from an on-time and on-budget mindset.

Gender-intelligent performance management systems are equally focused on where women place value—in the building and developing of alliances and skills that are replicable. They look not just at the short-term business goals, but also at the infrastructure women have been building along the way. Being goal-driven is a natural, wired-in capacity in men, and hugely complementary to a woman's inclination to build alliances, develop strong relations, and improve the capacity of people and processes networked along the way. Both goal attainment and relationship development are needed for success.

A woman CEO candidate for a Fortune 100 company attended a lavish four-day leadership-training course offered by a prestigious university in the northeastern United States. The course has been offered to executives in business and government for more than thirty years, and in order to refresh the materials and keep pace with the times, the developers have made slight updates to the courseware over the years, adding new case studies and new ways of articulating successful leadership traits.

The CEO candidate and the instructor were talking before the first day of classes when the woman asked, "I've noticed that the men and women on my teams practice their leadership differently. Will we be exploring gender differences in leadership over the next four days?" She'd observed that almost half the attendees were women, but saw only one model of leadership being discussed. Additionally, there were more individual assignments than group assignments.

The instructor replied, "Our focus will be on the principles of sound leadership, including having a vision, showing integrity, taking responsibility, building trust, and being goal-driven. These principles are shared by men and women alike."

The CEO candidate walked away unhappy with the response, beginning to think this wasn't the place for her. *I show my integrity and build trust in different ways,* she thought. *And being goal-driven is not my only focus. I share my leadership, and these four days are not designed for that.*

Balanced Leadership for Improved Organizational Performance

Studies show that in a business world that is becoming more and more fluid and uncertain, the quality of leadership needs to change to match that world and help the organization become more effective in this milieu. The dominant male model of leadership focuses on command and control, clear decision-making lines of authority, and vision and execution. All of these are important as a model of leadership, but as the example above demonstrates, studies also show that it's incomplete. More balanced leadership that amplifies the strength of men and women is producing more effective results in organizations worldwide.

As we now know, women and men share a different, though complementary, set of leadership behaviors that are crucial to overall organizational performance. As we first showed in presenting the business case for Gender Intelligence, McKinsey & Company's 2009 study surveyed nine thousand leaders and managers from around the world to measure the frequency of use of nine leadership behaviors that tend to improve organization performance.[57]

Their study revealed that women and men frequently apply a specific though complementary set of strengths:

Balanced Leadership

Women tend to apply more	• People development • Expectations and rewards • Role modeling
Women tend to apply slightly more	• Inspiration • Participative decision-making
Women and men tend to apply equally	• Intellectual stimulation • Efficient communication
Men tend to apply more	• Individualistic decision-making • Corrective action and control

It's important to note that this study reveals the tendencies of women and men in their approaches to leadership. You may know men who are as inclined as women toward developing, mentoring, and inspiring employees. And there are many women who like to make decisions alone and apply command-and-control principles to drive results.

Women and men—working in unison—bring these leadership behaviors together, enabling an enterprise to perform well across all of the organizational dimensions of favorable work environment, ethical values, motivation, accountability, and innovation.

This last area—innovation—is key for organizations looking to expand in the global information age. McKinsey's study also revealed that, although the five behaviors of Participative Decision-Making, Role Modeling, Inspiration, Expectations and Rewards, and People Development have become increasingly critical in addressing future global challenges, 70 percent of senior leaders admit that their companies' top executives lack those specific and critical leadership traits. This, of course, makes sense since most of the senior leaders are men. Enter again the value of women joining men with a seat at the leadership table.

Recent research conducted by Zenger and Folkman shows that on average, women excel over men in leading a majority of functions and in overall leadership competencies.[58] Below is their summary of their research drawn from a sample of more than seven thousand leaders who had their leadership effectiveness evaluated in 2011. It's worth noting that the Zenger Folkman study was not of a global random sample of leaders, but rather a sampling of male and female leaders from high-performing companies.

In terms of the leadership of functions, women were rated more positively in twelve of the fifteen listed. As noted by Zenger and Folkman, "some of the largest gaps were in areas that tend to be male-dominated, such as sales, product development, legal, engineering, IT, and R&D." According to the study, the proportion of women in these functions ranges from 13 to 30 percent.

COMPETENCY	MEN	WOMEN
Sales		•
Marketing		•
Customer Service	•	
Operations		•
HR, Training		•
General Management		•
Finance and Accounting		•
Product Development		•
Legal		•
Engineering		•
Information Technology		•
Research and Development		•
Facilities Management/ Maintenance	•	
Quality Management		•
Administrative/Clerical	•	

In terms of leadership competencies, women were rated more positively than men by managers, peers, and direct reports in all but one
area—Develops Strategic Perspective:

FUNCTION	MEN	WOMEN
Takes Initiative		•
Practices Self-Development		•
Drives for Results		•
Develops Others		•
Inspires and Motivates Others		•
Builds Relationships		•
Collaboration and Teamwork		•
Establishes Stretch Goals		•
Champions Change		•
Solves Problems and Analyzes Issues		•
Communicates Powerfully and Prolifically		•
Connects the Group to the Outside World		•
Innovates		•
Technical or Professional Expertise		•
Develops Strategic Perspective	•	

Note how so many of these leadership competencies are well designed
to drive the very innovation that studies are showing is lacking. This research, of course, raises the question, if women generally rate higher,
why aren't there more women in leadership positions overall? Why does
the glass ceiling still exist?

Theories abound. Among the more popular ones:

1. Due to family needs, many women don't want to take on senior leadership roles that have high demands for their time. It takes them too much away from their families.
2. General sexism or gender inequality (societal belief that women don't make good business leaders).
3. They typically don't have the required skills.
4. They aren't tough enough or lack the ambition.

While there may be some validity to the first two theories, we see little evidence for the last two. There are many highly skilled women who have an enormous desire to add value from a leadership role. This is not a skill or motivation issue, as some may suggest. We believe that the primary reasons have much more to do with the lack of Gender Intelligence. Without Gender Intelligence, male leaders promote in their own image. They seek and reinforce leaders who think and act the way they do.

The narrow and limited way in which leadership is thought of and the weeding out of leaders who don't fit the mold happens from the middle management ranks all the way to the top with a fair degree of unawareness. We have witnessed all too many occasions where relatively well-intentioned male leaders consider the women who report to them as not cut out for the job. We have also witnessed how women will hesitate to toot their own horn. They focus more on trying to be of service than on advancing their career. As a result, too many women get passed over time and time again. And it is not the male leaders doing it alone. Too often women with seniority in middle management talk younger women out of making an effort, in essence saying, "It's all men up there. You don't stand a chance."

In our view, the glass ceiling is not just a social justice issue, or just a talent issue. The bigger consequence of the glass ceiling is that upper management has difficult breaking its own mold and creating conditions where the organization can take advantage of the different leadership tendencies that women bring. These and other emerging studies point to an inescapable conclusion: if men dominate in leadership positions, a company will experience a limited set of leadership behaviors, thereby reducing an organization's capabilities. Organizations with balanced men and women in leadership also tend to have more balanced representation in critical thinking and decision-making, which then causes an increase in economic performance over time.

It's More Than Walking the Talk

The organizations that are on the path today to becoming gender-intelligent are recognizing that changing the mindset of leadership is not enough. They are recognizing that systemic change has to take place deep within the organization.

This is how organizations at Stage Five perform every day, infusing Gender Intelligence into all of their key functions, processes, and systems. Leaders and managers ensure there are no obstacles to the advancement of women in unity with men and use Gender Intelligence principles to shape their leadership mindset and create a gender-balanced company culture.

Some of the companies doing it best—American Express, Deloitte, and IBM—are sustaining cultures conducive to gender diversity and inclusiveness and are growing in their global competitiveness. They are attracting and retaining the best talent, making better strategic decisions, producing more relevant products and services, and, as a result, achieving superior financial results.

For many it's the bottom-line results that are the most encouraging, causing more companies to shift away from viewing gender diversity solely as a fair and equitable thing to do to finding the economic value of gender diversity just as compelling. And the business case becomes a powerful motivator for any company still doubtful about expending effort and energy on gender-intelligent infrastructure that allows for sustainable change.

9

The Economics of
Gender Diversity

The senior management team at one of the top retail chains in the United States, in an effort to assess the effectiveness of its stores, developed five criteria for success—a combination of metrics that most positively correlated with store revenue growth and employee satisfaction. They included customer satisfaction, time spent in store, employee morale, employee performance, and quality of in-store merchandising.

They found that out of all their more than nine hundred stores, there were eight that were consistently outperforming all others across all five criteria. What interested the senior team even more was that these eight stores were not all located in one major city or region of the country, but rather were dispersed across the United States. The senior team was curious to discover what these eight had in common.

What became immediately visible was the gender balance in management. Though the senior team had seen stores with far better ratios of female to male managers and some stores with virtually all-women management, what was different about these eight was the low turnover of women.

After interviewing the men and women managers in each of the eight stores, the team learned that it was more than just an equality in numbers that was creating success; it was also equality in value and contribution—a greater listening and blending of ideas for the best possible outcome. These eight stores were practicing Gender Intelligence. One winning idea that came from one of the management teams in one of the stores and spread to some of the others caught the attention of senior management.

A handful of stores had instituted a different approach to commission selling that was working very well. It was driven by a desire to be more customer-driven than commission-driven and was influenced by the female leadership, who generally have a higher appreciation and place higher value on the whole customer experience than their male counterparts do. Rather than jumping on shoppers as they entered the store and fighting for that commission, driven by a fuller view of the customer experience salespeople now share a group commission versus having individual commissions. Now they refer shoppers who are looking for information to the most capable salesperson in that particular area of interest. Shared versus individual commission has since been rolled out across all stores.

This movement away from individual to group commission, which positively affected most every one of the company's five criteria, was brought about by difference-thinking—the blending of women and men in problem-solving and decision-making. Women naturally bring a different line of sight into the workplace than men, and in this example, the difference was both palpable and completely additive to the beginning model.

There are two different economic insights that companies may have that propel them toward greater gender diversity. One is the insight that including women in the conversation broadens the company's reach in marketing, sales, and customer service. The second, much broader insight is that when they infuse Gender Intelligence in everything they do, they see results not in one function, such as marketing, but in areas of all functions, including operations, a bastion of male dominance in terms of representation. This company is a perfect example, demonstrating how, once companies open themselves to gender-intelligent thinking, it becomes infectious as other teams and divisions and departments seek to emulate the change and realize their own economic success through gender diversity.

Companies like American Express have broken through to the next level by infusing Gender Intelligence into as many activities and practices as possible—from critical decision-making at the CEO level.

This systemic shift is made possible when the argument for gender inclusion is not limited to what is fair and equal. In the business world, that's not enough. But some trailblazing organizations today are starting to ask, "What is the economic value of gender diversity?" They're seeing signs of the impact of women in both the workplace and the marketplace and they're moving the conversation in that direction. Companies must do more, however, than simply place more emphasis on how to attract and retain female talent, the argument for that being, and rightly so, that there's a huge talent pool of women out there and the companies that land this top talent will win the battle.

It's a start, but companies introduced throughout this book as well as many others are breaking new ground, shifting away from the fairness argument for gender diversity to the economic advantage and win-win outcomes made possible when empowering women and men together.

As more organizations actively seek ways to make gender diversity work for them, more and more consultancies and associations are conducting research into why and how women bring greater economic value to the equation. We think it's compelling what they're finding:

- Balanced leadership improves the bottom line of companies—in some instances dramatically.
- Gender-blended teams—from the boardroom to the shop floor—are more likely to achieve substantially greater outcomes in problem-solving and decision-making and greater productivity than teams containing only men or only women.
- Though women influence and control the clear majority of consumer spending globally, and they increasingly have the earning power to maintain control, the majority of women feel they aren't represented in the marketplace in product design, communication and education, or service.
- Many countries face considerable demographic challenges and talent shortfalls. While integrating women into their economies has always been the right thing to do, now it is the smartest way to dramatically improve a country's rate of economic growth.

Unfortunately, even when faced with this type of persuasive research, some companies are just not making the connection, missing what gender-intelligent people would consider some pretty meaningful signs. The problem is, they're not yet looking for the value in difference, denying it in the first place, then undervaluing it when it shows up.

What Would a Gender-Intelligent Leader Do?

Imagine a financial services company with sky-high profits and the adrenaline-pumping, everything's-on-the-line environment that can bring many people to the brink. In the bond trading division of this company we find two highly successful executives—one a man, one a woman—who, as you would expect, employ very different strategies to achieve success. The male executive targeted the wealthiest A-list investors and was constantly on the hunt for the *big* deals. The woman talked to many investors over the course of her day, forging strong connections with many and closing smaller deals, but more of them. In terms of numbers, their close rates and overall results were virtually the same.

When they let a big deal fall through, the ways they expressed their frustration and disappointment were nothing alike. The male trader just went off into a rage. Around the office, he stomped and cursed, confronted those he thought were responsible, and smashed a phone to pieces. For many people in the firm, especially the men, this behavior made him a hero. In fact, they used to collect his smashed phones in a closet and count them up each year, treating the pile like some sort of trophy. Women thought his physical outbursts were a bit over-the-top, but they also excused his flying off the handle as "passionate" and thought it simply demonstrated his concern for making money for the firm.

The female executive had been slowly reeling in a huge client, bit by bit, for weeks. Closing the deal would be a giant coup. One day, when the same deal fell through, she hung up the phone and rose from her desk in tears. In the moment, she was frustrated, was severely disappointed, and felt as if she'd wasted too much time.

If only she'd smashed her phone against the wall instead. Unfortunately, people at the firm badly misinterpreted her behavior. In the hallways, her colleagues expressed concern that she might have "reached a threshold" and was beginning to crumble under the pressure. The woman executive began picking up on the meta-messages from other people in meetings and lunchroom chatter that conveyed "She's not shaping up to be leadership material."

The false perception of the trader as weak by those around her proved too much to bear. She's since left, dealing a real blow to the firm in losing their second-highest producer. She had brought in a lot of money for the firm.

This company never made the connection. It completely misread the function and intent of the different emotional reactions of the male and the female leader. His outbursts helped him focus and zero in on a solution. Her tears tied back into a web of other emotions and memories that produced solutions for her. Both his and hers were powerful emotional reactions, both strengths in terms of helping them deal with disappointment, and both of equal value to the firm in keeping the traders productive and getting them back on track.

When the Leader Gets It . . .

Remember that in the Leadership Chain, Gender Intelligence is catalyzed by a shift and commitment in the attitude and behavior of the company's leaders. It begins with the mindset of the leader, who then changes his or her style of leadership, which positively affects the culture, which in turn causes the organization to achieve greater results.

Gender-intelligent leaders in varying positions understand how to build trusting, working relationships across gender. They walk the talk and build a coalition for change around them that takes root and is carried across the divisions, and becomes deeply ensconced in the fabric of the company.

The natural consequence is that more ideas are brought to the table and there's more discussion and interest in others' ways of seeing things. Internally, teams operate more effectively and efficiently and demonstrate greater Gender Intelligence externally in the marketplace, the source of greater economic value.

. . . Organizations Get It

Though leadership mindset and style are crucial to companies making a transformation, as organizations break through to Stage Five, Gender Intelligence is increasingly absorbed into the culture and is extended into the ongoing, recurring activities involved in the running of their business in a number of high-value ways, which we covered in depth in the previous chapter, including:

- Infusing Gender Intelligence into the functions most influenced by gender differences that stand to contribute the greatest economic return, including marketing, research and product development, sales, and customer service.

- Using Gender Intelligence to help employees derive the greatest value when engaging with one another as they conduct business throughout the day—particularly in how they interact, resolve conflicts, solve problems, and make decisions.
- Bringing gender-intelligent thought and design to all their employee development and enrichment systems, including hiring, performance management, compensation, and leadership and management training.

Companies on the path to Stage Five on the continuum understand the economic value in gender diversity and are starting to get results. We think the trend will only continue as more and more research is conducted on the value of gender-blending approaches in leadership, team productivity, marketing, sales, and customer service and as the world of business continues to be more and more uncertain, globally competitive, and fluid, requiring new and different ways to innovate.

Why Is Now the Time for Gender Intelligence?

We've said that we see a tidal wave of interest today in the economics of gender diversity. If we spent the last decades focused on the fairness of gender equality, what explains the popular shift to the economics of empowering women?

We've identified four major developments that have each and together encouraged a greater understanding of the dynamics taking place today. They are:

- Greater numbers of women with higher degrees
- More and more women and many men demanding that companies become Gender Intelligent
- Greater understanding of brain physiology and gender-based brain differences
- Upward trends in women's global buying power

Those four forces are causing leaders and their organizations to shift their thinking away from gender diversity in numbers to gender diversity of thought. Along with this, more research is being commissioned to make better sense of these societal-level changes and influences.

Since the 1980s, the number of women with undergraduate and graduate degrees in virtually every field has steadily grown, with women dominating in medicine, law, and business at universities across the globe. Even in countries in the Middle East, women represent the majority of college graduates. Just as those early feminists predicted, that flood of degreed women has spilled into organizations and companies on every continent.

This critical mass of women in education and business is forcing the conversation because despite their gains, the women's movement goals of the 1970s have not been achieved. After thirty-odd years making up half of middle management in organizations around the world, only one in five women is in senior management and one in ten at the CEO or board level. Countless thousands of women, voting with their feet as they walked out the door, have sent a powerful message to organizations.

Greater understanding of how brain physiology and hormonal chemistry influence gender-specific thoughts and actions has come to the forefront. In fact, a growing stream of findings has shown the dramatic variations that occur throughout the brain, informing and influencing the different ways men and women communicate, listen, solve problems, make decisions, handle emotions, deal with conflict, and manage stress.

In a way, it's refreshing to see the substantial data that explains, in large part, why we think and act as we do. So often, when the men and women we work with learn about the differences and their empirical root, there's a profound sense of relief. They could feel and observe the differences, but they either were encouraged not to address them or didn't even understand them on a level that would allow them to take action.

While the upward trend in women's global buying power is splashed all over the news, so many companies still believe they can afford to ignore women as a consumer group. While women have always held sway over market spending to a certain extent, the sheer strength of their influence has not been recognized until now. For instance, only in the past five to ten years has there been research conducted to reveal that, when it comes to marketing and advertising, women process information and make purchasing decisions differently than men. And yet, even though women influence and control the majority of spending decisions, they're still being marketed to as if they were men.

A large beer company felt they had connected with the men who favored their brand, and decided to go after the female market. History had proved, they thought, that a six-pack of their brew didn't excite women and so they told R&D to come up with something new. A new line of achingly colorful coolers and the like emerged, all meant to entice the female customer. Take it out of the can and make it pink, they thought; that will get the women buying.

The beer company invited us in to conduct a diagnostic and focus group with male and female consumers. Women showed complete dissatisfaction with the coolers concept; the pink wash hadn't worked. More interesting were the women's comments about the brand in general, one of the top beer brands in the world. It read as "blue collar," according to the women, and more disturbingly as "anti-women" and "stereotyping of women." The women went so far as to say they found the company's beer commercials "violently offensive."

The men in the marketing department found the women's reaction ir-relevant. "We do target-marketing branding," they told us. Those com-mercials weren't meant for the women. It only mattered if the men who drank their beer found them appealing.

What they didn't get was that even though the beer company was tar-geting men successfully with its "offensive" commercials, men weren't the ones picking up the beer at the store. It was the women who chose what to put in their carts and they were voting with their feet.

So many companies still do this today. They justify their marketing campaigns and advertisements because these have a certain target audi-ence. It's only natural that others don't get the marketing, they counter. It wasn't meant for them. They aren't targeting the very people who do the majority of purchasing or influence most purchases. Only in the past twenty or so years have leaders and their organizations grown to appreci-ate the significance of that transformation in the marketplace—a realiza-tion that's making companies stand up and take notice.

The Building Power of the Gender Intelligence Movement

Having practiced Gender Intelligence for more than twenty-seven years, working closely with over a hundred Fortune 500 companies, as well as educational institutions and governments around the world, we've helped our client organizations view gender equality from a strength-through-differences standpoint rather than as equality in numbers. As knowledge and power of the movement continue to grow, more companies are taking notice of the results their competitors are realizing from employing Gender Intelligence principles and are deciding they can no longer afford to sit on the sidelines while others join with other gender-intelligent companies to share strategies, stories, and results.

Our client organizations recognize that men and women bring different perspectives to the table. They're finding that the complement of gender differences in critical thinking, management, and leadership is sustaining the organization's growth and success in this highly competitive Information Age.

Our Gender Intelligence Summits feature recognized experts in neuroscience and psychology, accomplished leaders in business and government, and the sharing out of best practices among leading organizations in advancing Gender Intelligence. These gatherings and new and exciting conversations on gender outside of the summits are taking place across the globe—from Dallas to Denmark to Dubai.

When you add it all together—the critical mass, the continuing discoveries in brain science and chemistry, the impact of gender in the marketplace, and the Gender Intelligence movement and message—you begin to see what's prompting the inquisitiveness, encouraging companies to find out how they can improve their bottom-line results, and commissioning a growing body of research showing how gender diversity translates into economic value.

What the Research Is Showing

The research continues to confirm what we've experienced with organizations over the past quarter of a century, discovering there are clear advantages to greater gender balance and diversity of thought.

As we seek patterns in the information available, we find there are five areas where gender diversity is unleashing the greatest amount of economic value:

1. Balanced leadership
2. Gender-blended teams

3. Market responsiveness
4. Risk management
5. Talent utilization

Gender-intelligent organizations are discovering that the greater the gender diversity in each of these five areas—from leadership to marketing to talent management—the greater the contribution to the economic benefit for the organization.

BALANCED LEADERSHIP

The pattern of thinking for the past forty years held that men and women should lead in the same way (like men). But what business and scientific research is showing is that there is no truth in the belief that women want to lead as men do or need to do so in order to find success. The only truth is that there are many unfulfilled women not leading from a position of strength and with inside-out congruence. This is something that women in senior leadership are highly attuned to and men are beginning to understand.

Though there has been a shift in understanding since the 1980s, look into the executive conference rooms of many companies and you'll find that old paradigm is still very much in effect. Organizations need balanced leadership the most when they feel compelled to go back to the old ways of being and doing. Under conditions of ambiguity and uncertainty, humans often revert to what they know best, to what is comfortable. For men, this means employing a more "heroic" style of leadership that trades on command and control.

What society is focused on now is how to build the future paradigm of leadership—one that is more distributive and collaborative than centralized and unilateral. This is a world where the natural and often differing leadership proclivities of men and women work in unison, producing a synergistic effect that is all too rare yet sorely needed. Many books and articles have been written advocating this future paradigm, and there is generally a high level of buy-in into the fact that this is where society is going—indeed, it is where we have to go.

But what's not always acknowledged is that when you have a greater balance of women and men in leadership, you are actually accelerating that paradigm shift. That's the position we've taken for years, one backed up by the success found among our clients' leadership teams. As we explained in the previous chapter, the presence of women helps change the conversation and nudges the company toward a critical shift in thinking. The same is especially true at the top of the organization and at the board level.

Research conducted over the past ten years has repeatedly shown that companies with higher representation in their top management teams on average experience better financial performance than companies with the lowest representation of women. The more gender-blended teams provide a broader array of solutions, from which more balanced decisions are made.

Current research at the board level that studies the dynamics of the discussion and the quality of decision-making when women are present shows how the range of issues raised and discussed increases and includes usefully different perspectives when female board members are involved.

Research also shows that boards with women are more likely to pursue best practices in areas including board evaluations, codes of conduct, conflict-of-interest guidelines, and closer looks at executive remuneration arrangements—all areas that help shape company culture. Most persuasively for some, companies with women board directors post higher financial performance in three important measures:[59]

- Return on **equity**—on average, companies with the highest percentages of women board directors outperformed those with the least by 53 percent
- Return on **sales**—by 42 percent
- Return on **invested capital**—by 66 percent

The reason women make a powerful difference in the boardroom often ties back to the collaborative leadership style they bring. Their style benefits board dynamics by encouraging people to show up, listen more carefully, and focus on win-win problem-solving. Women are more likely to ask the tough questions and request direct, detailed answers.

Clearly it matters to corporate leadership and governance that women are on the boards. But is it the mere presence of women that's changing the dialogue and enhancing the decision-making process?

A number of studies reveal that the answer is: not exactly. While one woman can and often does make substantial contributions, and two women are more powerful than one, increasing the number of women to three or more enhances the likelihood that women's voices and ideas are heard. With three or more women, boardroom dynamics are palpably and substantially altered.[60]

Suddenly, having women in the board meeting becomes normative. You don't have one or two women representing "a woman's opinion" that could be more easily discounted. Three or more women on a board creates a critical mass where women are no longer seen as outsiders with *their* point of view, but are able to influence the content and process of board discussions more substantially.

How are we doing on achieving that critical mass? By all metrics, poorly. With all the legislative and corporate efforts to increase the relative number of boards with women—and in some Nordic countries that is now 30–40 percent—the percentage of boards with the optimal number of women remains quite low throughout Europe. The same is true in the United States. The chart below reflects the number of women on boards in 2012 in the Russell 3000, an index that measures the performance of the largest three thousand companies in the United States.[61]

Number of Women on Boards

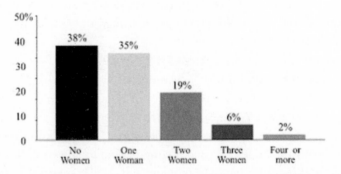

As you can see, a full 92 percent of the boards claiming to have gender representation have less than the critical mass of three needed to make a true difference. They still lack the female representation and perspective needed to spur true diversity of thought, where the content of board discussions is more likely to include the perspectives of multiple stakeholders, not only shareholders, but employees, customers, suppliers, consumer groups, and the community at large.

More work is necessary to create boards with a critical mass of women, ensuring that difficult issues and problems are explored in greater depth, which results in better conflict resolution, a broader field of solutions, and more informed decision-making. The culture of the boardroom needs to shift in order to better the relationship with top leaders. As the board moves toward a more open and collaborative dynamic, it helps management hear the board's concerns and ideas without defensiveness.

GENDER-BLENDED TEAMS

Since taking gender into consideration, research has consistently shown that teams containing a better balance of men and women achieve higher results in innovation and effectiveness. Behavioral studies show that in gender-blended groups where everyone feels comfortable and all opinions are heard, teams are more likely to challenge established norms and get the best ideas on the table, improving communication, ideation, problem-solving, and decision-making.

As we've learned and new research continues to show, men and women bring a different approach to team collaboration. They bring different viewpoints and experiences to the table and therefore add a richer collection of perspectives and values.

A recent study coauthored by MIT, Carnegie Mellon University, and Union College researchers, for example, documents the existence of collective intelligence among groups of people who cooperate well—more minds are better than one. The study shows that such intelligence extends beyond the cognitive abilities and contributions of the groups' individual members, and that the tendency to cooperate effectively in the first place is linked to the number of women in a group.[62]

Looking to expand the definition of intelligence based on the performance of individual tasks, the researchers set out to test the hypothesis that *groups*, like individuals, have a consistent ability to perform across different kinds of tasks. The researchers were looking to test how the group developed what they called "collective intelligence."

The groups worked together on tasks that ranged from visual puzzles to negotiations, brainstorming, games, and complex rule-based design assignments. The researchers concluded that a group's collective intelligence accounted for up to 40 percent of the variation in performance on this wide range of tasks.

That collective intelligence, they believe, stems from how well the group works together. For instance, groups whose members had higher levels of "social sensitivity"—how well group members pick up on each other's emotions—were more collectively intelligent. Conversely, in groups where one person dominated, the group was less collectively intelligent than those groups where the conversational turns were more evenly distributed.

Though they didn't set out to prove the benefits of group diversity, during the study the researchers discovered that teams containing more women demonstrated greater social sensitivity and, in turn, greater collective intelligence compared to teams containing fewer women.

Moreover, the researchers found that the average IQ of individual group members did not significantly predict the performance of their groups overall. Having a bunch of smart men in a group was not as valuable as having a blend of men and women, a significant finding given the hiring priorities of many organizations.

Other studies have shown similar results. This team-based research is challenging conventional thinking. It calls into question our whole notion of what intelligence means in this global, connected, highly interactive Information Age. What individuals can do all by themselves is important, but it's becoming less so by the day. What matters equally is the additive quality of gender diverse collaboration.

MARKET RESPONSIVENESS
Once they have Gender Intelligence, companies can't help but become more market responsive. The internal pressure from gender-intelligent leaders causes the organization to see the client or customer differently and question marketing objectives, strategies, and communications. Throughout this book, we've given a number of examples of organizations finding Gender Intelligence and becoming more market responsive.

In the preceding chapters we learned how Dove appealed to real women the world over, and about Deloitte's journey toward recruiting the best and brightest women and keeping them from its competitors. It may surprise you to learn that even fast-food franchises were able to find measurable economic value by changing their approach.

A fast-food brand that has reached into nearly every corner of the globe, McDonald's has always been quick to react to the changing needs and expectations of the marketplace. While most of the men in the company's leadership seemed satisfied with their Quarter Pounders and fries, the women in the company led the movement for healthier menu choices like yogurt parfaits, salads, and grilled chicken sandwiches. Because they constituted a critical mass at the company, the women were able to steer this global titan in a new, modern direction that satisfied their own needs as employees and appealed to them as mothers wanting the same for their children.

There are countless other companies finding economic value as more balanced leadership teams reverse-engineer the needs and expectations of the marketplace back into their organizations, a move in many cases launched by women. It would stand to reason that if 80 percent of the time a woman will influence the purchase of a company's product (or their competitor's), then the company should see that women are heavily involved in or leading the company's marketing direction and the management of its brands. Those organizations that ensure their companies mirror the marketplace give greater voice to their customers, and the company's success attracts talented women from other organizations who want to contribute to a company that understands and values gender differences.

RISK MANAGEMENT

Risk management as it relates to gender dynamics is less about reaching out and more about protecting the company from gender discrimination, but its value can't be overlooked. Considering the cost, many companies have every reason to fear sexual harassment lawsuits. Complainants today receive, on average, $250,000, if she or he wins at trial, not including attorneys' fees. Settlements avoid the cost of litigation but can still cost a company tens of thousands of dollars; verdicts that go against a defending company can cost millions![63]

The U.S. Equal Employment Opportunity Commission has received an average of 25,800 sexual harassment complaints every year for sixteen years from 1997 to 2012. Interestingly, the average has increased over the most recent five years to 28,800. In 2012 the number of complaints broke the 30,000 mark.[64]

Considering the ubiquity of diversity training programs since the 1990s, it would seem that the number of sexual harassment complaints would be declining, if the training programs were successful. While there are people and companies who engage in willfully bad behavior, many complaints are also the result of men behaving unintentionally or misunderstanding and poorly communicating their intentions. Each year, an average of 50 percent of the suits are dismissed, the judge determining there is no reasonable cause. The ones that do stick cost U.S. business more than $100 million annually in awards to plaintiffs.[65]

Those are just the dollar figures. The hidden costs include increases in sick leave and time away from work; decrease in individual productivity of the victim of sexual harassment; lost productivity by the victim's friends and associates; and job turnover, including transfers, being fired, and quitting. Moreover, the personal cost to plaintiffs is dire, and includes stress, depression, and other potentially severe emotional and physical consequences.

The repercussions of a lawsuit are deeply felt. Firewalls go up that prevent both women and men from acting naturally and being at their best. Companies adopt draconian policies aimed to prevent any chance of misconduct, such as prohibiting male supervisors from having closed-door meetings with female subordinates. Men become uncomfortable traveling with or even having a business lunch with a woman colleague. They don't want to be misunderstood for *any* behavior on their part. The forced separation only hurts women more, the sad irony being that the inability to meet privately or travel with the boss or with other male colleagues can limit a woman's chances for developing her career and finding the right mentors and sponsors to help her move up in an organization.

The benefits of risk management are not only found in saving money on sexual harassment lawsuits, but extend also to mitigating the loss of talented and highly skilled women, especially to competitive companies that then benefit from the women's expertise and institutional knowledge. Gender Intelligence helps save the cost of recruiting and training replacements in time and dollars, which, as we learned from Deloitte's example, can be considerable. Gender-intelligent companies also stem the immeasurable loss of valuable perspectives on the marketplace; they move forward while competitors remain disadvantaged and stuck.

TALENT UTILIZATION

In a world where many countries face serious demographic challenges from shrinking and aging populations, businesses don't have many options to achieve dramatically positive rates of economic growth with relatively little effort. Therefore, while the further integration of women into global economies has always been the right thing to do, the evidence now clearly indicates that it is the smart thing to do as well.

While there is no research as yet to prove its causality, we strongly believe that empowering women means a more efficient use of the talent pool, enhancing overall productivity and economic growth. Business and government alike also need to change and grow, rising to meet still-unforeseen challenges of the new Information Age. You can't force innovation; it requires new and unique ideas, and the best ideas flourish and flow in a gender-diverse environment.

Today, 76 percent of American women between the ages of twenty-five and fifty-four are in the workforce, compared to 87 percent in Sweden. If the United States could increase the workplace participation rate of women in each state to 84 percent, it would add 5.1 million women to the mix, the estimated equivalent of as much as a 9 percent GDP growth.[66] Increasing women's participation isn't just good for individual companies; it makes a difference in the relative economic success of entire nations, as we see from the chart below.

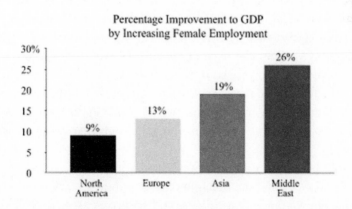

Percentage Improvement to GDP
by Increasing Female Employment

The chart indicates the approximate improvement to a nation's or a neighboring group of nations' GDP made by closing the female employment gap, in particular the gap in senior positions, wages, and leadership. A report by the United Nations Economic and Social Commission for

Asia and the Pacific found that restricting job opportunities for women is costing the region as much as $46 billion a year. Similar restrictions have imposed massive costs throughout the Middle East, where decades of investment have dramatically reduced the gender gap in education but haven't closed the gap in economic participation, which remains the widest in the world.[67]

The disparity between women's achievements in education and their absence in the workplace demonstrates that the solution is at hand. There's a talent shortfall in Asia and the Middle East, but not a talent scarcity—qualified women abound. The key here is that these countries need to see the shortfall as a talent opportunity and not get trapped in defensive posturing.

Talent utilization is unleashing the greatest amount of economic value for gender-intelligent companies as well by attracting women who want their work and personal lives to be congruent. Companies that value gender differences and authenticity offer enormous value to these women, translating into the fact that being an early adopter of Gender Intelligence in one's industry can make you a virtual magnet for talented women.

American business magnate, investor, and philanthropist Warren Buffett effectively and articulately reasoned the recognition, valuing, and blending of gender talents and skills in an article he wrote for *Fortune* magazine in which he noted, "Our country's progress since 1776 has been mind-blowing, like nothing the world has ever seen. Yet, America has forged this success while utilizing, in large part, only half of the country's talent. For most of our history, women—whatever their abilities—have been relegated to the sidelines." A firm believer in U.S. success, Buffett said, "We've seen what can be accomplished when we use 50 percent of our human capacity. If you visualize what 100 percent can do, you'll join me as an unbridled optimist about America's future."[68]

Considering that the United States constitutes just under 5 percent of the world's population, imagine the possibilities when we engage businesses, educational institutions, and governments across the globe in Gender Intelligence. Imagine the possibility of accelerating gender-intelligent thinking in the populous countries of India and China in addition to Europe, Australia, and South America.

The barriers and restrictions to women entering the workforce and advancing into leadership roles that require and value their unique contributions erode the abilities of women to participate fully in their economies, to support their families, and to pursue their own dreams and ambitions. When countries deny women access, they deny themselves the economic growth they need to build stronger societies and achieve greater prosperity as a whole.

The diagram below details the five areas where Gender Intelligence sustains a culture conducive to gender diversity and inclusiveness, accelerating the company's ability to reach maximum economic value. With Gender Intelligence, organizations are growing their global competitiveness. They're making better strategic decisions, producing more relevant products and services, securing and retaining the best and brightest men and women, and as a result, achieving superior financial results.

The Economic Value of Gender Intelligence

Gender Intelligence

Leadership Balance

Gender-Intelligent Teamwork

Market Responsiveness

Risk Reduction

Enhanced Talent Pool

Greater Economic Prosperity

The combination of balanced leadership, gender-blended teams, market responsiveness, and talent management results in greater economic value to organizations with reduced risk. When we see it happen with our clients the results are profound, as in the example set by eBay president and CEO John Donahoe. For everyone who has something to sell, there is a buyer. This was the premise that led to eBay's meteoric rise. John Donahoe was named CEO of eBay in 2008 and by the end of 2010, he was in the throes of pulling the organization out of its global-recession doldrums. As part of his plan, he committed the company to a multiyear strategic initiative to increase women's representation in eBay's leadership to ensure a competitive advantage in the industry. At the time, this was considered a radical move in Silicon Valley and by the start-ups and tech firms that call it home, the majority of whom were well known for a lack of diversity in executive ranks.

Donahoe set an excellent example as CEO and ignited the forward motion by exemplifying the commitment to the women's initiative in word, deed, and behavior. Human resources chief Beth Axelrod told us he was comfortable being the company's most forceful advocate and most visible spokesperson for the initiative. "It is clear he has taken on the role on his own at no one else's prodding. With John, it's authentic."

We find a prime example of this in the performance objectives set within the company. Not wanting to launch initiatives just for show, Donahoe asked his board of directors to hold his feet to the fire and hold him personally accountable for achieving the strategic goals of the corporate women's initiative, putting in place the programs that develop sustainable careers for women at eBay and personally mentoring five individual women leaders.

The CEO's example was enough to prompt the company's twenty-five senior vice presidents to commit to similar performance goals in 2012. The momentum spread throughout the leadership ranks of the company that same year, ensuring that all eBay employees at vice president level and above took ownership of the initiative.

Tasked to either mentor or sponsor five women, each vice president had a goal to "invite the conversation" with women teammates or subordinates. Axelrod says the goal was in "legitimizing the naming of whatever it is that will enable that woman to thrive within the organization," creating opportunity for better support.

If that resulted in an uncomfortable initial conversation, eBay was prepared to help people work through the rough spots and get to a more enlightened and open space for everyone. Months into the initiative, "the thrive conversation" had informally entered the lexicon and culture of eBay. Alan Marks, responsible for corporate communications across eBay, was effusive in naming Donahoe's leadership mindset and congruous behavior and style as having been instrumental in "making it okay to have these conversations." This, according to Marks, was no minor achievement.

The essential catalyst that continues to nurture the change remains leadership by example. Without it, said Axelrod, "nothing is possible." Of course, having commitment at the top "doesn't necessarily mean you will make progress, but in the absence of it, it's pretty clear that you won't."

Creating More Gender-Intelligent Organizations

The companies mentioned in our book are finding greater economic value through Gender Intelligence. And there are many other organizations that are striking out on their own and looking for ways to make gender diversity work for them. More and more companies today are finding greater economic value through balanced leadership, gender-blended teamwork in strategic thinking and decision-making, and more gender-intelligent market responsiveness.

In the next chapter, we'll give you a peek behind the scenes of some of these companies, allowing you to learn from the discoveries that caused them to make real changes that blended and amplified the voices of men and women.

10

Gender-Intelligent Organizations Today

Surveying the Landscape

As you have probably ascertained by this point, the organizations we work with are all over the board in terms of their attitudes toward gender diversity, how much they recognize the value in gender differences, and how much they really want to put in the hard work it takes. At all the companies we work with, once they know where they've been and know what's possible, their next questions are, What will it require of us? and What will it look like when we arrive?

Though we've showcased some wonderfully progressive organizations in the book, we think that most organizations today are barely aware of the value of a gender-diverse culture. What awareness does exist is often swaddled in platitudes that make for great sound bites in a speech or quotes on a website, but have little staying power overall. Many, by their own admission, don't even care to know the business potential of a truly gender-diverse culture. The needle hasn't moved much for this group in a number of years. The companies that make up this group are doing nothing to very little to become gender-diverse, or are approaching the process minimally and reluctantly. What is very clear is that those that do claim to care are approaching diversity as a by-the-numbers game.

Thankfully, a growing number of organizations are gender-aware, although still not yet gender-intelligent. Though they're moving forward with the best of intentions, they are too often misinformed in many of their efforts or are simply trying to replicate the strategies that work for other organizations but might not be the right fit for them. In many instances, these organizations lack the commitment of the CEO and full engagement of senior leadership.

And, finally, there is a small but growing percentage of organizations that have seen through their gender blind spots. They are noticing signs and reading studies of the impact of women in the workplace and marketplace. They're shifting away from token representation to mining the economic value of gender diversity by empowering women and men together. And the most advanced of this group are having breakthrough insights that are changing the culture of their organizations and bringing them greater success internally and in the marketplace.

Three Types of Organizations

As we look across the landscape today, around the globe, we can generally place organizations into one of these three types or groupings, each of which falls naturally on the Gender Intelligence Continuum express:

TYPE 1: Don't care or not interested (Stages Zero and One on the Gender Intelligence Continuum)

TYPE 2: Well-meaning but misinformed and unaligned (Stages Two and early Stage Three on the continuum)

TYPE 3: Genuinely committed—and leading the way to becoming a Stage Five organization (later Stage Three and Stage Four on the continuum)

Based on the totality of our experience, the chart on page 182 represents, by type, our estimated percentage of organizations around the world.[69]

As we explore all three types throughout the chapter and look at the dynamics in each, think of where your organization might fit and see if the dynamics that we describe match those you experience within your

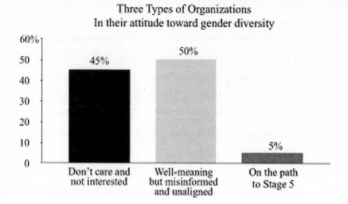

Three Types of Organizations
In their attitude toward gender diversity

company. Because you've come this far, we hope you are convinced and motivated enough to work toward Gender Intelligence in your own organization, regardless of whether you're in a position of senior leadership. At the end of the chapter, we'll share what we believe are the Five Conditions for Success that help keep companies on the path to becoming gender intelligent. We hope you use these conditions to evaluate your own organization.

TYPE 1: DON'T CARE AND NOT INTERESTED

Regrettably, many organizations today still don't know and don't care to know about the value of gender diversity. They may not believe there's a gender issue in their organization to begin with, or they may even think there's no room in their field for women or for men. Regardless, they're not interested in finding out about the value in difference-thinking. Leaders of these organizations often believe there are no differences between men and women or find the differences annoying, but not meaningful. You might say they are in the Dark Ages, hundreds of years away from any Renaissance thinking.

Over the course of our practice, we've found that Type 1 organizations fall into one of two camps—those that "don't know and don't care to know"—the most challenging—and those that are "aware but uninterested" in doing anything about it, or that chafe at the idea that anything more than minimal effort will be required of them.

These organizations have different priorities, with the result that developing gender diversity or Gender Intelligence would never occur to these

leaders on their own. The senior men and sometimes women in these organizations just don't think about gender. For many, if not most, the focus
is on the immediate business at hand—getting the deal or finishing the
project.

This camp also contains organizations that see themselves as having
a capacity issue; they're aware of the concept of gender diversity but
don't feel they can do any more than they're already doing. Others feel
they simply don't have any issues to work on. Type 1 organizations are
operating at a deficit in a number of ways. Their turnover of women is
frequently high. They're also sacrificing a competitive advantage in the
marketplace to the more gender-diverse and valuing companies.

Who are these people? Lumbering dinosaurs in the Information Age
led by less enlightened leaders from a different time? You may be surprised to learn that some of these companies are, in fact, led by young
people who many assume might be a little more gender-intelligent than
turns out to be the case.

One of the largest consumer software companies in the world today
is what we would describe as a Type 1 organization. They're steeped in
their denial to the point where we have found it difficult to even get an
entrée point to have the conversation about gender dynamics and their
influence on the bottom line. "We're so different," their chief diversity
officer seemed to suggest, that they are *post*-gender. "We're one of the
youngest organizations in the world in terms of the average age of our
employees. Gender issues don't even happen here. This is a company
that other organizations benchmark themselves against when they're considering building interactive work teams and creating an innovative and
inclusive culture." To suggest that this young company fell prey to any
old-boy-network shenanigans or hierarchical power plays was laughable.
The reason? This should, by now, sound familiar rather than innovative:

"Everybody treats each other the same and respects each other's culture."

"We're a team-based company."

And "we have work-life flexibility programs through the *roof*."

The reality is that this consumer software company is experiencing a
huge turnover of highly skilled women who seem not to find the work-
life programs and purportedly inclusive team culture as hospitable as
advertised.

When we asked the chief diversity officer about the high turnover of women, she acknowledged the fact, but then quickly followed up by saying that exit interviews showed that women were leaving for primarily personal or family reasons. It wasn't the company, it was the *women*.

You may recognize this company's attitude from the Gender Intelligence Continuum—yes, this company thinks they're a Five. They're looking at their gender diversity initiatives and they're not seeing any problems, but they are not seeing opportunities, either. In large part, women are leaving this software company for the same reason women leave all organizations that lack Gender Intelligence. They don't feel valued. They feel excluded from team meetings and decision-making, and they don't see opportunities for advancement.

The exit interviews don't tell the whole story. As discussed earlier, many women say that they are leaving the company for personal reasons. It's a common white lie that women tell to avoid burning bridges in what can seem like a very close-knit industry.

The second group of Type 1 companies may not have yet fallen prey to a precipitous exodus of women or a monumental dip in market share that can prompt serial "aha!" moments. Most of the men at the top of these organizations and even some of the women executives are used to the business model at hand and the conversation feels good to them. They're getting results in the marketplace and finding success, so the prevailing attitude is "Why spend time and money on something that isn't broken?"

The leaders believe their organizations are fair in their hiring practices; they have in place a meritocracy that ostensibly treats everyone the same and gives everyone equal opportunity. When a gender-related issue does arise, the leaders in this camp often feel that the best course of action is no action at all.

We recently conducted a diagnostic with a large consulting firm and uncovered some significant issues. The other leaders in the company asked to have a meeting with the incoming president to share the results of the diagnostic, having assessed every one of his soon-to-be direct reports.

We showed the scores of each senior leader to the president-elect and drew his attention to two male leaders who scored very low on their dominant patterns and derailers. This translated into their behavior lacking in collaborative insight and initiative, verging on resistance. If not handled properly, these two alone could derail any Gender Intelligence movement in the company. Thank you and please go away now, the incoming leader's reaction seemed to say. "I'm aware of the personalities of those two guys and I understand there may be some issues, but I'll look into it when I take office. I know both men and I have to say, they're two of the most valuable players on my team."

Though the dynamic these two offered to the group would directly affect his transition into leadership, the leader felt, "I can't afford upsetting the applecart the day I come on board, especially not in this economic climate." Furthermore, though he acknowledged they both had "questionable personalities" and were "difficult managers," he was willing to overlook these facts because they were top producers as well. "Just give me a few months to settle into the job," he said, "and maybe we'll put the leadership through some Gender Intelligence training after. We're approaching our busiest season."

This leader's reaction is typical for Type 1's. Unfortunately for him, not only did he fail to grasp the missed opportunity in working to change their behaviors and the culture of the firm; he also underestimated the risk ignoring Gender Intelligence can bring. A short time after that meeting, the behavior and actions of one of the two low scorers landed the consultancy in the middle of a gender discrimination lawsuit. By denying the problem and pushing it off, the incoming president let stand a ticking time bomb. Ignoring the issues to protect his "top producers" ended up costing them a great deal of time and money as well as low morale, lost talent, and unrealized opportunity.

We experienced a similar situation with a law firm in Chicago. We conducted an extensive diagnostic and during the company-wide presentation of the results, the women tried to add depth to the discussion by speaking to specific experiences of exclusion and not having their ideas heard. They also shared that most of the senior female attorneys saw no chance of making partner.

The men were dismissive and disrespectful, literally rolling their eyes during the meeting. But one woman had decided she'd had enough. Much like the consulting firm, this law firm faced a huge gender discrimination lawsuit from a female attorney who quit after putting herself up for partner four times and being denied partnership each time. She knew her results were better than those of the men against whom she competed. The reason she was given for not making partner was that she had "sharp elbows"— that she was too aggressive in her behavior.

She sued the law firm saying that over the twenty-four years she had been there, the culture and organizational mindset had molded her into being that person they later said didn't fit. They even hired an executive coach who groomed her on how to behave like an extreme version of the alpha-male partners in the firm. She won a huge settlement and started her own practice.

It doesn't take a lawsuit to know that it's unfortunate that the clear majority of organizations today seem satisfied with being Type 1. In many cases, half their workforce is composed of women, but as you move up the organizational ladder, invariably you see a precipitous drop-off in their numbers. They may have the lowest percentage of women in senior management, but Type 1 organizations tend to have the most experience with sexual harassment lawsuits and the opportunity cost is extreme.

TYPE 2: WELL-MEANING BUT MISINFORMED AND UNALIGNED

In comparison to Type 1 companies, Type 2 organizations show clear signs of progress, with most of it based on good intentions and an authentic sense of fairness. Nevertheless, some leaders and their organizations are still actively reactive and defensive. While they might be evolving from Type 1, some are doing so at a snail's pace that frustrates the employees and teams eager for more change.

Leaders will fund gender diversity efforts, for example, but may see it as a "nuisance fee," an attitude that reverberates throughout the company culture. For other leaders, it's guilt money for not appearing fair and equal. Gender diversity initiatives are relegated to HR or the head of diversity and are soon enough clearly just window dressing.

The remaining companies in this group approach gender diversity out of genuine human compassion and a sense of fairness, which is where the sense of guilt that permeates the leadership ranks remains strong. They'll point to positive metrics to show they're making progress, but the initiatives function like reparations instead of coming from the belief that gender diversity is linked to an economic advantage for the company. In all cases, they tend to focus on gender diversity and miss the bigger opportunity, namely Gender Intelligence

One organization we work with is a classic Type 2. They have all the right intentions and a strong, values-based company. They recognize they need to be more gender-aware and gender-balanced as well—they acknowledge their deficiencies. In our initial cultural diagnostic, leaders were shocked at how the senior leadership team was perceived by women and were dismayed by the many communication disconnects between the men and women in senior management. Moved to action, these good-hearted people declared in a senior management team meeting that their values required company change and a course correction.

All too soon, other, more pressing and immediate issues edged the emerging conversation around Gender Intelligence off the to-do list. The quarterly results were showing signs of weakness and a new product line was about to be launched, and they couldn't see the connection between either thing and gender balance. Then a conversation around layoffs and a restructuring of the business grabbed their leaders' attention and never let it go. Despite good intentions, the conversation around Gender Intelligence died out.

That is the critical missing link for Type 2 organizations; because gender intelligence is still not yet a strategic imperative, diversity efforts will give way to other priorities. Guilt or good intentions won't keep them present with leadership. Instead, these companies end up with a few well-meaning initiatives and the effort too often ends there, the company spinning its wheels.

As we discussed in earlier chapters, another downfall of companies like these is that they still view gender diversity from a representational standpoint. They then establish goals to have representation at all levels of management and leadership in part to show the world they are diverse. When goals are not met, they may attribute it to hiring or management bias. Unconscious bias training for management might cause a modest amount of movement, but be costly in time, money, and resources. And still the gender diversity gap remains, with high turnover rates for women at the senior levels. The cause? The absence of Gender Intelligence.

We've worked with many organizations in Type 2. It often begins with chief diversity officers or heads of HR who attend a Gender Intelligence Summit and hear what other companies are doing. They admire the progress these companies are making and love the message of Gender Intelligence. Their excitement about bringing this new level of awareness to their organizations doesn't necessarily correlate with leadership's mindset. We've seen this pattern play out so many times, and sadly, this experience has become predictable.

Mary, a senior vice president of HR and global diversity for a Fortune 100 company, had dreamed of making her organization gender-intelligent for the longest time. She was in sync with the research, the message, and the values and committed to bringing change to her company. After several meetings with us, one including the CEO and members of the executive team, Mary was given the green light to proceed. She hired Patricia as vice president of diversity to own and spearhead the initiative.

A good deal of preparation went into conducting the diagnostics and presenting the results to senior management. A gender diversity town hall was held at headquarters and streamed through the corporate intranet. Senior executives attended the first Gender Intelligence workshops and were amazed at the insights gained. And although the manager-level workshops in the Americas, Europe, and Asia were voluntary, the collaborative spirit and sincere commitment of the managers to become more gender-intelligent was getting the attention of the company's leaders. The percent of women in senior management was ticking upward and sticking. The head of the sales division even started to see application in his area and envisioned "Gender Intelligence in Sales" workshops.

But all that changed when the strategic priorities of the company shifted budgetary resources and the entire program was put on hold. Mary and so many other leaders in the organization—true believers in the value of gender intelligence and difference-thinking—were devastated. But while they saw the potential for true growth through Gender Intelligence, the leadership mindset didn't see it as a strategic imperative.

Some think that it might have been better never to have started down the road at all, because the raised expectations created enormous disappointment on the part of Mary and so many others. We disagree. We have witnessed more than one case where a company starts the process and it dies down temporarily, only to be resurrected later by leaders who were inspired in the early efforts and want to see it continue. Once promoted to a higher position of authority, those previously engaged took it upon themselves to resurrect the effort.

Some leaders will try to bring gender diversity into the organization under a larger umbrella of general diversity, another Type 2 tactic we haven't yet seen work well. Many will do this out of a sense of guilt for placing one diversity initiative over another and will focus on racial and ethnic diversity as well as gender in a combined strategy.

We've seen the reaction of one individual push the fear-of-bias button for diversity leaders and broaden a gender-strategic initiative to include all types of diversity.

A few years ago, we sat down and began our meeting with tough questions for ourselves:

- Among the organizations we'd worked with all these years, which ones had truly made authentic progress in Gender Intelligence versus those still approaching it as window dressing?
- In spite of many of our clients having won awards for their diversity initiatives, why had most not made significant progress as a company toward being a Type 3 organization?

As we suggested and then crossed off company after company, the list got very small and our meeting grew quiet. We have been pushing Type 2 organizations up a hill to become more gender-intelligent for almost three decades and today often feel the same frustration as Mary.

In the end, receiving this wake-up call that morning has only convinced us even more that pursuing diversity through representation doesn't produce a transformational shift in culture. It may shift a culture from being biased to less biased and from closed-minded to open-minded, but it doesn't necessarily change the male-dominant paradigm. In order to achieve real and lasting change, an organization must commit and aspire to being Type 3.

TYPE 3: GENUINELY COMMITTED

When an organization becomes aware of the economic power of men and women working together with self-confidence and authenticity, the mindset of its leaders changes, the culture shifts, and the organization as a whole begins to behave more productively and effectively. Gender Intelligence permeates how it markets and sells its product; how functions relate to one another; how human resources are managed; how talent is selected, hired, and used; and how leaders lead.

There are a number of highly successful organizations today instilling what we call a *culture of difference-thinking*, fueled by Gender Intelligence. These Type 3's are genuinely committed to Gender Intelligence

and are on a path to change. They recognize gender diversity as a strategic imperative; they clearly get the business case; and they're doing a
number of things that, together over time, are creating a transformational
shift in the culture. Here are three examples of gender-intelligent organizations leading the way today.

When American Express examined its workforce at the end of 2008, it
discovered that, while women constituted more than half of its employee
base and held one out of every three of the company's top five hundred
positions, they were still woefully underrepresented at its seniormost
levels and virtually absent at the very top. To its credit, leadership set out
to investigate why.

One finding across the studies was perplexing and its potential solution elusive. "Across all the findings, one surprising observation kept
reappearing, and we didn't know how to tackle it," says Valerie Grillo,
American Express's chief diversity officer. "We found the higher a woman
rose in the company, the more male-influenced the environment became
around her—with the expectation she would alter her behaviors to fit
this norm."

We began our diagnostic process, where we seek to discern the attitudes and general beliefs among male and female managers and executives and learn whether and how these factors affect the balance of
representation. Through that work, we found that after fifteen years of
driving for gender equality, the gender balance had not changed at American Express precisely because of the culture at its seniormost levels. We
made a detailed presentation of our findings to senior management and
recommended Gender Intelligence as a solution. The senior leadership
immediately understood the impact and committed American Express to
becoming a Gender-Intelligent organization—starting with its executive
committee.

After participating in their own Gender Intelligence workshops, the
senior leaders required every manager to commit to learning and leading
gender-intelligent teams. Subsequent workshops were conducted within
each line of business to get at issues specific to that business or group.

"In historic companies like ours, it can be easy to rely on approaches
that have worked in the past," says Valerie. "But by taking the time to
teach our leaders, we shifted mindsets. It was an 'aha!' moment for many
of the attendees, and almost immediately we started to see a positive
change."

With this consciousness as the first step, senior leaders were then strongly encouraged to model the commitment to Gender Intelligence—taking charge of the follow-up dialogue as Gender Intelligence cascaded down the organization. Now that the conversation is "out in the open," there is increased comfort and understanding. "We found communication is more productive now between managers and employees, especially during performance reviews," says Grillo.

Within two years, Gender Intelligence had permeated through the company culture. Both the men and women of American Express had learned a deeper and more generous style of listening than they had been accustomed to in the past. The result was an organization where no employees feel stifled or made to act in incongruous ways that run counter to their authentic selves. "As a customer-centric organization, creating an inclusive culture is the only way for us succeed," Grillo wisely notes. "We have a lot of diverse talent here—both in ideas and background—ensuring they can be their true selves has helped us to connect with and better service our customers in innovative ways."

Today, American Express has the best numbers in its industry in terms of the percentage of women in its senior management and leadership ranks. And leadership at the top remains invested and interested. President Ed Gilligan is unabashed in saying, "We know in order to succeed we must create a workplace that embraces diverse opinions and empowers all employees to reach their highest potential. This spirit of inclusiveness enables us to make better decisions today to accelerate our growth for tomorrow."

Gilligan, considered one of the most gender-intelligent leaders in the credit services industry, made it his personal commitment to embed Gender Intelligence throughout the company's culture. It was he who assumed responsibility for change and wasn't afraid to keep pressing. While you will often hear, "Are we being gender-intelligent about this?" asked at meetings at American Express, it was Ed Gilligan who coined the phrase.

BMO Financial Group—Canada's first bank and the eighth-largest bank in North America—first got on board in the 1990s. In 1992, then CEO Tony Comper formed a task force to look at how the North America–based financial services provider could more effectively advance its women employees into leadership roles. In 2012, BMO renewed efforts that have resulted in a multipronged and ongoing set of initiatives aimed not just at aggressive numerical targets—like the goal of 40 percent female representation in the senior leadership by 2016—but also at shifting the current mindset and company culture.

Those initiatives have worked, according to current CEO Bill Downe, not just in achieving what he describes as "better financial performance," but also in keeping the organization working "continually" to "address the underlying attitudes that get in the way of progress."

Again, sustained commitment and attention from the top is critical to success. "It doesn't happen by itself," says BMO's chief talent officer, Lynn Roger. To make it happen, BMO has laid out what Roger calls "an aggressive diversity and inclusion agenda," described by Sonya Kunkel, managing director for diversity and inclusion, as "applying business discipline to the practice of talent management to ensure that diverse talent rises to the top." The agenda focuses equally on accelerating the development of diverse talent and holding leaders accountable for finding and advancing those individuals in their own talent pools.

While the latter function "used to be HR's role," according to Roger, we've seen the effects of relegating initiatives to HR without leadership support. Over the past twenty-four months in particular, a push to develop the "talent mindset" of leaders so they can do the finding and advance women more effectively has paid off. An enterprise-wide Diversity Renewal Council comprises representatives from all businesses and all functional groups and creates action plans to integrate diversity more deeply into the talent pools of each.

Barbara began her journey with BMO in its Capital Markets group with CEO Tom Milroy, who continually displays his authentic commitment to focus on the advancement of women.

As previously noted, gender-intelligent sponsorship has a lot to do with who is selected and groomed to enter senior management ranks. Chief administrative officer Valerie Sorbie knew that sponsor-to-protégé relations are a natural occurrence between men; she also knew that asking men to sponsor female protégés might at first seem awkward, even loaded. Knowing this area was key to advancing women, Sorbie persisted.

"The program prescribes sponsorship of women at the middle level," she told us, "Women are selected from across geographies, levels, and business groups to be sponsored by both men and women from our executive committee. The result has been a stunning shift in mindset for both men and women—a shift in culture." The sponsorship experience itself within BMO Capital Markets has served as a positive example of how changing leadership mindsets can expand gender balance at the senior level, as is now being rolled out through the rest of the enterprise.

Guardian Insurance, one of the largest mutual life insurance companies in the United States, recently declared that they want to be the first company in the insurance industry to be gender-intelligent. They recognize that the world has changed and that more women are becoming target customers—from millennials remaining single longer and self-sustaining even in marriage to boomer widows seeking personal insurance policies.

Guardian used to be led by a hard-charging, hard-driving male CEO with whom many of the women leaders and insurance representatives couldn't align. Even the men tended to put up with him rather than see him as a role model. The company then took on a new, female CEO who rapidly became known for her inclusive, transparent, hands-on style and very collaborative tendencies as a leader. While they have only recently declared their intention to become a gender-intelligent organization, if they follow it up with concerted effort over the coming years and with commitment from the top, Guardian, we feel, will unfailingly attract the best women and men in the industry, and their collaboration will create better products, communications, and customer service to serve a changing—and increasingly female—marketplace.

Each of these Type 3 companies and the many others we've profiled in previous chapters, including Deloitte, IBM, eBay, SAP, and Nissan, have undergone imperative "aha!" moments that helped eradicate their blind spots and led to breakthrough insights. Other Type 3 companies are still working to identify and abolish their blind spots but remain committed on the path to Gender Intelligence.

A few years ago during that difficult meeting where we had our own "aha!" breakthrough, we sat down and looked at the companies that succeeded and the companies that failed; we sought to find a pattern that explained the difference. Through careful examination and frankly, a fair bit of soul-searching where we faced head-on our own contribution to some of the failed attempts, a clear pattern began to emerge as to what we consider to be the five conditions necessary for true Gender Intelligence.

The Five Conditions for Success

Every company, Type 1 to Type 3, that seeks to implement gender-intelligent culture encounters challenges, ups and downs, and frustrations along the way. Certain barriers can't hold back an organization bent on change.

Yet in our experience, organizations cannot become gender-intelligent and fully benefit from the economic value that comes to the organization and the personal and professional growth that comes to their employees without the presence of certain conditions.

We define these as the Five Conditions for Success of a Gender-Intelligent Organization:

1. The CEO's authentic commitment
2. Led by a powerful and influential coalition
3. Approached systemically and not as a singular initiative
4. Approached with enterprise-wide resolve
5. Guided by Gender Intelligence

As we explore each of these conditions, ask yourself what it would take for each of these conditions to be present in your organization.

1. THE CEO'S AUTHENTIC COMMITMENT

Many CEOs say what they think people want to hear, but in the end, actions always speak louder than words. Authenticity is key. These leaders must possess the ability to look in the mirror, to be reflective, to have a high level of learning agility and a willingness to see their own blind spots.

The first condition for success is very clear and dovetails with the principles of the Leadership Chain. The CEO must demonstrate clear vision, a strong business case, and plans for growth through change with Gender Intelligence. It has to become a strategic business imperative of the organization and cannot be confined to an initiative with accountability two or three levels into the organization.

Most important, the CEO must own it. It's not an HR initiative but a *leadership* initiative that is tied to the strategic priorities of the organization, preferably one of the top three. The CEO acts with a sense of urgency and resolve.

As the company's diversity officer, Hala was committed to Gender Intelligence and she tried for years to have her CEO put more of his efforts behind creating an organization that values the differences between its men and women. Unfortunately, he read her repeated requests less as strategic than as whining and complaining.

Barbara met with the CEO, who expressed his interest and concern. "I'm making the investment, I believe in the movement. But I don't know what Hala is asking of me. What more can I do?"

Barbara made clear to him that it would require his authentic and visible involvement as well as that of the senior team. It was not enough to make his CDO, Hala, accountable for the initiative. She shared with him that Hala was having a difficult time getting the other executives to commit. In essence, bolstered by the knowledge of what worked and what didn't to meaningfully sustain a transformation to Gender Intelligence, Barbara told him he had to empower Hala and provide air cover. Nothing less would work.

Without hesitation, the CEO slapped the desk and said, "You've got it!" The following week, he convened a meeting with his executive team and declared that the company would become a gender-intelligent organization and that the effort would be a strategic initiative linked to bottom-line results. He said that each senior executive would partner with Hala, but he, the CEO, would be accountable for progress.

Once the CEO is authentically committed, he or she realizes that the only way to instill and sustain culture change is for all of the company's leadership to make the same authentic commitment and create a coalition for change.

2. LED BY A POWERFUL COALITION

The CEOs leading Type 3 organizations recognize that the only way to change the culture to one that values the differences between men and women is to bring together a coalition responsible for spearheading the effort, if possible, a coalition with this profile:

- A team composed of eight to fifteen influential, high-level leaders from across the organization
- Empowered to function outside the normal hierarchy and to challenge standard business practices

- Reports directly to the CEO or to someone whose leadership gives the coalition weight, credibility, and urgency
- Leaders establish milestones and present progress reports to the CEO and company
- Is committed to leading and sustaining the change effort throughout its life cycle, promoting learning, awareness, and practice
- Actively learns in order to continue modeling the new attitudes and behavior

BMO Financial Group offers an excellent example of the coalition becoming active learners as each executive on the team treats his or her own learning as part of the process. And it shows in meetings through the quality of engagement, the general inquisitiveness, and the group's agility in learning.

The coalition as a group was curious about gender blind spots and invited us to do an in-depth diagnostic of each coalition team member. We conducted one-on-one interviews to help uncover personal and cultural perceptions. Members then used the feedback to discuss their personal progress as gender-intelligent individuals. They asked us to help them investigate their own attitudes, beliefs, and behaviors and then used what we uncovered as a beginning point in their own learning. There was no defensiveness—they just ran with it.

CEO Bill Downe and his coalition are now advancing Gender Intelligence throughout the organization with the ultimate goal not just of better financial performance, but of sustaining that performance by continually addressing the underlying attitudes that get in the way of progress.

A coalition is most powerful and influential when it is made up of a representative sample from across the organization, and does not have to be made up entirely of execs. At BMO, this group partners with the CEO, diversity, HR, as well as the leaders and influencers involved in all the key activities in the organization needed to move this forward. Together, the team makes judgments and decisions about how to promulgate transformation within the organization.

3. APPROACHED SYSTEMICALLY

Gender Intelligence cannot be an initiatives-based undertaking. As we outlined in Chapter 8, it needs to be infused into the key aspects of the organization. Organizations don't have to execute total system change at once but they do have to initiate enough specific actions, changes, and learning processes to tip the scales and produce a meaningful shift.

To summarize what we covered in depth in Chapter 8, key functions include marketing, R&D, sales, and customer service. In management practices, it is critical to address the way conflict and problems are confronted and resolved as well as how decisions get made. Overall, there needs to be greater understanding of the way men and women talk to one another, increased empathy, and listening.

Finally, in order to produce and infuse Gender Intelligence throughout the organization, communication, technology, and human systems all need attention. The preponderance of these systems reside in HR and include identifying gender-balanced characteristics and attributes and looking in diverse pools for new talent, taking differences into account for performance management and compensation systems, and looking at the diversity of thought in senior leadership as well as how it is cultivated. Gender-intelligent leaders tend to make the efforts of HR departments more aligned with and connected to the strategic initiatives of the organization, and as a result, gender-intelligent HR departments become a tremendous value for the business units they serve.

The work we did with a global financial institution demonstrates why the systemic is a necessary condition for success. You couldn't fault them for thinking big in one area—leadership decided to put every one of its ten thousand managers around the globe through Gender Intelligence workshop training.

The CEO of the bank also committed to the workshops—and he even attended eight of them. The workshops themselves were very successful, and at one point there was a two-year waiting list to participate. While the popularity of the workshops was powerful and generated a lot of awareness, in the end they amounted to nothing more than a useful training exercise. Without systemic shifts the company had no systems in place to generate sustainable change and it wasn't understood what efforts needed to be undertaken in talent management.

Based on our experience, we predict that a program of this magnitude and cost, given the same conditions, ultimately won't work. Though effective at targeting the heart of the organization's culture and introducing gender-intelligent concepts and practices at the management level, experience shows it will eventually collapse under its own weight and cost.

For the initiative to make a meaningful and sustainable impact, it must be linked to the strategic initiatives of the organization.

4. APPROACHED WITH ENTERPRISE-WIDE RESOLVE

It makes no difference if a company has a fully committed chief diversity officer if Gender Intelligence is not infused throughout the organization and made one of the top three enterprise-wide priorities, immune to budgetary vagaries and leadership whims. Placing the initiative at that high a level guarantees it a strategic imperative and holds the CEO accountable in leading the entire cultural change effort—from the executive level to each new hire. Moreover, the effort must include clear and measurable goals that indicate progress.

With these aims, gender diversity is no longer a game of representation, but a value-based, organizational change effort that attracts and unites top talent and aligns itself with an increasingly diverse marketplace.

5. GUIDED BY GENDER INTELLIGENCE

Although this condition appears last in the list, in some ways it is actually required, a priori, in order for any of the others to follow. As you've seen throughout the book, our experience is that when leaders truly get Gender Intelligence—are able to really look in the mirror and honestly evaluate if they are modeling its tenets—the other conditions flow naturally. The fifth and most critical condition for Gender Intelligence success is that there is an authentic and open commitment of learning and active practice throughout the entire organization. When leaders understand and model Gender Intelligence, they no longer accept the management practices, behaviors, and policies that presented barriers to understanding and diversity of thought. They see their past actions as reflections of blind spots and limited beliefs, and they actively pursue more effective ways of being, thinking, and acting. This condition really requires that all leaders adopt and practice the six gender-intelligent behaviors we outlined first in Chapter 7, and which, when modeled, ripple through the many functions and their teams.

Sustaining the Change Effort

While an authentic commitment on the part of the CEO is the critical starting point (for which the behaviors above are crucial), even that alone is not enough to create a critical mass for change and carry the effort throughout the organization.

The CEO's mindset and style of leadership are incredibly influential in setting the tone, but Gender Intelligence is never about one person, or even a handful of people at the top. Instead, the leader and the change coalition must work to build an enterprise-wide commitment and effort to create a gender-intelligent culture. No CEO will stay at the helm forever; the only way for organizations to stay the course after a CEO is gone is through the coalition and support of the executive team working to make every team, every employee gender-intelligent.

It doesn't happen overnight. Research has shown that a full cultural transformation in a large organization can take several years, depending on the given size of the organization and how deeply embedded the existing culture may be. Nevertheless, our experience is that the process can be accelerated if companies can post and internally communicate some quick wins that demonstrate the economic value of gender diversity and work to get more people invested in sustaining the change.

This culture change effort is not for the faint of heart. If, however, you're one of those companies that recognize the potential and power of Gender Intelligence and are ready for it and committed to carrying it through, the next chapter will give you greater guidance for how to find your own path and stay the course.

Part Four
Conditions for Success

11

How to Get Started

Bill McGruber, the managing partner of one of the top law firms in the United Kingdom, had read all the books on gender diversity. He knew, more than most, how women were an important asset to his firm. Yet, like many in his position, he led a staff of mostly male senior partners, and his orientation to business, to the legal profession, and to leading in general was decidedly male. One evening, that all shifted.

Bill's "aha!" moment came while at the dinner table with his wife and two daughters home from college. In the middle of what turned out to be a lively discussion, he could hear himself discounting their perspectives. He realized, at that moment, that he wasn't even making an attempt to listen and may have been dismissive of his daughters all their lives. He never knew that of himself until then. Their line of reasoning, so different from his own, had often come across like complaining to him and he would tune out of the conversation or turn their voices down in his mind and not open himself to their points of view.

He started reading books on gender differences and the biological and cultural influences on those differences. He took those insights to his law firm and realized that he was hiring men in his own image and treating women attorneys as he would his wife and kids at the dinner table. He used to think the women in the firm, in particular his direct reports, complained a lot about nothing, but when he started to drop his assumptions and defenses and truly listen, he heard paths to solutions he would most likely never have considered, and in many instances they showed better outcomes.

Bill wanted to spread his Gender Intelligence across the law firm and educate his existing male senior partners or hire new ones who reflected his views in valuing difference-thinking. His singular efforts began to make a difference. At the end of the year, while assessing the annual performance of branch offices, Bill discovered a surprise in the data. Five law offices were financially outperforming the firm's dozens of other large practices scattered throughout Europe, particularly in employee and client retention. Four men and one woman made up the team of senior partners running those branch offices. He wanted to uncover what it was that was separating these best from all the rest.

To Bill's deep satisfaction, his newly found Gender Intelligence had genuinely influenced the five leaders, particularly the men, who were becoming quite enlightened themselves about gender differences and always mining for value in those differences, especially during client meetings. Each of the men said they had read about the science behind gender differences and spoke of how it showed up in their personal lives with their spouses and children, particularly with their daughters. They each made the connection to their professional lives as Bill had.

Each of the four men had loosened up the business processes they were using for making strategic decisions, building client relationships, and networking—all those areas that, up until now, had been approached from a very rigid, very male perspective.

Each let the men and women attorneys in their offices build their client bases in their own way. It may have taken a little longer for the women to close deals, but those relationships were turning out to be the longest lasting.

It was a reaffirming data point to Bill to learn that the five law offices also showed the lowest turnover of women attorneys and the highest per-cent of women as partners.

Many leaders today look out over their employee ranks and recognize not only that half of their middle management are women, but that so few are in leadership positions after years of quotas and targeted recruitment efforts. They're also realizing that the decision makers in the marketplace are predominantly women. They're beginning to see the economic value of women in leadership positions but have difficulty finding women to fill those positions or stay once hired into the organization. They're beginning to question all the time and money spent chasing quotas and the revolving door of talented women coming into and leaving their companies.

Many are coming to understand Gender Intelligence, genuinely want to be part of the new conversation about gender, and are asking, "Where do we start?"

Our answer is always the same: You start with yourself as a leader. You begin with a willingness to be uncomfortable. Getting on the path to becoming a Stage Five organization will require some discomfort, some looking into the mirror. Leaders need to realize that the culture that they're now leading and want to transform requires that they come to terms with themselves and their own leadership first. With eyes wide open, they are more able to recognize how their leadership has shaped and influenced the leadership and management style of their direct reports and on down through the company—actually creating the culture that they desire to change.

Once that is recognized and accepted, the next step is to find their company's path to Gender Intelligence and pursue that path by getting an accurate pulse of the men and women in the organization and the issues in need of addressing.

Over the years, we've discovered time and again that existing employee survey data often doesn't show how leadership behavior is what's alienating many of the women in the organization and driving some of them away. The issue of alienation is not showing up because the surveys are not explicitly asking employees about it. Nor are the few women in senior positions raising the issue. They're so glad that they've arrived that they don't want to ruffle any feathers. Besides, they have plenty on their plates already. And so this at times amorphous but powerful feeling of exclusion on the part of women goes unchecked. It doesn't show up in survey responses or in performance reviews. Women driven to the brink don't even raise the issue in exit interviews, oftentimes afraid that telling the truth might come back to haunt them. They're getting out—easier and better to just move on.

Though it's the conduct and character of the leaders and managers in many companies that's driving top talent away, many are not looking at it as a culture problem. But that's exactly what it is, and it's preventing the

company from making a necessary cultural shift to greater gender awareness and appreciation, the type of shift that would drive real results.

Thus far we've shared numerous examples of companies that have at-
tempted to tackle the issue of gender diversity but either started by addressing factors that predictably have little effect or put all of their
attention on a singular element like representation. Systemic problems
don't shift that easily.

Organizations are also failing to take advantage of a real opportunity
in the form of employee surveys. What leaders say to us is that the
surveys say they're doing fine. Their employee surveys (or the way they
analyze them) don't indicate to them that there are differences in the
experiences of the men and women in the company, or even that there
are differences in one department. Part of the reason for that is that
management often asks the same formulaic questions, year after year.
Moreover, they often don't act on what they learn. The result is dwin-
dling employee attention, where those who have taken the same survey
for years routinely check the boxes to get it done.

Often, companies misread this employee disinterest as tacit success.
While the companies continue to experience high turnover of women,
because the surveys don't say otherwise they assume it has to do with
family or personal issues for the women themselves. They put a real effort
behind their diversity initiatives year after year in areas such as targeted
recruitment, work-life programs, mentoring, and leadership training, and
expect to see some really improved numbers of women in management,
but they rarely if ever do and continue to wonder why.

Symptoms Versus Cause

Many CEOs that we meet sense there's an underlying reason they can't
retain talented and experienced women, but they seldom recognize their
own contribution to the problem or that of other men on their executive
teams. All they tend to see are the symptoms, such as women in fewer
senior management positions, or women so unhappy they file suit. The
CEOs that we speak of are not alone. So many companies have good
intentions but can't see past topically treating the symptoms. It creates

an initiatives frenzy, which seems like progress, even while it leads them further away from the true cause: organizational culture.

After we have our "symptom versus cause" discussion with organizations and begin to lift the veil of denial and unawareness, leaders willing to do more ask us, "So, where do you start?" First, this is where we *don't* start: by fixing the women and setting numeric goals for progress.

We encourage leaders to start by forming a deep understanding of the organization—its hiring and promotion practices, its culture, its leadership, its key systems and processes, and the associated results such as turnover and financial success. In other words, to do an organizational diagnosis.

Getting down to the details, we ask for the following data points to the extent they are available to help us do a thorough diagnostic. In all cases, it is preferable to have data in each of the areas below dating back five years, or at least three years. Through this data, we seek to discover any relevant trends or patterns that show over time. The data includes:

1. Employment opinion surveys
2. HR survey results
3. Leadership surveys such as 360 surveys or other surveys that measure leadership effectiveness
4. Representation of all demographics at all levels
5. Turnover data by level by demographic
6. Exit interviews by level by demographic
7. Gender diversity strategies or initiatives as well as talent management strategies and processes
8. Overt expressions of company values and leadership competencies
9. Recruitment strategies
10. Interview methodologies
11. Any discrimination or sexual harassment history (lawsuits, grievances, etc.)
12. Culture surveys that measure the nature of the culture
13. Any studies done on the company, such as by *Harvard Business Review* or other case studies
14. Awards received or applied for that relate to leadership or company culture

Number two on the above list receives special attention; our approach to looking at employee surveys is particularly unique and, we believe, crucial. We apply a gender-intelligent lens to the existing employee opinion survey data, filtering employee responses through specific categories to get to the root issues and reveal causes leadership was unable to see. We cut the data by gender, by levels of leadership and management, and by region. We then cull out specific questions that reveal potential patterns in the culture, especially as it relates to gender dynamics.

To supplement the data from the surveys, and to help put all of the data in context, we also conduct one-on-one executive interviews and senior-level, male and female focus groups where we ask direct, gender-specific questions designed to draw more insight out of leadership's responses and create dialogue around certain issues. Here's a sampling of the kinds of questions we use in executive one-on-one interviews and focus groups:

- To what extent do you feel the culture is inclusive?
- Does that culture of inclusiveness change the higher up you go in the organization?
- To what extent do you believe women and men face different challenges for promotion?
- To what extent are different views and ideas welcome here?
- Why is it that the higher up you go in this organization, there are fewer women than men?
- What three things are you most appreciative of in this organization related to inclusiveness for both genders?
- What three things most concern you that you would want to see change?

From all of this, the true causes behind the organization's problems begin to emerge. Through the honest exchanges that take place in interviews and focus groups, and in the way we look at the data, we see standard patterns revealed again and again. The important difference is in how at this point the leaders themselves suddenly start thinking differently about their gender issues. They begin to see deviations between men and women that challenge the company's prevailing assumptions about gender balance as well as the direct or sometimes indirect consequences of those deviations.

The Gender Intelligence Diagnostic Survey

The next most important step in the diagnostic process is to supplement what we've learned with our Gender Intelligence survey. This allows us to delve deeper into the culture of the organization, capturing gender-specific perceptions and experiences at each managerial and leadership level.

On the following page is a typical graph from our diagnostic survey process showing the perception of employees along a number of dimensions that meaningfully affect their levels of satisfaction. The 100-point scale gives a very precise sense of differences derived from asking people to rate the degree to which they agree or disagree with a number of statements on a 10-point scale. Higher numbers toward the center of the graph indicate stronger results. This visual is the compilation of four multinational companies, each representing a different industry, to capture a business-wide point of view. It measures the separate responses of men and women in eleven categories, selected and designed to reveal the presence of gender differences:[70]

- Opportunity for Advancement
- Work-Life Flexibility
- Dignity and Respect
- Diversity and Inclusiveness Are Valued
- Ethnic Diversity Is Valued
- Gender Diversity Is Valued
- Openness
- Personal Accountability
- My Manager
- Satisfaction and Commitment
- Training and Guidance

The men's scores on the graph are represented by the inside gray line, closest to the center of the wheel. The women's scores for each item are represented by the outside black line. In large sample sizes such as this one, we typically interpret differences of two points or more as meaningful and differences of five points or more as quite significant.

In studying the gaps between the men's and women's scores, you'll discover what are typically the most meaningful deviations for many organizations: Gender Diversity Is Valued, Opportunity for Advancement, Openness, and Dignity and Respect. Women tend to score each of these categories considerably lower than men do. Interestingly, though many companies would say women are far more dissatisfied with work-life balance, oftentimes we see Work-Life Flexibility has the least deviation among the categories, as below.

The Gender Intelligence Diagnostic

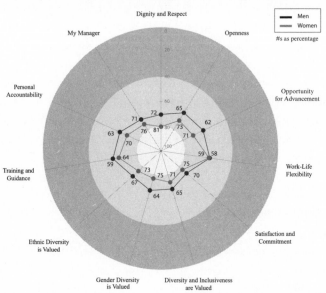

Once we've homed in on where the largest deviations are occurring, we look to determine what's causing the deviations in each category. Are the barriers and challenges imposed by the culture of the organization, or are they self-imposed limitations that can be coached and mentored through?

Let's take you through a sample diagnostic as we look at many of these categories and offer a sampling of the kinds of statements we ask men and women to react to in doing our work. For each category, you will be able to see for yourself where the gaps are and why they exist, beginning with Opportunity for Advancement, a critical issue for many organizations seeking to increase the number of women in their senior management ranks. For each, we show you three or four examples of statements we use when assessing that particular category.

OPPORTUNITY FOR ADVANCEMENT:

- I get the challenging assignments that will provide me opportunity for advancement.
- I get ample opportunity to grow and develop skills necessary for my career at this company.
- With focus, talent, drive, and determination, anyone can get to become a leader at this company.

Opportunity for Advancement looks at how men and women perceive their chances for promotion based on their capability and competence. Men typically feel there's ample opportunity because they witness plenty of examples of people being promoted and they see this for men and women alike. Data also consistently shows the common perception on the part of men, especially in the senior management ranks, that because of quotas, women are given preferential treatment and more opportunities for advancement than men.

Interestingly, that perception often doesn't bear out for women. The women often don't believe they're receiving preferential treatment or more opportunities than men at all; in fact, many think just the opposite. Many of the women we survey cite counterexamples in the form of all men or the preponderance of men on executive teams in the different divisions in their companies or statistics on how few women CEOs and board members there are.

This category also reflects the dynamic where men, more often than women, will create opportunities for themselves by demonstrating what is considered leadership behavior in many male-dominant cultures. This includes engaging in greater self-promotion and taking clear credit for their successes, which often lead to promotion based on one's perceived potential. Women, who tend not to be as self-promoting or even as boastful as men, will most often be promoted based on proven experience rather than the perception of their potential. The net effect is that often there are fewer opportunities for advancement for women.

When we ask men and women to respond to the statement "I get the challenging assignments that will provide me opportunity for advancement," a huge deviation appears, with women uniformly scoring that statement extremely low. The question remains—why?

As we dig deeper in interviews and focus groups, we often ask women if they seek out those assignments or wait to be given them by their managers. Therein lies the common pitfall for women: not being more proactive in requesting the challenging assignments. This is the expectation of those who believe that women should approach challenging assignments as men do.

This doesn't take into account what we learned back in Chapter 2 about men's and women's approaches to risk. Men don't have to be 90 percent sure that they can deliver on an assignment in order to throw their hat into the ring. Because of the way they're wired, they often believe they will figure it out along the way and find the right support in order to get it done.

Oftentimes when leaders are looking at the numbers, they see balanced representation in middle management and even as much as 20 percent women in the executive ranks and think they're doing okay. But when we look at the representation data by positions that have profit-and-loss responsibility versus support-related functions that don't, we find that a dominant number of women executives who make up that 20 percent are in the latter group. So even when companies think they have balance in numbers, they still have an imbalance in function.

Many people often ask, Is that necessarily a bad thing? We want to ask a different question: Is it women who are making this choice and do they feel empowered and engaged in their existing roles? Through the one-on-one and focus group interviews, we often hear the answer is no.

We find that there are underlying assumptions about women that cause male leaders to tell us women are happy and content being relegated to HR, diversity, communications, or public relations. They assume that women are risk averse, that they don't want to travel, and that they are not as committed as men. They point to the fact that some have family-related responsibilities to the degree that men don't typically have.

Other organizations are challenging their assumptions. They're looking at the research showing the economic value in gender diversity and are thinking differently about how they view line and staff functions. Sales, for instance, is a prime example of a line function where companies tend to attract primarily men, most of whom are driven to make as much money as they can. These processes and measures in the sales function tend to support the hunter mentality many men exhibit, and the rewards reinforce the behavior. Looking at the disparity offers organizations a chance to review the win-at-all-costs drive so often valued in the sales function, and which is so often a turnoff to women. If it benefits the company to have diversity of thought in the sales function, companies can ask themselves, "What if that traditional sales process is too limited and narrow given the makeup of the marketplace today?"

WORK-LIFE FLEXIBILITY:

- My work schedule gives me sufficient flexibility to meet my personal and family needs.
- I am aware of the work-life flexibility tools available to me.
- I feel free to use work-life flexibility programs without consequences to my career.

The dimension of Work-Life Flexibility is another trend we're seeing in our diagnostics, and these three example statements reveal some interesting dynamics.

In measuring the responses to the Work-Life Flexibility statements, we usually see very little difference between men's and women's desire for and pursuit of work-life flexibility, though the *effect* of the lack of work-life flexibility negatively affects women more than men.

Another dynamic here bears mentioning. When everything is measured on performance and face time in the office, men and women alike feel they can't participate in work-life flexibility programs without consequences to their careers. However, there is a difference in how each manages the commitments they do have outside the office.

When women have personal commitments, they tend to vocalize the details of those commitments. For example, a woman may say to her supervisor or colleagues in a meeting, "I have to leave now to take my daughter to the orthodontist." Men don't often offer an explanation, and will simply say as they leave, "I have a prior commitment." If they do offer details, peers and supervisors laud them. "He must be a great

dad!" is often the response, and seldom do peers or bosses alike question a man's commitment to the company or the project he's on if he
tends to his family. Conversely, when a woman leaves to take her child
to the orthodontist, few colleagues and bosses are thinking, *What a
great mother!* Instead, they often wonder if she is really committed to
her work.

DIGNITY AND RESPECT:

- People are treated with respect, regardless of race, gender, religion, or
  lifestyle preference.
- I feel genuinely heard and understood by members of the opposite
  gender.
- I feel like I'm treated as a real asset to this company.

This is one of the areas we see significant deviations—differences that
often depend upon the quality and style of leadership and the nature of
the company. Often, we'll see differences in the perception of dignity
and respect at different levels in the organization, with less dignity and
respect shown to women in upper levels of management or in specific
departments or areas of the business such as strategic planning or sales.
While there are many behaviors managers can exhibit to make employees
feel a lack of respect, it's often a reflection of senior leadership's inability
to demonstrate and reinforce the values they espouse.

Healthy companies care deeply about the degree to which all employees are respected and don't accept managers behaving in ways that produce feelings to the contrary. They maintain this commitment to their
values by weeding out the problem managers by letting them go and take
greater care to not hire them in the first place.

We have found that more than most factors, the health and well-being
of the organization depend on the tensile strength of leadership's commitment to have the conduct and character of their managers *matter.* The
simplest and most effective way for managers to show respect is by appreciating the work of their employees. Women will sometimes feel less sure
of how well they're doing in their roles, especially because of the unease
created by having to fit into their organization's male-influenced culture.

Getting that direct, confirming feedback can help bolster their confidence and cause them to experience theirs as a workplace that values and respects their contributions.

DIVERSITY AND INCLUSIVENESS ARE VALUED:

- The executives in this company clearly demonstrate that they value diversity.
- The leadership within this company recognizes and respects the value of differences—they welcome diversity in all its forms: visible, lifestyle, viewpoints, etc.
- In this company, leaders actively promote gender diversity.
- In this company, leaders actively promote racial/ethnic/cultural diversity.

In this category, we break diversity down into three component parts: diversity and inclusiveness in general, gender diversity, and ethnic diversity. The sample statements shown here help us distinguish between the kinds of diversity that are most valued and promoted. We don't see a lot of deviation between men and women in valuing racial, ethnic, and cultural diversity. That all changes when it comes down to gender.

In our diagnostics, when we ask men and women their take on the statement "The executives in this company clearly demonstrate that they value gender diversity," men often react in a positive way. Even if they know the company isn't where it should be, they speak to the intention of the organization and their intentions as well. In the company's quest to be gender diverse they assert, "We're doing better than most," or tell us, "We have a meritocracy that's fair and equally applied to all," or feel "We have a culture here where differences are valued."

While men speak to the intent and potential for the diversity policies that are in place, women often speak to the lived reality. They say that leaders pay a lot of lip service to diversity in general, but also offer this: "I don't have the experience in conversations with some of the leaders here that they're valuing *me*."

There are many reasons they might feel this way. Women often say that there's an old boys' network still in effect, with a counterpart among younger male colleagues, where men develop informal bonds with one another that solidify those relationships. Through these bonds, men share a set of assumptions about how business is conducted, and build trust over time that reinforces those assumptions and the bonds between the men. In order to fit in, women need to adopt that set of assumptions and act like one of the guys. "I can't be myself," women tell us; "therefore I don't feel valued because I can't bring my whole self to work."

Men speak to their intentions to be inclusive, but the reality is that many men are more comfortable being around and interacting with other men. Women often misinterpret this as an intentional exclusion, while for men it is more from the natural comfort and familiarity they get from hanging out with the guys.

This is true for women as well, a cultural norm lived out by most of us since childhood. Visit any elementary school playground to see it in effect: boys playing dodgeball with other boys and girls socializing with girls in groups. There is a ritual and a norm and naturalness around this that makes sense to us as children. It stands to reason that the way we naturally behave throughout our lives when we're not in the office would hold true in our interactions at work. To some degree, men and women tend to engage in similar-track thinking, have similar observations of life, appreciate the same humor, and demonstrate a similar prioritization of work effort, problem-solving, decision-making, conflict resolution, and on and on.

Where men and women are more equally represented, there is less of a problem. Women often indicate that inclusiveness is better at the lower levels of the organization than it is higher up. Problems occur when you apply that dynamic to a work environment with a dominant number of men in leadership positions. This naturally creates a feeling of an old boys' network toward the top of the organization that is less inclusive of women and provides informal barriers to their advancement and promotion. (The converse is often true in companies led primarily by women.)

This is why we often challenge "women's networks" as a strategy to improve gender diversity. While fulfilling on one level for women in the workplace, women's networks do nothing to break apart the segregated "club" to which women feel they are not invited to belong.

OPENNESS:

- I have the freedom to safely express my views and opinions.
- My opinions and ideas are readily sought.
- I feel amply included in the process of solving problems and making decisions.

When we talk about Openness we refer to men and women having the freedom to safely express their views and opinions at work. The category also speaks to employees feeling that their ideas are encouraged and their differing opinions are welcome and openly discussed. In each of the three sample statements above, women—especially women higher up the organization ladder—usually offer lower scores than do men.

Perhaps not surprisingly, women who give Dignity and Respect a low score will also show low scores in Opportunity for Advancement, clearly showing a correlation that is often missed in the way companies typically analyze their data. This all tends to translate into women saying, "I don't feel safe. I don't feel I can speak my mind here."

Women as well as men can determine equally the degree of Openness felt in an organization's culture, as demonstrated by the following anecdote.

Barbara was recently invited to meet with three high-level female executives of a technology company with headquarters in Italy. Two of the women reported directly to the CEO. All three of the women were experiencing high turnover of women at the executive level and were looking for solutions. Here is what Barbara experienced, in her own words:

I often strive for interaction during my presentations, especially in more informal, small groups, but the interruptions and rudeness of these women were surprising. It was abundantly clear to me they weren't looking for dialogue and an exploration of solutions. They came to the meeting with closed minds.

I thought to myself, I wouldn't want to work for this company either if these three women were demonstrating its culture. I could see why they had a turnover problem. They had taken on that militaristic, command-and-control mentality we often find among the first women to break into the top ranks of a male-dominant organization. I was witnessing what we call "first woman syndrome" in its fullest expression! Since I sensed they weren't really benefiting from the material I had prepared, I stopped in the middle of my presentation. "I don't see that you're receiving any value from this discussion," I told them honestly. "Should I stop or should we continue?"

They all urged me to continue, though they also told me they had it all figured out. "We hire the best and the brightest women and we have our hiring targets and percentages for the next year. All we need to do is hire more women and it will be resolved."

Out of respect for their time and a desire to alter their perspective I decided to confront them directly: "You will never get there from here. With all due respect, I have never seen, in almost thirty years of practice, any correlation between recruiting women into the kind of culture I sense from your behavior and having them stay and advance. I don't believe you're ready yet for Gender Intelligence."

As I packed up my materials and stood up to leave, the women began to shift in their seats. I had a feeling they were shifting their mindsets as well. Perhaps they were beginning to understand how women can sometimes be their own worst enemies by adopting a male model of command and control, unaware of how closed they truly had become. Given my experience with these leaders, you can imagine how the women who worked for them might be hesitant to name the problem or confront them directly. They may feel their only option is to leave.

We often come across organizations where Openness exists in certain departments while others feel less safe, all because of leadership differences exhibited in different pockets of the same company. In one such company, we worked with a business unit leader, Jack, who is very open in his leadership. He doesn't make decisions quickly, but instead asks questions and invites differing views. Jack creates an atmosphere of candor where team members can challenge decisions and each other and pose differing opinions in a collaborative and constructive way. His style of leadership permeates his business unit and we saw his direct reports behave in much the same manner.

In another part of the organization, Bill, also a leader, exhibits a very different style. Bill is very smart, and frequently makes snap decisions with little input from others. We observed him use his intelligence and quick wit as a sort of defensive mechanism, sometimes to the point of humiliating people who disagree with him. However, Bill is valued because of his intelligence and knowledge about the industry and its customers. As a result, senior management tends to forgive him for his lack of openness. The problem is, he tends to get the lowest scores in employee surveys, and there are fewer women in his business unit.

Kathy, who reports to Bill, had an experience that demonstrated how his leadership behavior affected feelings of trust and safety. She had been trying to complete a massive, complicated compliance document that required input from Bill before she could finalize it. During the meeting, Bill kept interrupting her and became frustrated, telling Kathy, "You're obviously not managing this correctly." Kathy was still furious in our one-on-one. "This is the first time in my thirty-year career with the company where I became emotional," she told us. "I know more about this compliance request than anyone else in the organization, and it's completely under control. It was Bill who lacked an understanding of all the things I was doing and who I was working with, including policy makers and lawyers." He didn't get the complexity and had no time for explanations. "He had zero attention or bandwidth for this."

Two hours after the meeting, Bill called Kathy back to his office and apologized. She told him that he was a great man to work for, but she had never felt so *not heard* in her entire career as in that compliance meeting. "My wife says the same thing," Bill admitted. "When I get overwhelmed with something I don't understand, I take it out on her in the same way."

In the area of Openness, it is critical that there be congruity between intentions and behavior. It takes a higher level of commitment, attention, and care to ensuring leadership's actions match their thoughts, beliefs, and values to produce a truly open environment that feels safe to everyone involved.

PERSONAL ACCOUNTABILITY:

- I often witness behavior conducive to a respectful and inclusive work environment.
- People readily intervene when they see noninclusive or disrespectful behavior.
- I feel encouraged to raise concerns about inclusiveness.

When we talk about personal accountability we build on the behaviors that create an open environment and take them one step further. If someone else had been in the office with Kathy and Bill, how would they have responded to his treatment of her? How did leadership respond to Bill's reputation, knowing it wasn't known for demonstrating inclusivity? The results of our diagnostics show that men tend either not to notice or to ignore behavior that is not conducive to a respectful and inclusive work environment. When seen, men rarely call it out. Part of the reason for this has to do with a powerful unspoken rule in male culture where you don't call out other guys for inappropriate behavior, especially in front of other people.

For the first two hours of a Gender Intelligence workshop, James was the only person who couldn't see how his behavior was so typically male. From his sports and war strategy analogies, to his aggressiveness in making his points heard, to his slightly off-color humor, none of his behaviors allowed for different points of view or any level of comfort for the women who worked with him.

During our break for lunch, we were standing in line to place our meal order when we overheard two men from the workshop talking.

"Did you hear James during the session?" one of them said, incredulous. "It's the same old James," he chuckled. "No one would ever call him gender-intelligent. Someone should tell him."

His colleague, who was laughing in agreement, stopped short. "I'm not going to tell him!"

"I'm not going to tell him, either," replied the first man. "No way. I'm not going there! If I do, I'll be voted off his island."

The male code—never betray the pack—is deeply ingrained in the psyche of men. What might look outlandish or openly disrespectful in teenagers looks different once those same men appear in the boardroom or in key meetings. Rarely do we see mature men objectifying women, and if they do, it's not in public, except on rare occasions. The gender insensitiveness we see nowadays is much less crude. Instead, what we see are men behaving consistent with a set of rules for how decisions are made and problems solved—which can be alienating in their own way.

These are unwritten, unconscious rules, difficult for men to call out because they seem so natural to their ways of being. They range from speaking in short, declarative sentences to focusing narrowly on one aspect of a problem. They include men's tendencies not to self-reflect and to avoid vulnerability. Men keep their eyes on the prize, don't apologize, and in general act more confident than they really are. And they discredit women more passively, in their decisions about whom to hire or promote, than they did overtly in yesteryear.

Because the male code still lives and breathes in the hearts of men, they perpetuate and reify the rules of male-dominated business culture. A fair number of women also don't challenge behaviors they see as problematic, fearing they may lose out on opportunity by speaking up, or that they may be subtly (or not so subtly) excluded from the boys' club.

But men feel that and something more, something much more primal that speaks to complete rejection from the pack. (Remember *West Side Story*: "When you're a Jet, you're a Jet all the way, from your first cigarette, to your last dyin' day. . . .") Because of this feeling, you rarely see men challenging other men in public. If you do, they are often visibly uncomfortable.

Women, on the other hand, tend to notice the presence or lack of respect and inclusion, and not just for themselves but also for other races, ethnicities, and cultures that may feel slighted. Although hesitant to speak as well, many women are ultimately moved to make a stand. As with men, it's much more than just a business issue. Women are more sensitive to the culture around them and to the relationships of the people who operate within a given culture. This is one of the reasons we believe that Gender Intelligence and the presence of women in leadership tend to accelerate all diversity. Companies that have a better blend of women and men at all managerial levels foster an environment where broader cultural diversity efforts can take root and an inclusive culture can grow.

MY MANAGER:

- When making key decisions, my manager gets plenty of input from others, regardless of gender.
- My manager provides me with direct and helpful feedback.
- My manager provides me with the coaching and guidance I need to improve my performance.

We include My Manager as one of our categories because people often leave organizations because of their manager and the items we include in the survey such as those above help us understand why. For so many workers, their daily experience of the workplace is so significantly shaped by their relationship with their manager that it deserves special attention. Managers can create a welcoming environment for their team, even within a broader culture that is less supportive. In the same vein, it's often a great manager who keeps people from leaving an otherwise unwelcoming organization.

There are several statements in this category where women assess their manager as very low compared to how men assess. One is in their confidence that their manager will visibly challenge the disrespectful behavior of others. If their managers are men, we've just covered why that might be the case. Women, compared to men, also often feel that their managers are not as welcoming of differing ideas and opinions.

Additionally, women tend to give managers low scores in providing guidance on improving performance and receiving direction. The feedback loop is key to good manager-employee relationships and is also greatly affected by gender differences in very important ways.

Women seek more feedback than men not only because they engage in more self-reflection and focus more on self-improvement. On average, women tend to need and want more feedback than men because they are part of a minority in a business-wide majority-minority dynamic. When you're a part of the minority in any environment, you need a little more guidance and support in order to feel comfortable, as least initially. In working in male-dominant environments, women want more cues and reassurance that their actions and behavior are correct, because the environment feels less familiar and comfortable to them. However, the dynamic that plays out is often the opposite. Men tend to shy away from giving direct, confronting feedback to women, afraid the women will have an emotional response.

Additionally, women, more than men, tend toward collaboration rather than an individualistic approach to business. This style is characterized much more by a give-and-take in which feedback becomes the way in which they can mutually adjust to create better shared outcomes. Without the feedback, the collaboration doesn't occur quite as powerfully. Therefore, women offer and ask for feedback to produce that mutual adjustment process.

In the end, the experience of one's manager affects not only the person but the culture of the team, and it is both the manager and the culture of one's direct team that powerfully shape the experience of working in the company. And yet, because those very same people affect one's hiring or promotion, it is difficult to confront the way one's manager or peers behave, so the patterns related to how a manager behaves often go unaddressed, especially in companies that lack Gender Intelligence.

SATISFACTION AND COMMITMENT:

- Women feel a high sense of satisfaction in working here.
- Men feel a high sense of satisfaction in working here.
- If I had a daughter with the right skills and experience, I would encourage her to work at this company.
- If I had a son with the right skills and experience, I would encourage him to work at this company.

The issue of Satisfaction and Commitment helps to frame the organization as a healthy culture for the men and women who work there. Having women and men react to these sample statements as well as others gives us a new line of sight into the culture of the organization.

As with diversity issues, when speaking for themselves, women, in general, tend to be less satisfied than men. When we ask women and men to score satisfaction not just for themselves, but for the other gender, women will often score men as being higher in satisfaction and women lower. In contrast, men often score both men and women very high. This raises the interesting question: Why don't men see that some women are dissatisfied? Through our experience, we've noted a number of common reasons:

1. The women aren't saying they are unhappy in terms that men can easily hear. For example, women have a tendency to be more suggestive than directive when collaborating on a team.
2. Sometimes women aren't saying they are dissatisfied at all, even though they feel strongly dissatisfied.
3. Some men don't want to hear the dissatisfaction.
4. Some men, when they hear it, don't believe it is true. They discount the feedback as "complaining."

The end result is that dissatisfaction is not addressed and women eventually vote with their feet—hence higher turnover rates. Or they "quit and stay." We see a clear picture of the degree to which men understand that women might be less satisfied with business as usual. When asked to respond to, "If I had a daughter with the right skills and experience, I would encourage her to work at this company" and "If I had a son with the right skills and experience, I would encourage him to work at this company," men typically score their response to the hypothetical of their daughter working in their organization a bit lower than they do having a son work for the company. This suggests that men may have some inkling that the organization may not be as fulfilling a work environment for women. At a conscious level, men believe it's equally satisfying for both men and women to work in their company while at a somewhat unconscious level, revealed by their lower scores, they start to show their underlying awareness that the organization may not be a satisfying place for women.

It follows that the net effect of "less satisfaction" is that women are somewhat equally "less committed" to the company than men are. When we pose the statement "I feel satisfied here, and as a result, I intend to stay in the foreseeable future," women's lower scores reflect the effect on their commitment, and, ultimately, their loyalty.

In 2003, researchers introduced the concept of a Net Promoter Score (NPS) as an alternative to traditional customer satisfaction research.[71] The NPS measures the loyalty that exists between a provider and a consumer. More recently, NPS practitioners have developed more discerning ways to discover causes of NPS being higher and lower. They are finding it in data about employee engagement and commitment, revealing the now well-understood principle that engaged employees create workplaces that often translate into greater customer loyalty and commitment.

Moreover, while greater dissatisfaction affects customer loyalty, it also affects so much more, to the point that satisfaction is also one of the twelve categories that the Gallup Organization uses in their Q^{12} Employee Engagement Survey to measure engagement at the workgroup level, which gives them insight into where engagement is strong and where it can improve.[72]

Not surprisingly, therefore, satisfaction is a crucial area of insight that we always include in our diagnostic. In a way, it provides a summary of all the other indicators by getting to the matter of loyalty. There is more turnover of women throughout the ranks of industry and, in parallel, less workplace satisfaction felt by those women. However, Satisfaction and Commitment is a revealing measure only if the leaders accept its conclusion.

Our organizational diagnostic process reveals a slew of gender phenomena, almost all born out of the presence or lack of Gender Intelligence, which in turn affects satisfaction and commitment to a great degree. The following is a recap of the ones that we most often see emerge in our assessments, suggesting that the phenomena below are not just the result of one particular organization and its history or culture, but the confluence of many larger forces in society as well:

- Women quitting and staying. They're delivering good work but they no longer have the aspiration to advance.
- The creation of networks and training for women that are not necessarily gender-intelligent
- Leadership and management behaviors that are incongruent with the organization's policy and value statements
- Great initiatives embarked upon with great passion that end up as window dressing
- Meaningful parts of the company—senior leadership or sectors like IT and sales—that remain predominantly male
- Women in senior management who are seldom in positions with P&L or line responsibility, but rather in support sectors such as HR, diversity, and communications
- Senior women leaders often not wanting to make diversity an agenda item, to avoid pushback

- Hiring and promoting practices that tend to favor men
- Promoting practices based on sameness

Making the Connection for Leaders

When we are invited into an organization and conduct our diagnostic, we are able to make the connection for leaders between inclusiveness and their employees' scores on openness, satisfaction, and commitment with the attenuating results—turnover, promotion patterns, representation patterns, and more. We are then able to remind leaders of the Leadership Chain and talk about their very fundamental role in setting the tone.

After all, if employees are leaving their workplace, dissatisfied, most likely that stems from the culture of the organization, which in turn directly flows from the mindset of the leader. Leaders' attitudes and beliefs inform and influence their leadership style and behavior, define their company's culture, and ultimately affect the results of the organization—be that in a positive or negative way.

Not everyone is ready to hear what we have to say. We've experienced leaders who, at the end of a diagnostic process, will simply deny the data out of hand. "We're either not hiring enough women," they tell us, or "we're simply hiring the wrong kind of women. We need to hire women who are more committed." More and more, these leaders are the exception to the rule.

Today's leaders are like you—ready to listen and take responsibility. They're recognizing that you don't start at the symptom level but instead look at the cultural level to see the connections to the outcomes the data reveals. Instead of becoming defensive, they're having their "aha!" moments and looking inward toward their own mindset and behavior and toward the culture of the organization. They are honestly assessing their own leadership and recognizing the importance of congruity between their intentions and their behavior.

Their willingness is smart and driven by the bottom line—they want to benefit from the economic value in Gender Intelligence and create cultures that are personally and professionally satisfying for both the men and the women in their organizations. And their beginning point in effective change is to look in the mirror.

Our diagnostic is just the beginning point. From there, a clear transformation plan is needed, framed by the insights gleaned from the diagnostic. Here is where the heavy lifting begins. When designing an organizational transformation plan, it is crucial to have a thought process for how to get from the current condition to the desired future. Since we know it takes powerful effort to make sweeping organizational changes, we developed the concept of levers.

The mathematician Archimedes is known to have said, "Give me a lever long enough and a fulcrum on which to place it, and I shall move the world." And indeed, a lever is a powerful machine. The word comes from the French *lever*, meaning "to raise." Of course, a lever works to amplify an input force to provide a greater output force; hence the concept of "leverage." Simply put, think of the initiatives and actions crucial for effecting change as levers. Put in place the correct levers and they become the key elements to the transformation plan, amplifying your efforts throughout your organization.

Many think that the most important lever to pull is hiring, operating from the belief that gender imbalance ties back to the talent pool from which men and women are selected. But if you place good people into a gender-unintelligent culture, you will never get the best out of them. Good women will flounder, get frustrated, despondent, and eventually leave. Before hiring, an organization must take the crucial first step of leadership and learning.

For most companies, to become an authentic gender-intelligent organization, we see nine critical levers that together produce a profound transformation. Below we've listed these crucial levers, along with sample strategies or initiatives and measures an organization might put into place. Of course, the needs of each organization are unique—please treat this as a list of possibilities rather than as a targeted plan.

LEVER 1. Make Gender Intelligence a strategic imperative
- set clear goals and expectations
- make a compelling business case that even the most cynical observer can buy into

Example measure: the linking of gender-intelligent goals to the larger strategy map for your company

LEVER 2. All leaders are gender-intelligent—their conduct and character are exemplary.
- conduct gender-intelligent leadership 360s or embed Gender Intelligence into your 360s
- create annual leadership reviews with embedded Gender Intelligence criteria
- provide Gender Intelligence leadership coaching for leaders

Example measure: a raise in the overall 360 Gender Intelligence leadership average

LEVER 3. Embed Gender Intelligence in all hiring processes and practices
- diagnose the hiring practices of the organization
- provide insights and tools on how to hire gender-intelligent men and women
- provide insights and tools on how to make the hiring process more gender-intelligent

Example measure: consistency in the outcome of people who go through Gender Intelligence training

LEVER 4. Embed Gender Intelligence in all promoting practices, including succession planning
- provide training on removing blind spots in promotion

- examine and change the promotion process so it is infused with Gender Intelligence
- examine the high-potential pool to make sure it's gender balanced at each succession level

Example measure: consistency in the outcome of people who go through Gender Intelligence training

LEVER 5. Declare your intention to be a leading gender-intelligent organization and brand your organization accordingly (note: this may have to go before number 5, as it will help attract more women)
- Reshaping the message
- Organizing summits
- PR

Example measure: changes in marketing collateral

LEVER 6. Generate a stronger female leadership pipeline
- explore creative methods for widening the lens
- agree on targets for the pipeline

Example measure: increased number of potential women leaders

LEVER 7. Provide support, guidance, and leadership training for women
- focus on training for women that identifies the potential pitfalls and being more self-initiating in navigating their careers

Example measure: satisfaction level of targeted women who participate in the training

LEVER 8. Generate gender-intelligent understanding and behaviors throughout the organization
- promote Gender Intelligence training throughout the organization, starting with leaders and managers

- examine typical decision-making and problem-solving strategies and offer alternatives that are more gender-intelligent and more inclusive

Example measure: number of people who participate in the workshops and their satisfaction levels; organization survey designed to measure changes in practice

LEVER 9. Embed Gender Intelligence in all customer-facing efforts
- examine assumptions behind the way the organization relates to customers
- analyze the key needs of clients and assess what the organization is doing against those needs
- discover how Gender Intelligence can enhance customer-facing efforts
- train in gender-intelligent relationship building and selling

Example measure: client survey feedback

After a diagnostic has been conducted, it becomes abundantly clear to the organization that it will need to embark on a number of initiatives and actions crucial to effect transformational change. The concept of levers becomes most helpful then in determining what critical elements to undertake and their order of importance. Though the prioritization will be different for each organization, what we usually start with is some kind of learning process that educates key leaders and decision makers on Gender Intelligence, enough so that they can thoughtfully determine which levers to push and pull and in what order. This, in effect, becomes the basis of their plan. Included in the plan are also communication strategies to keep the organization apprised, as well as a guiding coalition, which we spoke of earlier in Chapter 9, to ensure consistent effort.

Once the plan is in place, execution becomes paramount, as is the understanding that plans are not static. Instead, they are living, breathing instruments that adapt and change as the organization learns and grows. Staying power then becomes a crucial condition for success. Given that a cultural transformation of this nature will take time, the profile of management will change as leaders come and go—including the CEO. Therefore, the coalition becomes not only the guiding force for change but also a constant that ensures the transformation endures.

Once the critical elements have begun, the scope of change can seem overwhelming at times to leaders and managers. Other priorities can sometimes take precedent, and without stick-to-it-iveness, Gender Intelligence can become the flavor of the month. Our experience is that embedded in the plan must be opportunities for quick wins so everyone in the organization can begin to see demonstrable evidence of the power of Gender Intelligence.

Our Dream

We set out on this journey twenty-seven years ago to lift the veil on our gender blind spots and misunderstandings and raise the level of appreciation for our gender differences. Our desire was and remains a gender-intelligent world where books like this one are no longer required. The reality is that we may not get there anytime soon.

We wrote this book with an intention to inspire leaders whose hearts are in the right place but who may not know how to start or what it really takes to create a gender-intelligent organization. Our desire is to shift the mindset of leaders who are missing important elements in their thinking and in their actions, allowing them to move their organizations forward. If you are a leader or organization with the integrity, courage, and commitment to start down the path to enlightenment now, we hope this book will serve as your guidepost, and Gender Intelligence as the powerful lens of truth.

We dream of a world where someday all people can bring their full selves to everything they do and to every aspect of their lives. Imagine the possibilities of a world where men and women, boys and girls are valued authentically. Imagine a world where we are not trying to change one another or make one another something we are not, but are truly honoring and appreciating our unique attributes.

As we look into the future, we can't help but imagine what the world would be like if it were filled with men and women—at all levels of leadership and in all walks of life—possessing such Gender Intelligence. What if we understood, appreciated, and valued each other well enough and genuinely enough to the point where men could speak for women and women could speak for men?

Imagine the spirit of collaboration, creativity, and productivity that would permeate the global business environment. Visualize the amazing economic impact the full engagement of highly educated yet underutilized women would have, particularly in those countries facing talent shortages expressly because their traditional cultures undervalue half their populations.

Imagine couples living in fulfilling relationships and finding greater love through an enhanced understanding and appreciation for each other. Envision gender-intelligent parents raising sons and daughters to be cooperative, confident, and compassionate individuals with the freedom and direction to live authentic and satisfying lives.

Imagine national leaders with open minds and softened hearts, working to end forever the maiming and killing of their young girls and the suppression of their women.

We believe all of these scenarios are Gender Intelligence in action—men and women seeing the world through each other's eyes and valuing each other's line of sight, turning difference into value.

Throughout our book, we shared how Gender Intelligence is effectively bringing greater economic value to organizations. And we demonstrated how this new conversation about gender extends well beyond the bottom line by helping men and women find greater success in their careers and happiness in their personal lives.

This journey began with one person at the start who changed the course of our practice and accelerated the growth of Gender Intelligence. The initial motivation was to spread Gender Intelligence through keynotes and workshops in public forums. We were reaching many individuals, but not attaining the critical mass we needed. And we were not reaching enough men.

That individual was the late Dr. Willis Harman, an influential social thinker and futurist, whose concern had always been the constructive role of business in transforming society. He immediately recognized the beneficial value of Gender Intelligence in positively and permanently shifting the social discourse. Willis's recommendation at the onset of our practice was that we bring Gender Intelligence to the finest corporations in the world—the breeding ground of future leaders.

The movement grew! For years, we've been working with countless organizations on the path to Gender Intelligence, and as we write this book, we are now pursuing breakthroughs in Gender Intelligence well beyond the business arena. Influenced by the improvement in the personal lives of countless men and women in organizations, our vision is to take this movement beyond transforming corporate cultures and contribute to the betterment of society. Our dream now is to take Gender Intelligence to a larger scale and positively affect the lives of people and communities across the globe.

We're starting on many fronts but none provides a more solid foundation and greater hope for the future than bringing Gender Intelligence to our younger generation and parenting our children to be authentic boys and girls, and have them grow into confident, emotionally strong men and women.

Unfortunately, in some parts of the world, it's more rudimentary than that, as we find that we must first transform the global mindset in how we value women and girls. One of the most powerful yet somber statistics found in Nicholas Kristof and Sheryl WuDunn's brilliant book, *Half the Sky*, is that more girls have been killed in the last fifty years, particularly in China, India, and Pakistan—simply for being girls—than all the men who died in all the wars of the twentieth century. Imagine if families and communities valued the birth of a daughter the same way they valued the birth of a son.

This change is slowly but surely taking place as countries realize and embrace, as equals, their greatest undervalued and underdeveloped economic resource—the female half of the population. We believe the engagement of women in developing countries for their balanced voice in business and government will be one of the greatest breakthroughs for humankind in the twenty-first century.

We're seeing more and more female leaders emerge as presidents and prime ministers, and as senators and members of parliament, bringing their own authentic expression of power and leadership. We've had strong women leaders in governments before. Yet, in many instances, their leadership echoed traditional male leadership traits. It's continuing to evolve from that now as gender differences in leadership and governance are showing the way for the next generation of women leaders to express their own authentic voices.

Gender Intelligence is taking governments to a new level of interaction and problem-solving, beyond partisanship and posturing to the blending of the powerful, unifocal thinking of men with the equally valuable, expansive thinking of women. We believe this natural complement of gender strengths is the right path and offers the best solutions to social issues.

The blended voice of men and women in governments has the potential to bring countries together to solve global issues, break the impasse on seemingly endless disagreements, encourage deeper and more meaningful dialogue, and forestall violent conflicts and wars. The solution right under our noses is in bringing the best brains of both men and women together to create a better, more stable world—both economically and socially. Imagine how different our world would be right now if women had been at the table just in the last fifty years.

Even more important, imagine the possibilities of the world we could leave for our next generation by taking the path to Gender Intelligence now.

We're doing more than imagining; we're taking action. Established in 2005 by President Bill Clinton, the Clinton Global Initiative (CGI) convenes global leaders to create and implement innovative solutions to the world's most pressing challenges. This year marks the first in which CGI and Barbara Annis & Associates will work together to empower women along the corporate value chain, to address gender gaps in governance, and to increase development solutions in urban areas around the world.

We've already created powerful partnerships with a number of influential organizations and individuals in commerce and government. They include the Impact Center, a premier leadership development organization in Washington, D.C., and the Women and Public Policy Program in collaboration with the Center for International Development at Harvard's Kennedy School of Government and their global initiative, Closing the Global Gender Gap. They include alliances with Sheryl Sandberg of the *Lean In* movement; with EDGE Certified, a Swiss foundation fostering equal opportunities through a global certification system for gender equality; and with Dr. Alan Richter of QED Consulting and the Global

Gender Intelligence Assessment. It also includes partnering with the World Economic Forum, committed to improving the state of the world by engaging business, political, academic, and other leaders of society to shape global, regional, and industry agendas.

And we're striving to create even more alliances wherever we can with like-minded men and women leaders intent on accelerating Gender Intelligence and bringing a balanced voice to our world. There's a global movement afoot and more powerful partnerships are being created every day.

We wholeheartedly invite you to participate! And with your commitment in your own life to Gender Intelligence and the world in which you live, you will be joining a growing mass of people who have taken a stand for a better world.

Acknowledgments

We wish to thank our senior editor, John Fayad, for his dedication and hard work and Leslie Miller for her careful crafting of language that made the final manuscript sing. We also wish to thank the many thousands of men and women who have participated in this work and have ensured that it made a lasting difference in their lives. Thank you to Colleen Lawrie and the team at HarperCollins, and to our literary agent, Carol Mann, for bringing this work into the world. We also want to acknowledge our friends, colleagues, and clients for having made tremendous contributions in their spheres of influence.

I wish to thank Lee Akazaki, Kenchiro Akiyama, Jane Allen, Jennifer Allyn, Shahla Aly, Greg Van Asperen, Beth Axelrod, Robin Baliszewski, Clare Beckton, Jim Beqaj, Jill Beresford, Megan Beyer, Gina Bianchini, Maryann Bloomfield, Lynda Bowles, Stephanie Hanbury Brown, Woody Buckner, Victoria Budson, James Bush, Dr. Larry Cahill, Susan Cartsonis, Kenneth Chenault, Jennifer Christie, Stephane Cotichini, Judy Dahm, Geena Davis, Christa Dowling, Nancy Elder, Carol Evans, John Fallon, Dr. Helen Fisher, Stacey Fisher, Nancy Forsyth, Gaby Giglio, Ed Gilligan, Neena Gupta, Dr. Ruben Gur, Bruce Haase, Nadine Hack, Jane Hewson, Jan Hill, Arianna Huffington, Swanee Hunt, Dr. Joseph Jaworski, Elisabeth Jensen, Michael Kubina, Sonya Kunkel, Dr. George Labovitz, Stan Labovitz, Carolyn Lawrence, Bruce Leamon, Chuck

Ledsinger, Dr. Marianne Legato, Maria LeRose, Elizabeth Lesser, Renee Lundholm, Anne Madison, Susanna Margolis, Ramón Martín, Marguerite McLeod, Graciela Meibar, Dr. Keith Merron, Dr. Anne Moir, Betsy Myers, Constance Peak, Paola Corna Pellegrini, Kerrie Peraino, Phyllis Stewart Pires, Allison Pogemiller, Jennifer Reynolds, Dr. Alan Richter, Adel Rickets, Hubert Saint-Onge, Eiko Saito, Janet Salazar, Sheryl Sandberg, Nicole Schwab, Maria Shriver, Dr. Janet Smith, Jim Hagerman Snabe, Val Sorbie, Pernille Spiers-Lopez, Erin Stein, Claudia Studle, Kate Sweetman, Dr. Deborah Tannen, Rachel Thomas, Aniela Unguresan, Dr. Karin Verland, Dr. Elena Vigna, Emily Viner, Lara Warner, James Ward, Donna Wilson, Marie Wilson, Oprah Winfrey, Dr. Sandra Witelson, Anka Wittenberg, Dr. Jeannette Wolfe, and Janet Wood.

A special thank-you to: John Hart, CEO of the Gender Intelligence Institute and the Impact Center, whose dedication and commitment to advancing Gender Intelligence and Collaborative Leadership ranges from the White House to our powerful emerging leaders; to all the amazing, deeply committed women and men leaders and staff at the Women's Leadership Board at Harvard's Kennedy School; to the Gender Equality Project Geneva and EDGE Certified Project. I am honored to partner with you in creating a world where men and women are equally valued and respected in all aspects of economic, political, and social life. To the Clinton Global Initiative for bringing Gender Intelligence to its global efforts to create and implement innovative solutions to the world's most pressing challenges; to the remarkable board members of the Institute for Women's Studies in the Arab World (IWSAW) at Lebanese American University, Beirut, for their enduring contribution to empowering women in the Arab world through development, programs, and education; and to all the organizations and their men and women embracing Gender Intelligence for the sake of working and succeeding together including:

American Express, Baker Tilly, Bank of America, Bentley University, Blake, Cassels & Graydon, BMO Financial Group, Choice Hotels International, CIBC, Costco, Crayola, Credit Suisse, Danish CEO Network, Dassault Systemes, Deloitte, the Department of Justice, the Department of National Defense, Deutsche Bank, Disney, Dove-Unilever, eBay, EDS, Electrolux, Federal Business Development Bank, Financial Times, Ford Motor Company, Fordham University, Gender Equality Project Geneva, Goodman & Carr, Greenberg Traurig, Guardian Life Insurance, Harvard

University, HSBC Bank, IBM, IKEA, Imperial Oil, Industry Canada, Kellogg's, Kvinfo, Johnson & Johnson, Lever Ponds, Levi Strauss, Mattel, McDonald's, Microsoft, Molson, Motorola, National Defense Canada, Nissan, Novartis, Oliver Wyman, Pax World, Pearson Education, Pfizer, Prentice Hall, PricewaterhouseCoopers, RBC Financial, RBC Investment Group, SAP, Scotia Bank, SMBC, Sunlife Insurance, Swedish Chamber of Commerce, Symcor, Tambrands, Technip, Toshiba, Treasury Board, UBS Investments, Unilever, Wells Fargo Women of Influence, Wood Gundy Securities, and Xerox.

—*Barbara Annis*

First and foremost, I want to thank my coauthor, Barbara Annis, for her tireless dedication to the cause of Gender Intelligence, for inspiring the movement this book represents and for trusting me fourteen years ago to become her business partner, coauthor, and friend. Without her this book could not have been written. Along the journey of my life, I have had many who have challenged my thinking and who have contributed meaningfully to the body of work that this book represents. Among them, I include my mentor and friend, Bill Torbert; my past business partners, Grady McGonagill and Mike Mckeon; and the crew at Spencer, Shenk, and Capers. I wish to thank my men's community for their support, love, and encouragement with a special nod to my close friends and colleagues Rick Kutten, Tim Kelley, Lion Goodman, Michael Lipson, and David Wilcox, who have been there with me through thick and thin.

This book could not have been written with such care and heart without the support and encouragement of my colleagues Bill Stevens, Steve Tennant, Marty Kaplan, Martha Borst, Mark Voorsanger, Paul Downs, and a cast and crew of hundreds more from whom I have received the grace of their presence, guidance, and love.

And I wish to offer special thanks to my ex-wife, Tina Benson, and my two children, Josh and Maya, who have been there through thick and thin and who have without exception have been supporters of our work at Barbara Annis & Associates. I also wish to thank my stepmother, Chrissa Merron, for her commitment to the field of organization development; she has been a true example of a woman who played life by her own rules while honoring others in doing the same. Finally, I want to thank my father for his love and guidance, and my mother, who I believe more than anyone in my early life was a model for a powerful woman of integrity. It is as a result of their love and example that I am who I am today.

—Keith Merron

Notes

1. U.S. Department of Education, 2011, UNESCO Institute for Statistics, Percent of Women in Education, 2010.
2. The World's Women 2010: Trends and Statistics, United Nations Department of Economic and Social Affairs, http://unstats.un.org/unsd/demographic/products/Worldswomen/wwwork2010.htm.
3. "Scaling Up: Why Women-Owned Businesses Can Recharge the Global Economy," Ernst and Young, 2011, p. 6, http://www.ey.com/Publication/vwLUAssets/Scaling_up_-_Why_women-owned_businesses_can_recharge_the_global_economy/$FILE/Scaling%20up%20-%20why%20women%20owned%20businesses%20can%20recharge%20the%20global%20economy.pdf.
4. "Emotional Intelligence," http://danielgoleman.info/topics/emotional-intelligence/.
5. Gender Surveys, Barbara Annis & Associates, 2005–2012.
6. Michael Gurian and Barbara Annis, *Leadership and the Sexes: Using Gender Science to Create Success in Business* (San Francisco: Jossey-Bass, 2008), p. 7.
7. Dr. Helen Fisher, *The First Sex: The Natural Talents of Women and How They Are Changing the World* (New York: Ballantine Books, 2000), pp. 5, 284.
8. "Recovery of Stroke Victims," Doreen Kimura, "Sex Differences in the Brain" (2002), http://www2.nau.edu/~bio372-c/class/behavior/sexdif1.htm.
9. Murray Goldstein, "Decade of the Brain: An Agenda for the Nineties," *Neurology,* 1994, pp. 239–41, http://www.ncbi.nlm.nih.gov/pmc/articles/PMC1011403/pdf/westjmed00061-0033.pdf.
10. Michael Gurian, *What Could He Be Thinking?: A Guide to the Mysteries of a Man's Mind* (New York: St. Martin's Griffin, 2004), p. 129, http://www.michaelgurian.com/what_could_he_be_thinking.html.
11. Louann Brizendine, *The Female Brain* (New York: Three Rivers Press, 2007), pp. 64–65.
12. J. Decety and P. L. Jackson, "The Functional Architecture of Human Empathy," *Behavioral and Cognitive Neuroscience Review* 3, no. 2 (2004): 71–100.

13. Brizendine, *The Female Brain*, pp. 64–65.

14. Ibid., p. 120.

15. Zeenat F. Zaidi, "Gender Differences in the Human Brain: A Review," *Open Anatomy Journal* 2 (2010): 37–55, http://www.benthamscience.com/open/toanatj/articles/V002/37TOANATJ.pdf.

16. Stephan Hamann, "Sex Differences in the Responses of the Human Amygdala," *Neuroscientist* 11, no. 4 (2005): 288–93.

17. Deborah Blum, *Sex on the Brain: The Biological Differences Between Men and Women* (New York: Viking, 1997), p. 63.

18. Linda Babcock and Sara Laschever, *Women Don't Ask: The High Cost of Avoiding Negotiation—and Positive Strategies for Change* (New York: Bantam, 2007).

19. Uri Wolf, Mark Rapoport, and Tom Schweizer, "Evaluating the Affective Component of the Cerebellar Cognitive Affective Syndrome," *Journal of Neuropsychiatry and Clinical Neurosciences* 21, no. 3 (2009): 245–53.

20. Detlef Heck and Fahad Sultan, "Cerebellar Structure and Function: Making Sense of Parallel Fibers," *Human Movement Science* 21 (2002): 411–21, http://keck.ucsf.edu/~houde/sensorimotor_jc/DHeck02a.pdf.

21. "Thirteen Surprising Facts About Testosterone," http://healthyliving.msn.com/health-wellness/men/13-surprising-facts-about-testosterone-1.

22. Tori DeAngelis, "The Two Faces of Oxytocin," American Psychological Association, *Monitor on Psychology* 39, no. 2 (February 2008), http://www.apa.org/monitor/feb08/oxytocin.aspx.

23. Elizabeth Scott, M.S., "Cortisol and Stress: How to Stay Healthy," September 22, 2011, http://stress.about.com/od/stresshealth/a/cortisol.htm.

24. "The Physiology of Stress: Cortisol and the Hypothalamic-Pituitary-Adrenal Axis," *Dartmouth Undergraduate Journal of Science*, February 3, 2011, http://dujs.dartmouth.edu/fall-2010/the-physiology-of-stress-cortisol-and-the-hypothalamic-pituitary-adrenal-axis.

25. Vikram Patel, Alistair Woodward, Valery Feigin, Stella R. Quah, and Kristian Heggenhougen, eds., *Mental and Neurological Public Health: A Global Perspective* (San Diego: Academic Press/Elsevier, 2010), p. 5.

26. C. Otto Scharmer, *Theory U: Leading from the Future As It Emerges* (San Francisco: Berrett-Koehler, 2009), p. 50.

27. Grant Thornton International Business Report, 2012, http://www.gti.org/files/ibr2012%20-%20women%20in%20senior%20management%20master.pdf, p. 9.

28. Gender Surveys, Barbara Annis & Associates, 2005–2012.

29. Grant Thornton International Business Report, 2012, p. 9.

30. Paul Hastings, "Breaking the Glass Ceiling: Women in the Boardroom," 2011, http://www.paulhastings.com/assets/pdfs/Gender_Parity_on_Corporate_Boards.pdf, p. 11.

31. Gender Surveys, Barbara Annis & Associates, 2005–2012.

32. Stephen P. Kelner, C. A. Rivers, and K. H. O'Connell, "Managerial Style as a Behavioral Predictor of Organizational Climate," 1994, McBer & Company.

33. Avista Consulting Group, Inc., © 2001. Various versions of the concept of the Leadership Chain have been around for decades. Most of the original effort was led by David McClelland in his pioneering work on motivation and the work of his colleagues, George Litwin and Robert Stringer. See, for example, *Motivation and Organization Climate*.

34. Gender Studies, Barbara Annis & Associates, 2005–2012

35. "Collective Intelligence: Number of Women in Group Linked to Effectiveness in Solving Difficult Problems," *Science Daily,* October 2, 2010, http://www.science-daily.com/releases/2010/09/100930143339.htm.

36. Alliance of Communication Agencies 2010 Study, sponsored by the Marketing to Women Conference, http://www.she-conomy.com/report/marketing-to-women-quick-facts.

37. Proprietary Boston Consulting Group survey, 2009.

38. Impact Research Center: "62 Studies on Gender and Leadership Traits" (2011), www.baainc.com.

39. University of California, Hastings College of Law, Center for WorkLife Law, 2010.

40. Roy D. Adler, "Women in the Executive Suite Correlate to High Profits," Glass Ceiling Research Center, 2001, http://www.w2t.se/se/filer/adler_web.pdf, p. 5.

41. "The Dove Campaign for Real Beauty," 2004–2010, http://www.dove.us/social-mission/campaign-for-real-beauty.aspx.

42. Jone Johnson Lewis, "Women and Work in Early America," http://womenshistory.about.com/od/worklaborunions/a/early_america.htm.

43. Rick Wartzman, "Women and the Knowledge-Work Trend," February 19, 2010, http://www.businessweek.com/managing/content/feb2010/ca20100212_117706.htm.

44. "The Future of Work: A Golden Age for Working Women," August 24, 2012, http://www.forbes.com/sites/jennagoudreau/2012/08/24/are-women-the-future-of-work-jobs-economy/.

45. "Revealed: The Best and Worst Places to Be a Woman," http://www.independent.co.uk/news/world/politics/revealed-the-best-and-worst-places-to-be-a-woman-7534794.html.

46. Proprietary Boston Consulting Group survey, 2009.

47. Alliance of Communication Agencies 2010 study, sponsored by the Marketing to Women Conference, http://www.she-conomy.com/report/marketing-to-women-quick-facts.

48. Ruthie Ackerman, "Women and Investing: Why Many Advisors Are Missing Out," April 8, 2012, http://www.satorifin.com/wp-content/uploads/2013/05/120408-InvestmentNews.com-Women-and-Investing.pdf.

49. "The Sheconomy: A Guy's Guide to Marketing to Women," http://www.she-conomy.com/facts-on-women.

50. "Why Aren't More Women Selling Cars?" *Dealer Communications,* October 15, 2012, http://dealer-communications.com/dealer-management/why-arent-more-women-selling-cars/.

51. "Women in Senior Management: Still Not Enough," Grant Thornton International Business Report, 2012, http://www.internationalbusinessreport.com/files/ibr2012%20-%20women%20in%20senior%20management%20master.pdf.

52. "Nissan Motor CEO Carlos Ghosn Is Turnaround Hero," *Stanford Business,* November 11, 2002, http://www.gsb.stanford.edu/news/headlines/vftt_ghosn.shtml.

53. Gender Surveys, Barbara Annis & Associates, 2005–2012.

54. "CIOs' View of the IT Tasks Where Women in IT Have Most Positive Effect," Harvey Nash, CIO Survey, 2012, http://media.harveynash.com/usa/media center/2012_US_CIO_Survey.pdf.

55. "Women Still Earn Less 50 Years After Equal Pay Act," *CBS This Morning,* June 2013, http://www.cbsnews.com/8301-505263_162-57588459/women-still-earn-less-50-years-after-equal-pay-act/.

56. "The Gender Wage Gap Around the World," *New York Times*, March 9, 2010, http://economix.blogs.nytimes.com/2010/03/09/the-gender-wage-gap-around-the-world/?_r=0.

57. "Female Leadership, A Competitive Edge for the Future," McKinsey & Company, 2009.

58. "A Study in Leadership: Women Do It Better Than Men," Zenger Folkman Strength-Based Leadership Development, 2011, http://www.zfco.com/media/articles/ZFCo.WP.WomenBetterThanMen.033012.pdf.

59. Nancy M. Carter, PhD, and Harvey M. Wagner, PhD, "The Bottom Line: Corporate Performance and Women's Representation of Boards," *Catalyst*, http://www.calpers-governance.org/docs-sof/marketinitiatives/resources/bottom-line-corp-perform-and-womens-representation-on-boards-2004-2008.pdf.

60. "The Power of Three," Forum of Executive Women, http://www.forumofexecutivewomen.com/SiteData/docs/CoverStory/01d4349c76a7ea79/Cover_Story_The_Power_of_Three[1].pdf.

61. "Critical Mass on Corporate Boards: Why Three or More Women Enhance Corporate Governance," http://www.wcwonline.org/pdf/CriticalMassExecSummary.pdf.

62. "Collective Intelligence: Number of Women in Group Linked to Effectiveness in Solving Difficult Problems," *Science Daily*, October 2, 2010, http://www.sciencedaily.com/releases/2010/09/100930143339.htm.

63. Sex Discrimination and Sexual Harassment, http://www.catalyst.org/knowledge/sex-discrimination-and-sexual-harassment-0.

64. U.S. Equal Employment Opportunity Commission, Charge Statistics: FY 1997–FY 2012, http://www.eeoc.gov/eeoc/statistics/enforcement/charges.cfm.

65. Sex Discrimination and Sexual Harassment, http://www.catalyst.org/knowledge/sex-discrimination-and-sexual-harassment-0.

66. The Global Gender Gap Report, 2011, Harvard University and the World Economic Forum, http://www3.weforum.org/docs/WEF_GenderGap_Report_2011.pdf.

67. Report by the United Nations Economic and Social Commission for Asia and the Pacific, http://www.unescap.org/pdd/calendar/CSN-MDG-NewDelhi-Nov-2011/MDG-Report2011-12.pdf, p. 36.

68. "Warren Buffett, "Warren Buffet Is Bullish . . . on Women," *Fortune*, May 2, 2013, http://money.cnn.com/2013/05/02/leadership/warren-buffett-women.pr.fortune/index.html.

69. Gender Surveys, Barbara Annis & Associates, 2005–2012.

70. Ibid.

71. "Measuring Your Net Promoter Score," Bain & Company, http://www.netpromotersystem.com/about/measuring-your-net-promoter-score.aspx.

72. "Five Questions You Must Ask Your Team," *Gallup Business Journal*, May 2013, http://businessjournal.gallup.com/content/162794/five-questions-ask-team.aspx.

Index

If You Like What You've Read and Want to Grow in Your Gender Intelligence . . .

Arrange for keynotes or seminars with Barbara Annis and Keith Merron. Schedule Gender Intelligence workshops for your company or organization. The "aha!" moments will astound you! Take the Global Gender Intelligence Assessment, a valuable online self-assessment tool designed to help you better understand gender, become more inclusive, and improve your effectiveness in the workplace. Learn more about how Gender Intelligence diagnostics and workshops are helping organizations uncover their gender blind spots and discover breakthroughs in leadership, diversity, and the bottom line.

Visit **www.baainc.com**.

About the Authors

B arbara Annis, founder and CEO of Barbara Annis & Associates Inc., is a world-renowned expert on Gender Intelligence and inclusive leadership; she works with Fortune 500 companies and many organizations worldwide. Since 1987 Barbara Annis & Associates has facilitated more than eight thousand corporate workshops, keynotes, and executive coaching sessions. Barbara is the chair emeritus of the Women's Leadership Board at Harvard Kennedy School and was recently conferred with the International Alliance for Women Lifetime Achievement Award. She is the author of three books, including *Same Words, Different Language*; *Leadership and the Sexes*; and *Work with Me*, cowritten with John Gray.

K eith Merron, a senior associate with Barbara Annis & Associates, is an organizational effectiveness and executive development specialist; he has more than thirty years of experience assisting executives and managers in business, government, and education. In partnership with his clients, he has successfully conducted more than twenty-five large-system strategic-, cultural-, and technical-change efforts. Keith received his doctorate from Harvard University in 1985; his studies there spanned the fields of human and organizational development. He teaches at the Hult International Business School and is the author of four books on organizational change: *Riding the Wave, Consulting Mastery, The Golden Flame*, and *Inner Freedom*.